C INSTRUMENTS

Volume II

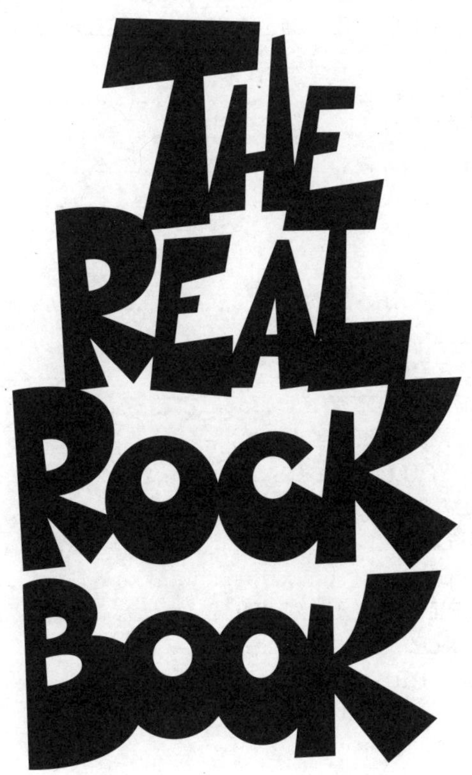

ISBN 978-1-4234-3853-3

7777 W. Bluemound Rd. P.O. Box 13819 Milwaukee, WI 53213

Visit Hal Leonard Online at
www.halleonard.com

MED. JAZZ WALTZ
BEING WITH YOU (IN PARIS)
- STEVE VAI
INTRO - SOLO
Fmaj7
Csus2/4
Fmaj7
Csus2/4
PLAY 4 x
HEAD
Fmaj7
Bbmaj7
Fmaj7
Csus2/4
Fmaj7
Bbmaj7
Fmaj9
Csus2/4
Bbmaj7
Ebsus2
Eb/Ab
Dbmaj7
C-7
C7
Fmaj7
Bbmaj7
Fmaj7
Csus2/4
Fmaj7
Bbmaj7
Fmaj9
Csus2/4
Bbmaj7
Bb-6
A-7
D-7
G-9
C7sus4
C7
Fmaj7
Csus2/4
Fmaj7
Csus2/4
SOLOS
Fmaj7
Csus2/4
Fmaj7
Csus2/4 REPEAT AS DESIRED

(MED.)
ABRACADABRA
—STEVE MILLER
INTRO
A-
G A- G A
(GUITAR)
VERSE
A-
D-
E7#9
I heat up, I can't cool down, you got me spin-nin' a -
I feel the mag-ic in your ca - ress. I feel mag - ic when I
A-
D-
round and 'round. 'Round and 'round and 'round it goes,
touch your dress. Silk and sat - in, leath-er and lace,
E7#9
A-
where it stops no - bod - y knows. Ev-'ry time you
black pan-ties with an an - gel's face. I see mag-ic
D-
E7#9
A-
call my name, I heat up like a burn - ing flame.
in your eyes, I hear the mag - ic in your sighs.
D-
E7#9
Burn-in' flame, full of de - sire, kiss me ba - by, let the fire
Just when I think I'm gon-na get a - way, I hear those words that
(*A-)
A-
CHORUS
D-
get high - er.
you al-ways say.
Ab - ra, ab - ra - ca - dab - ra.
*2nd X ONLY
E7#9
A-
I wan - na reach out and grab ya. Ab - ra, ab - ra - ca - dab -
D-
E7#9
A-
- ra. Ab - ra - ca - dab - ra.

VERSE
A-
D-
E7#9
You make me hot, you make me sigh.
Ev - 'ry time you call my name,
You make me laugh, you
I heat up like a burn -
A-
D-
To
make me cry.
- in' flame.
Keep me burn - in'
Burn-in' flame,
for your love
full of de - sire,
E7#9
A-
CHORUS
A-
with the touch of a vel - vet glove. Ab - ra, ab - ra - ca-dab -
D-
E7#9
A-
ra.
I wan - na reach out and grab ya.
Ab -
D-
E7#9
A-
D.S. AL
ra, ab - ra - ca-dab - ra.
Ab-ra-ca-dab - ra.
E7#9
kiss me, ba-by, let the fi-re get high - er.
Yeah, yeah.
GUITAR SOLO
A-
D-
1.,2.,3.
E7#9
A-
4.
E7#9
INTERLUDE
A-
G A- G A-
(GTR.)
OUTRO
REPEAT AND FADE
A- (GTR. CONT. SIM.)
G A- G A-
I heat up, I can't cool down, my sit-u-a-tion goes 'round and 'round.

(SLOW) AFTER THE LOVE HAS GONE

PRE-CHORUS
PLAY 2nd X ONLY
Some-thin' hap-pened a - long the way; what used to be hap-py was sad.
Some-thin' hap-pened a - long the way; yes-ter-day was all we had.
Some-thin' hap-pened a - long the way; what used to be hap - py is sad.
Some-thin' hap-pened a - long the way, and yes-ter-day was all we had.
CHORUS
And oh, af-ter the love has gone, how could you lead me on
and not let me stay a - round? Oh,
af-ter the love has gone what used to be right is wrong. Can love that's lost be found?
For a while Oh.
OUTRO-SAX SOLO
Oh, af-ter the love has gone, what used to be right is wrong.
REPEAT AND FADE
Can love that's lost be found? Oh.

12
AGAINST ALL ODDS
(TAKE A LOOK AT ME NOW)
(SLOW)
— PHIL COLLINS
INTRO
Eb-7 Absus4 Ab Eb-7 Ab
(KEYBOARDS)
VERSE
Bb-11 Bb-7 C-7 Dbadd9 Eb-11 Eb-7
How can I just let_ you walk a-way, just let you leave with-out__ a trace, when I
Gbadd9 Gb Ab/Gb F-7 Bb-
stand here tak - ing ev - 'ry breath_ with you?__ Ooh._______ You're the
Eb- Ab
on-ly one who real-ly knew me__ at all.______
VERSE
Bb-11 Bb-7 C-7 Dbadd9 Eb-11 Eb-7
How can you just walk a-way from me, when all I can do is watch you leave?_ 'Cause we've
wish I could just make you turn a-round, turn a-round and see me cry.__ There's so
Gbadd9 Gb Ab/Gb F-7 Bb-
shared the laugh-ter and_ the pain,__ and e-ven shared_ the tears.__
much I need to say_ to you,___ so man-y rea - sons why.____
You're the
Eb- Absus4 Ab
on-ly one who real-ly knew me__ at all.______ So take a look at me now, _
CHORUS
Db/Ab Eb7/Ab
well, there's just an emp-ty space.____ And there's noth-ing

13
Bb-
Gb
Eb-
Absus4
left_ here_ to re-mind____ me, just a mem - 'ry of__your face.___
Ooh, take a look at me now,_
Now, take a look at me now,_
Db/Ab
Eb7/Ab
well, there's just an emp-ty space.___ And you com-ing back_
'cause there's just an emp-ty space.___ But to wait_
Bb-
Gb
1.
Eb-
Absus4
Ab
__ to me__ is a-gainst_the odds,_ and that's what_I've got_ to face._____ I
__ for you_ is all__ I can do,_ and that's what_
2.
Eb-
Absus4
Ab
Db/Ab
I've got to face.__ Take a good look at me now, 'cause I'll___ still be
Eb7/Ab
Bb-
Gb
stand-ing here._____ And you com-ing back___ to me____ is a - gainst_ all odds,_ it's the
Eb-
Absus4
Ab
chance I've got - ta take.__________
OUTRO
Eb-7
Absus4
Ab
Eb-7
Ab
Take a look at me now..
Eb-7
Dbsus2
Absus2/C
Gbadd2
Ab
RIT.

ALL RIGHT NOW
(MED. ROCK)
—ANDY FRASER/PAUL RODGERS
INTRO
(GUITAR)
VERSE
There she stood in the street, smil - in' from her head to her feet. I said a, "Hey, now, what is this? Now, ba - by, may - be, may - be she's in need of a kiss." I said a, "Hey, uh-huh, what's your name, ba - by? May - be we can see things the
to my place, watch - in' ev - 'ry move on her face. She said, "Look, what's your game, ba - by? Are you try'n' to put me in shame?" I said a, "Slow, don't go so fast. Don't you think that love can last?"

A5
D/A
A5
same. Now don't you wait___ or hes - i - tate.___ Let's move
___ She said, "Love?___ Lord a - bove.___ Uh, now___
Dadd9 4/A
D/A
A5
be - fore they raise the park - ing rate."
___ you're try'n' to trick me in love."
Ow!___
CHORUS
A5
G5/A
D/A
A5
All right now.___ Ba - by, it's all___ right___ now.___
G5/A
1.
D/A
___ All right now.___ Ba - by, it's all___ right___ now,___
INTERLUDE
A5
3
A5
D/A
A5
___ whoa.___ Let me tell ya now.
Dadd9 4/A
D/A
A5
2.
D/A
A5
I took her home___ ___ right___ now.___
GUITAR SOLO
A
(BASS)
G
D/F#
PLAY 10X
E
OUTRO-CHORUS
A5
G5/A
All right
D/A
A5
REPEAT AND FADE
now.___ Ba - by it's all___ right___ now,___ yeah.___

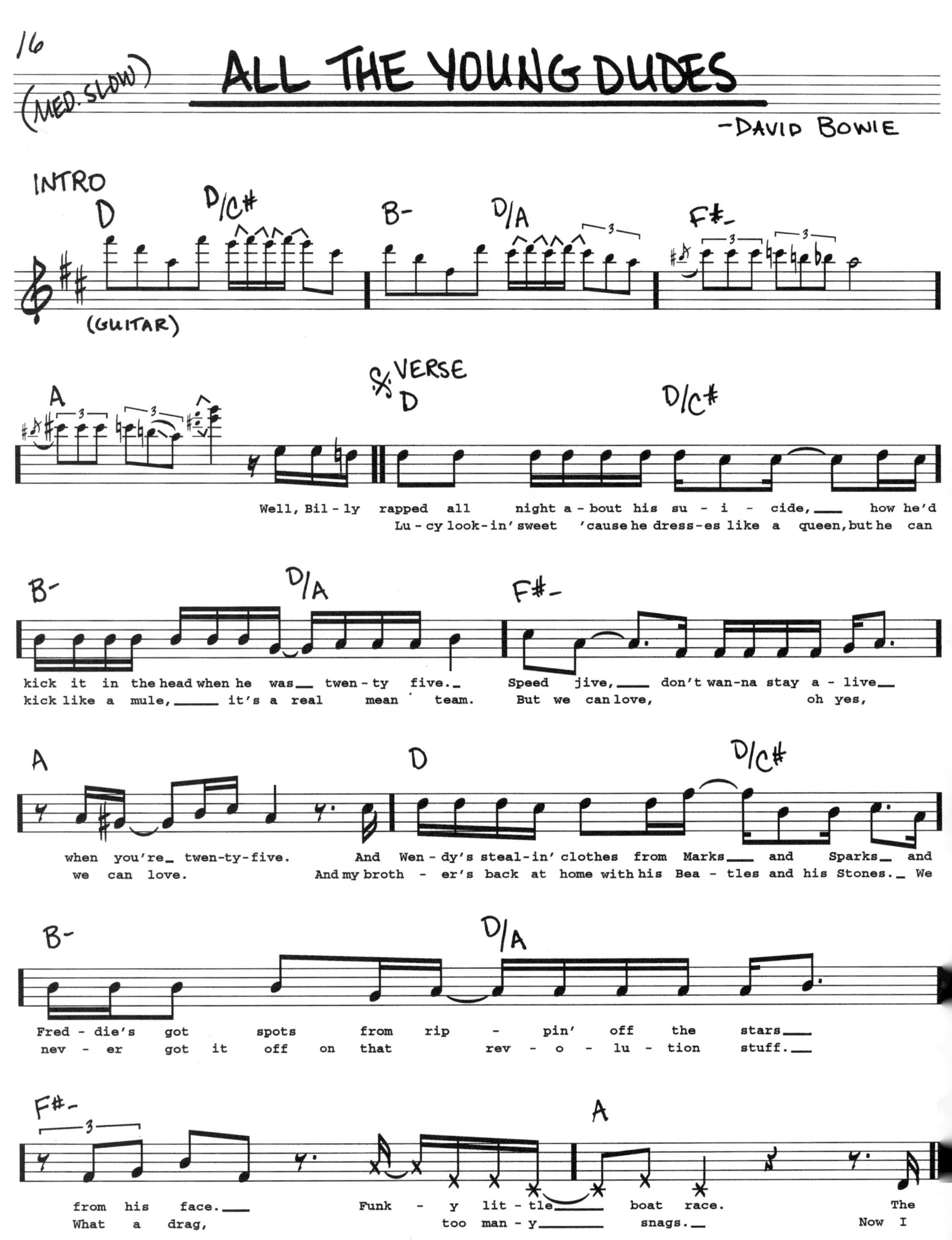
16
ALL THE YOUNG DUDES
(MED. SLOW)
-DAVID BOWIE
INTRO
D D/C# B- D/A F#- A
(GUITAR)
VERSE
D D/C#
Well, Bil - ly rapped all night a - bout his su - i - cide, how he'd
Lu - cy look - in' sweet 'cause he dress - es like a queen, but he can
B- D/A F#-
kick it in the head when he was twen - ty five. Speed jive, don't wan - na stay a - live
kick like a mule, it's a real mean team. But we can love, oh yes,
A D D/C#
when you're twen - ty - five. And Wen - dy's steal - in' clothes from Marks and Sparks and
we can love. And my broth - er's back at home with his Bea - tles and his Stones. We
B- D/A
Fred - die's got spots from rip - pin' off the stars
nev - er got it off on that rev - o - lu - tion stuff.
F#- A
from his face. Funk - y lit - tle boat race. The
What a drag, too man - y snags. Now I

PRE-CHORUS
E-7
F#7
B-
B-/A
tel-e-vi-sion man is cra - zy, say-in' we're ju - ve - nile de-lin - quent wrecks. Oh, man,
drunk a lot of wine 'n' I'm feel-in' fine, got to race some cat to bed. Oh, is
G
D
A
I need T V when I got T - Rex. Oh, broth-er,
there con-crete all a - round, or is it in my head?
TO ⊕
CHORUS
W/ LEAD VOC. AD LIB.
D
D/C#
B-
D/A
you guessed, I'm a dude, man.
Yeah! I'm a dude, dad.
(All the young dudes carry the news.
A-
G
F
C/E
C
G
C
A
D
D/C#
Boo - ga - loo dudes car - ry the news.
All the young dudes
B-
D/A
A-
G
F
C/E
C
G
C
A
D.S. AL ⊕
car - ry the news. Boo - ga - loo dudes car - ry the news.)
⊕ OUTRO-CHORUS
W/ LEAD VOC. AD LIB.
D
D/C#
B-
D/A
(All the young dudes car - ry the news.
A-
G
F
C/E
C
G
C
A
REPEAT AND FADE
Boo - ga - loo dudes car - ry the news.)

18
(MED.)
AND I LOVE HER
-JOHN LENNON/PAUL McCARTNEY
INTRO
F#-
E6
(GUITAR)
VERSE
F#-
C#-
I give her all my love,
She gives me ev - 'ry - thing
Bright are the stars that shine,
F#-
C#-
F#-
that's all I do.
and ten - der - ly.
dark is the sky.
And if you saw
The kiss my
I know this
C#-
A
B
my love
lov - er brings
love of mine
you'd love her too.
she brings to me.
will nev - er die.
I love
And I love
And I love
E
TO
1.
2.
her.
her.
her.
BRIDGE
C#-
B
C#-
G#-
A love like ours could nev - er die
C#-
G#-
B
B7
D.S. AL
as long as I have you near me.
(GTR.)

GUITAR SOLO
G-
D-
Bb
C
F
VERSE
Bright are the stars that shine,
dark is the sky.
I know this love of mine will nev-er die.
And I love her.
(GTR.)
OUTRO
F6
D

ANGIE
(MED. SLOW)
—MICK JAGGER/KEITH RICHARDS
INTRO
A-
E7
Gsus4
Fsus4 F
Fsus2
C
G/B
HARM.
(GUITAR)
P.M.
VERSE
An - gie,
An - gie,
when will those clouds all dis - ap - pear?
An - gie, you're beau - ti - ful, yes,
but ain't it time we said good - bye?
An - gie,
An - gie,
An-gie,
I still love you.
where will it lead us from here?
Re - mem - ber all those nights we cried?
CHORUS
With no lov - ing in our souls and no
All the dreams we held so close seemed to all
An - gie, don't you weep, all your kiss
mon - ey in our coats,
go up in smoke.
- es still taste sweet.
you can't say we're sat - is - fied,
Let me whis - per in your ear,
I hate that sad - ness in your eyes,
but An - gie,
Whispered: "An - gie
but An - gie,
An - gie,
An - gie,
An - gie,
you can't say we nev - er tried.
where will it lead us from here?"
ain't it time we said good - bye?
TO INTERLUDE
(GUITAR)

E7
Gsus4 G Fsus4 F
1. Fsus2 C G/B
2. Fsus2 C
D.S. AL ⊕ (NO REPEAT)
Oh,
⊕ INTERLUDE
A- E7 Gsus4 G Fsus4 F Fsus2 C
8VA
LOCO
(STRINGS)
With no
CHORUS
G D- A-
lov-ing in our souls and no mon-ey in our coats,
C F G
BRIDGE
D-
you can't say we're sat-is-fied, but An-gie, I still love you, ba -
A- D- A-
- by. ev-'ry-where I look I see your eyes.
D- A- C F
There ain't a wom-an that comes close to you. Come on, ba - by, dry your eyes.
G
OUTRO
A- E7
But An-gie, An - gie,
Gsus4 Fsus4 F Fsus2 C G/B A-
ain't it good to be a - live? An-gie,
E7 Gsus4 Fsus4 F Fsus2 C
An - gie, they can't say we nev-er tried.

(MED.)

AT THE HOP

– ARTHUR SINGER/JOHN MADARA/DAVID WHITE

INTRO

Ab6 F- Db Eb7 Ab6

(BASS & PIANO)

Ba, ba, ba, ba. Ba, ba, ba, ba. Ba, ba, ba, ba. Ba, ba, ba, ba, at the hop.

𝄋 VERSE

Ab6 Ab7 Db7 Ab6 Eb7 Db7 Ab6

1.Well, you can rock it, you can roll it, do the stomp and e - ven stroll it at the hop. When the rec - ords start a - spin - nin', you cha - lyp - so and you chick - en at the hop. Do the dance sen - sa - tions that are sweep - in' the na - tion at the hop.

(2.,4.) swing it, you can groove it, you can real - ly start to move it at the hop. Where the jock - ey is the smooth - est and the mu - sic is the cool - est at the hop. All the cats and the chicks can______ get their kicks_ at the hop.

CHORUS

Ab6 Ab7 Db7 Ab6

Let's go to the hop! Let's go to the hop! (Oh, ba - by.) Let's go to the hop! (Oh, ba - by.) Let's go to the hop!

Eb7
Db7
TO
1.
Ab6
Come on, let's go to the hop! 2. Well, you can
2.
Ab6
let's go to the hop!
PIANO SOLO
Ab6
Ab7
Db7
Ab6
Eb7
Db7
Ab6
3. Well, you can
VERSE
Ab6
rock it, you can roll it, do the stomp and e - ven stroll it at the hop.
Ab7
Db7
When the rec-ord starts spin-nin', you cha - lyp-so and you chick-en at the
Ab6
hop.
Eb7
Do the dance sen - sa - tions that are
Db7
Ab6
D.S. AL
sweep-in' the na - tion at the hop.
4. You can
Ab6
let's go to the hop!
OUTRO
Ab6
F–
Ba, ba, ba, ba. Ba, ba,
Db6
Eb7
Ab6 N.C.
ba, ba. Ba, ba, ba, ba. Ba, ba, ba, ba, at the hop.

24
(MED.)
BABY, I LOVE YOUR WAY
—PETER FRAMPTON
INTRO
(GUITAR)
VERSE
Shad-ows grow so long before my eyes and they're mov-ing a-cross the page.
Moon ap-pears to shine and light the sky with the help of some fire-fly.
I can see the sun-set in your eyes, brown and grey, and blue be-sides.
Sud-den-ly the day turns in-to night far a-way from the cit-y.
Won-der how they have the pow-er to shine, shine, shine. I can see them under the pine.
Clouds are stalk-ing is-lands in the sun. Wish I could buy one out of sea-son.
But
PRE-CHORUS
don't hes-i-tate, 'cause your love won't wait, hey.

CHORUS
G D A-7 C G D
Ooh, ba-by, I love_ your way,_____ ev-'ry day._ Want to tell you I love_your way,_
A-7 C To ⊕ G D A-7 C
_____ { ev-'ry day._ ooh._ ooh._____ } Want to be with you night and day,_____ hey._____
1. INTERLUDE
G Dadd4/F# E- Dadd4 C B-7 A-7 A-9/D
(ELEC. PIANO)
2. SOLO
G Dadd4/F# E- Dadd4 C F9 G Dadd4/F# E- Dadd4 C F9
(ELEC. PIANO)
But
PRE-CHORUS
B-7 E7 A-7 D7 D.S. AL ⊕
don't hes-i-tate,_ 'cause your_ love_____ won't_ wait._____
⊕ G D A-7 C
Want to be with you night_ and day._____
G D A-7 C
Ooh, ba-by, I love_ your way,_____ ev-'ry day._
G D A-7 C
Want to tell you I love_ your way,_____ ooh._____
G D A-7 C
Want to be with you night_ and day,_ yeah._____
OUTRO
G Dadd4/F# E- Dadd4 Cmaj7 G/B A-7 G
(ELEC. PIANO)

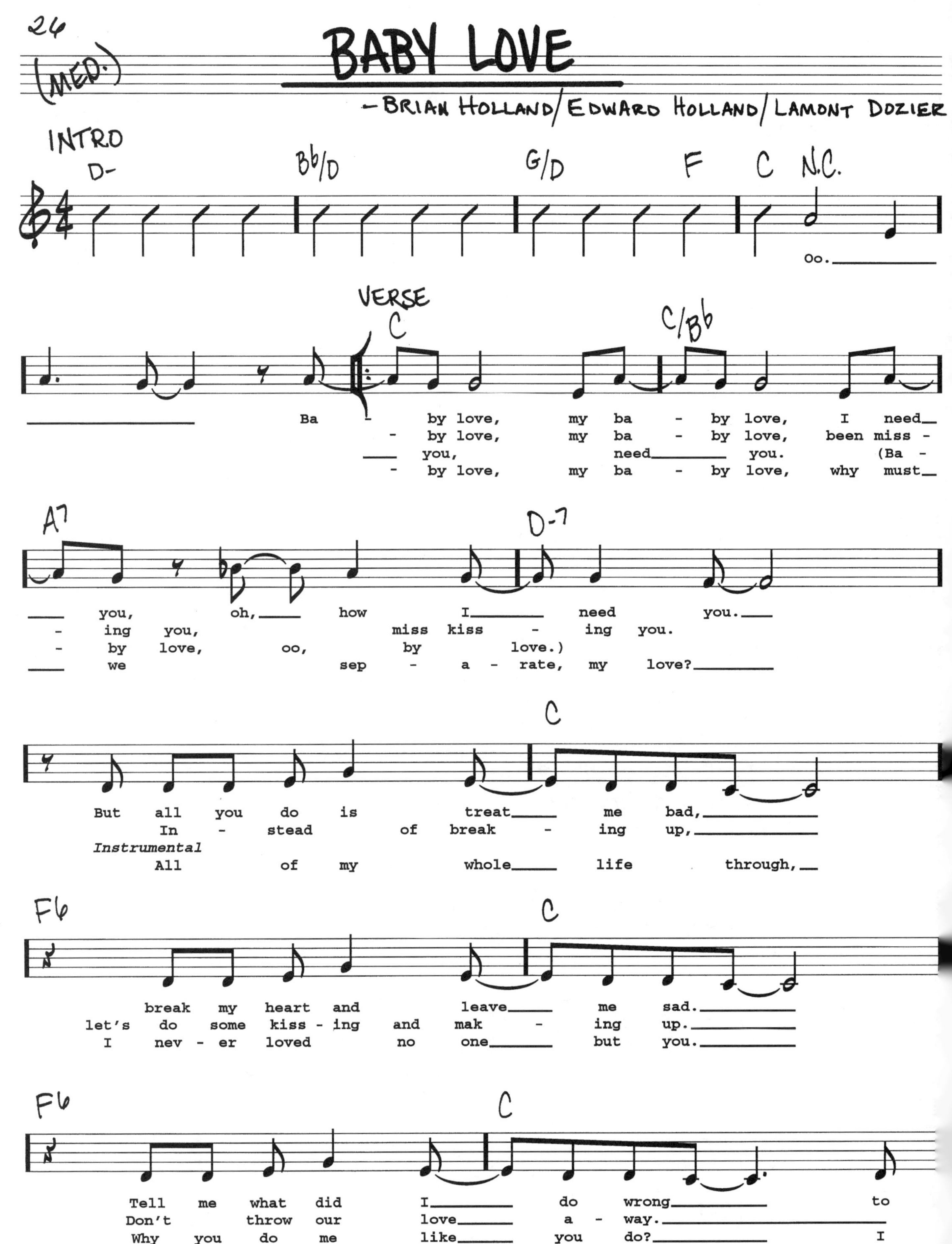
24
(MED.)
BABY LOVE
—BRIAN HOLLAND/EDWARD HOLLAND/LAMONT DOZIER
INTRO
D- Bb/D G/D F C N.C.
Oo.
VERSE
C C/Bb
Ba - by love, my ba - by love, I need
- by love, my ba - by love, been miss -
you, need you. (Ba -
- by love, my ba - by love, why must
A7 D-7
you, oh, how I need you.
- ing you, miss kiss - ing you.
- by love, oo, by love.)
we sep - a - rate, my love?
C
But all you do is treat me bad,
In - stead of break - ing up,
Instrumental
All of my whole life through,
F6 C
break my heart and leave me sad.
let's do some kiss - ing and mak - ing up.
I nev - er loved no one but you.
F6 C
Tell me what did I do wrong to
Don't throw our love a - way.
Why you do me like you do? I

F C/E D-7 G7 PLAY 4x

make you stay a - way so long? 'Cause ba -
In my arms why don't you stay? Need
get this need.
Instrumental ends Ba -

Db

Oo, oo. Need to

VERSE

Db Db/Cb

hold you, a, once a - gain my love, feel your
my love, my ba - by love, I need
hurt - in' me 'til it's hurt - in' me, oo,

Bb7 Eb-7

warm em - brace, my love.
you, oh, how I need you.
ba - by love.

Db

Don't throw our love a - way.
Why you do me like you do
Don't throw our love a - way.

Gb6 Db

Please don't do me this way.
af - ter I've been true to you?
Don't throw our love a - way. *Fade out*

Gb6 Db

I'm not hap - py like I used to be.
So deep in love with you,

Gb Db/F Eb-7 Ab7 REPEAT AND FADE

Lone - li - ness has got the best of me
ba - by, ba - by, oo, 'til it's

BABY WHAT A BIG SURPRISE

(MED. SLOW)

—PETER CETERA

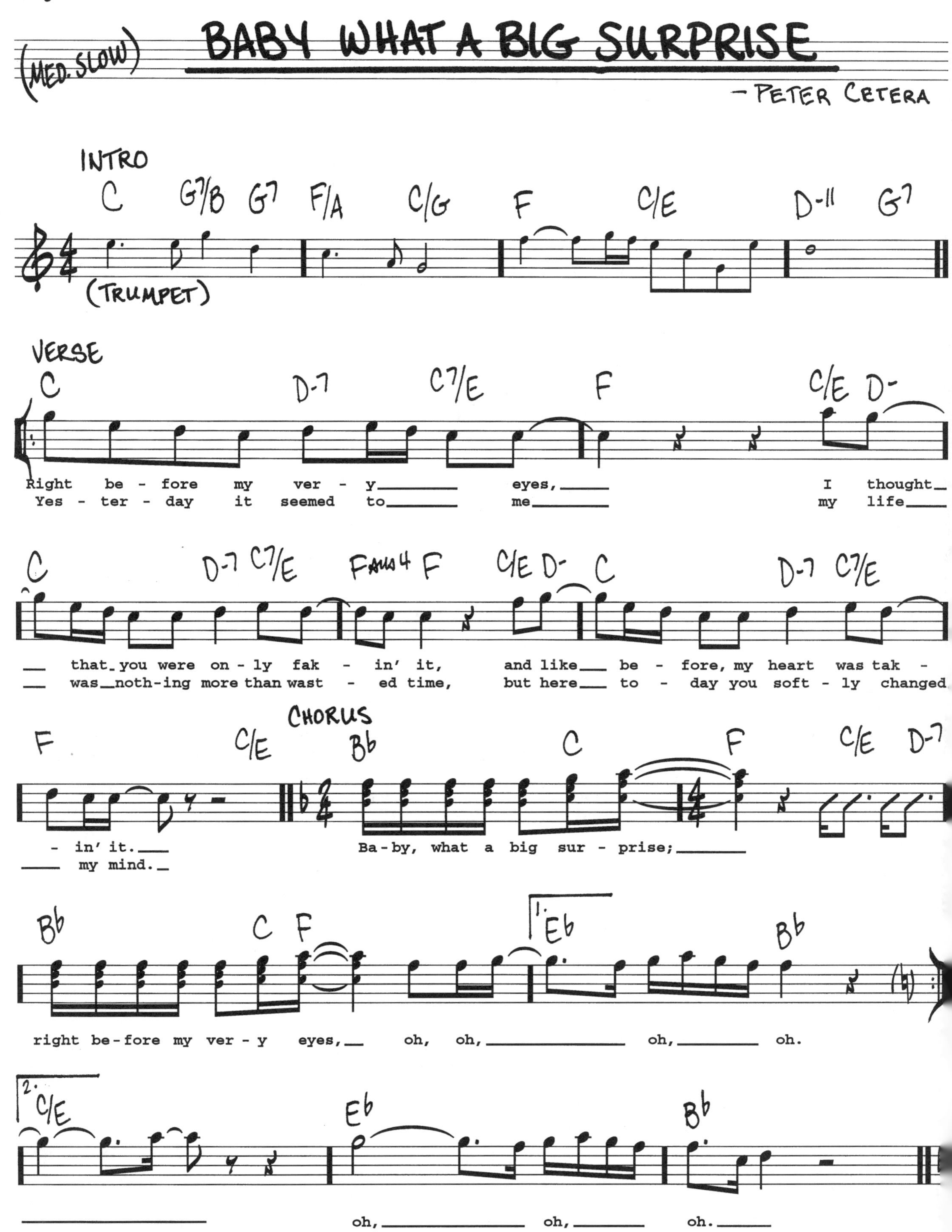

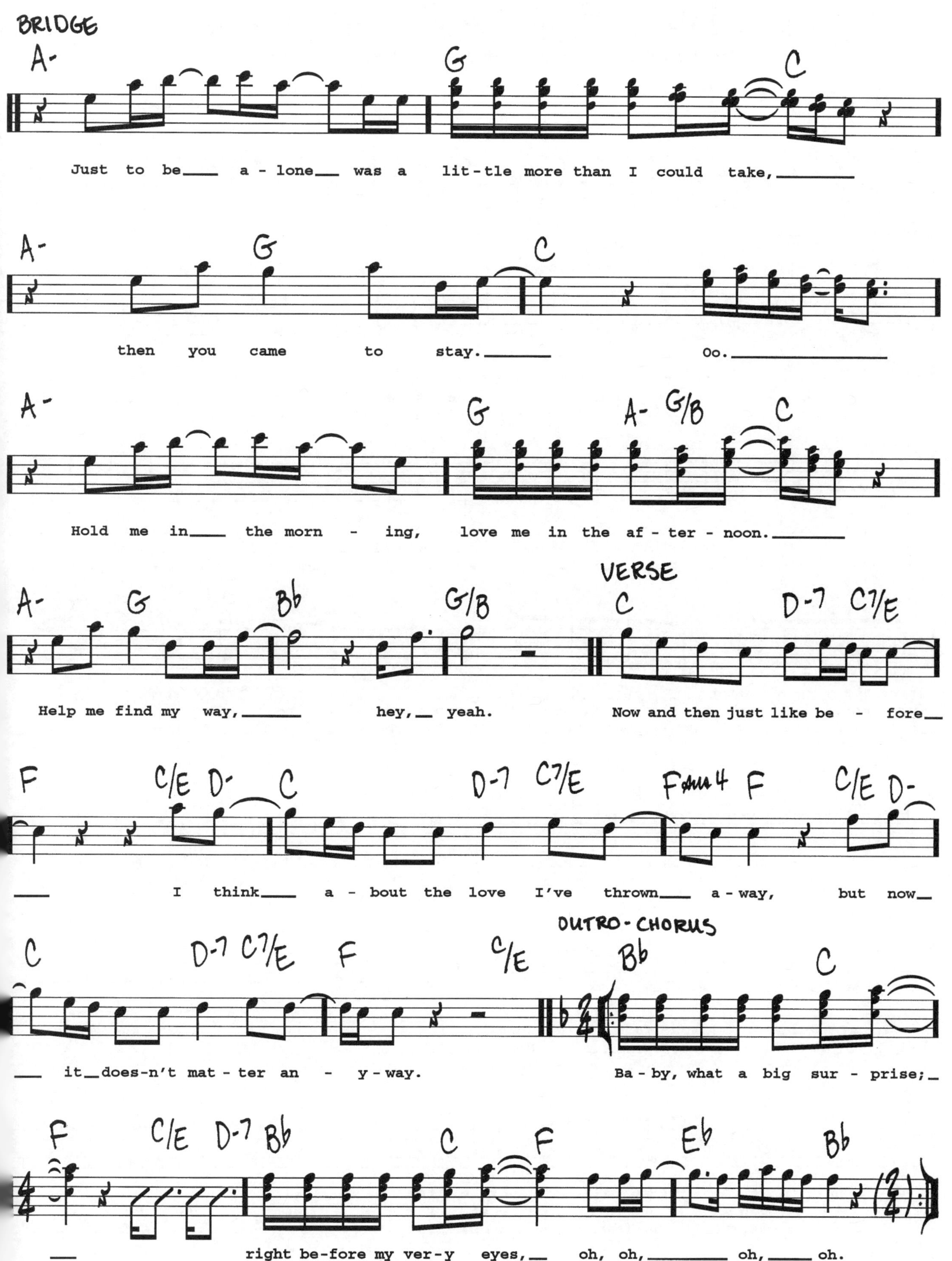
BRIDGE
A-
G
C
Just to be a - lone was a lit-tle more than I could take,
A-
G
C
then you came to stay.
Oo.
A-
G
A-
G/B
C
Hold me in the morn - ing, love me in the af - ter - noon.
VERSE
A-
G
Bb
G/B
C
D-7
C7/E
Help me find my way, hey, yeah.
Now and then just like be - fore
F
C/E
D-
C
D-7
C7/E
Fsus4
F
C/E
D-
I think a - bout the love I've thrown a - way, but now
OUTRO-CHORUS
C
D-7
C7/E
F
C/E
Bb
C
it does-n't mat - ter an - y - way.
Ba - by, what a big sur - prise;
F
C/E
D-7
Bb
C
F
Eb
Bb
right be-fore my ver-y eyes, oh, oh, oh, oh.

(MED. FAST)

BAD, BAD LEROY BROWN

-JIM CROCE

INTRO

G

1.

8VB (PIANO)

2.

D7

8VB

VERSE

G

Well, the south__ side of Chi-ca - go____ is the bad -
- roy, he a gam - bler and he like_
- day 'bout a week__ a - go__

A7 B

- dest part of town____ and if you go down there,_ you bet-ter
___ his fan - cy clothes__ and he like____ to wave___ his
Le-roy shoot-ing dice.___ And at the edge of the bar sat a

C D C G

just be - ware___ of a man______ named a, Le - roy Brown._
dia - mond rings__ in front of ev - 'ry - bod - y's nose.
girl, name of Do - ris and, a, ooh, that girl___ look nice.__

D7 G

__ Now, Le - roy, more than trou - ble. You see he
He got a cus - tom Con - ti - nen - tal._ He got an
__ Well, he cast__ his eyes__ up - on____ her__ and the trou-

CHORUS
1st x: Bkgd. Voc. Tacet
D C G D7 G
mens just call him "Sir."
ra-zor in his shoe.
of a jeal-ous man.
And he's bad, (Bad,) bad (bad.) Le-roy Brown,
A7 B
bad-dest man in the whole damn town.
Bad-der than old King Kong,
C D C G 1., 2. D7
and mean-er than a junk-yard dog.
Now, Le-
Well, Fri-
3. D7
VERSE
G
Well, those two men took to fight - in' and when they
A7 B C
pulled them from the floor
Le-roy looked like a jig - saw puz - zle with a
D
OUTRO-CHORUS
G
cou-ple of piec-es gone.
And he's bad, bad Le-roy Brown,
A7 B
bad-dest man in the whole damn town.
Bad-der than old King Kong,
C D C G 1. D7 2.
and mean-er than a junk-yard dog.
And he's bad,
Yeah, he was
B C D G
bad-der than old King Kong,
mean-er than a junk-yard dog.

(MED. FAST)
BEAT IT
–MICHAEL JACKSON
GTR. & BASS TUNE DOWN 1/2 STEP; PLAY IN E-.
INTRO
N.C.
(SYNCLAVIER)
1.
2. (DRUMS IN)
5
(GUITAR 2)
N.C (Eb-)
(Db)
(Eb-)
(Db)
(GUITAR 1 & BASS 8VB)
(Eb-)
(Db)
(Eb-)
(Db)
(GTR. 1 & BASS CONT. SIM)
VERSE
Eb-
Db
They told him, "Don't you ev - er come a - round here. Don't
They're out to get you. Bet - ter leave while you can. Don't
Guitar solo
Eb-
Db
Cb
wan-na see your face; you bet-ter dis-ap-pear." The fire's in their eyes and their
wan-na be a boy; you wan-na be a man. You wan-na stay a-live; bet-ter
Db
Eb-
Db
words are real-ly clear. So beat it, just beat it.
do what you can. So beat it, just beat it.
Eb-
Db
Eb-
You bet-ter run; you bet - ter do what you can. Don't wan-na see no blood. Don't be a
You have to show them that you're real-ly not scared. You're play-in' with your life. This ain't no
Db
Cb
Db
ma-cho man. You wan - na be tough; bet - ter do what you can. So
"truth or dare." They'll kick you, then they'll beat you then they'll tell you it's fair. So

CHORUS
(GTR. 1 W/ INTRO RIFF)
Eb-
Db
Eb-
beat it. But you wan - na be bad.
beat it. But you wan - na be bad. Just beat it, (Beat it.)
Solo ends
Bb-7
Eb-
Bb-7
beat it. (Beat it.) No one wants to be de-feat - ed. Show -
Eb-
Bb-7
Eb-
- in' how funk-y, strong is your fight, ah. It does-n't mat-ter who's
Bb-7
1.
Eb-
Db
wrong or right. Just beat it, (Beat it.) just beat it, (Beat it.) just
Eb-
Db
2., 3., 4.
Eb-
beat it, (Beat it.) just beat it. (Beat it, uh!) beat it, (Beat it.)
Bb-7
Eb-
Bb-7
beat it. (Beat it.) No one wants to be de-feat - ed. Show -
Eb-
Bb-7
- in' how funk - y, strong is your fight, ah. It
Eb-
TO
Bb-7
does - n't mat - ter who's wrong or right. Just
INTERLUDE
(3X, GTR. 2 W/ INTRO RIFF)
Eb5
1. beat it.
1., 2. Beat it.
1.- 3.
Db5
4.
Db5
D.S. AL
2., 3. Beat it.
Bb-7
D.S.S. AND FADE
wrong or right. Just

(SLOW)

BENNIE AND THE JETS

–ELTON JOHN/BERNIE TAUPIN

INTRO
Gmaj7
Fmaj7
(PIANO)
VERSE
A-7
D
Hey, kids, shake it loose to - geth - er. The spot -
Hey, kids, plug in - to the faith - less. May -
Instrumental solo
G
G#o7
- light's hit - ting some - thing that's been known to change the weath - er.
- be they're blind - ed, but Ben - nie makes them age - less.
A-7
D
3
We'll kill the fat - ted calf to - night, so stick a - round.
We shall sur - vive; let us take our - selves a - long,
E-
You're
where we fight
A-7
B-7
gon - na hear e - lec - tric mu - sic sol - id walls of sound.
our par - ents out in the streets to find who's right and who's wrong.

CHORUS
C
Gmaj7
Solo ends
Say,
Oh,
Oh,
Can - dy and Ron - nie, have you seen them yet, ooh,
A-
C
but they're so spaced out. B - B - B - B - B - Ben-nie and the Jets. Oh,
Gmaj7
but they're weird and they're won - der - ful. Oh, Ben -
A-
- nie, she's a real - ly keen. She's got e -
C
D
lec - tric boots, a mo - hair suit; you know I
E-
E-/D
read it in a mag - a - zine, oh.
C
Bb/C
C
Gmaj7
B - B - B - Ben-nie and the Jets.
(PIANO)
Fmaj7
PLAY 3x
OUTRO
Gmaj7
Fmaj7
REPEAT AND FADE
Ben-nie, Ben-nie, Ben-nie, Ben-nie and the Jets.

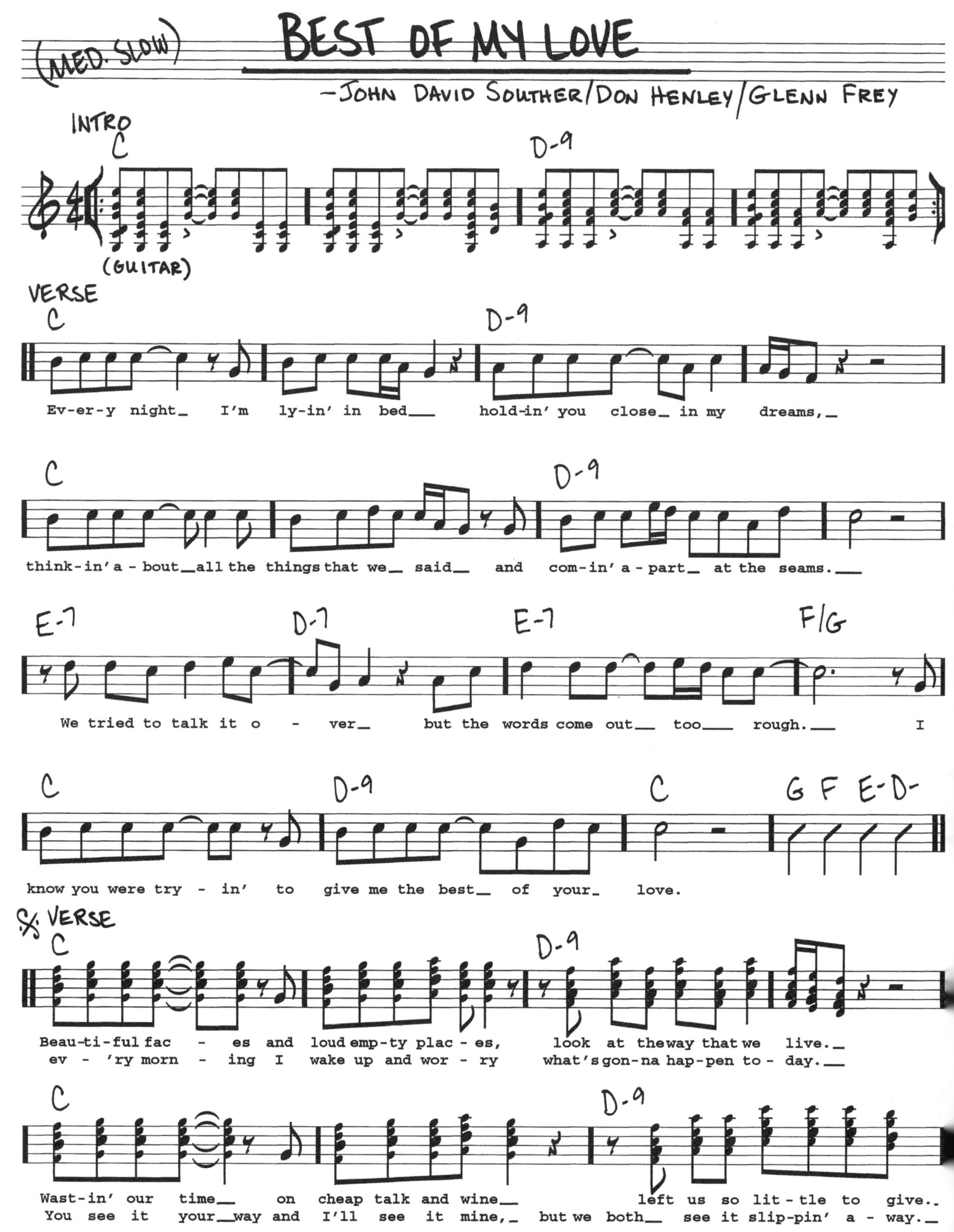
(MED. SLOW)
BEST OF MY LOVE
—JOHN DAVID SOUTHER/DON HENLEY/GLENN FREY
INTRO
C
D-9
(GUITAR)
VERSE
C D-9
Ev-er-y night_ I'm ly-in' in bed__ hold-in' you close_ in my dreams,_
C D-9
think-in' a - bout_all the things that we_ said_ and com-in' a - part_ at the seams.__
E-7 D-7 E-7 F/G
We tried to talk it o - ver_ but the words come out_ too__ rough.__ I
C D-9 C G F E-D-
know you were try - in' to give me the best_ of your_ love.
VERSE
C D-9
Beau-ti-ful fac - es and loud emp-ty plac - es, look at the way that we live._
ev - 'ry morn - ing I wake up and wor - ry what's gon-na hap-pen to - day.__
C D-9
Wast-in' our time__ on cheap talk and wine__ left us so lit - tle to give.
You see it your__way and I'll see it mine,_ but we both__ see it slip-pin' a - way._

E-7
D-7
That same old___ crowd___ was like a cold dark cloud___ that
You know we al-ways had each oth - er, ba - by.
E-7
D-7
G7
C
we could nev - er rise a - bove.____
I guess that was-n't e - nough.____
But here in my heart,__ I
Oh,__ oh, but here in my heart,__ I
D-9
C
G F E-
D-
TO ⊕ CHORUS
C
give you the best_ of my__ love.
give you the best_ of my__ love.
Whoa,_____ sweet dar -
D-7
- lin,'
(You get the best of my__ love.
you get the best of my love._
Whoa,______
CMaj7
D-7
sweet dar - lin',
You get the best of my love.)__
you get the best of my__ love.
BRIDGE
F-7
CMaj7
(Oo.)
I'm go-in' back in time__ and it's a sweet__ thing._
It was a
F-7
D-7
G7
D.S. AL ⊕
qui - et night, and I would be al - right if I could go___ on sleep - ing. But
⊕ OUTRO-CHORUS
C
D-7
sweet dar - lin',
you get the best of my love._
Whoa,______
CMaj7
D-7
REPEAT AND FADE
sweet dar - lin',
you get the best of my__ love.
Whoa,______

(FREE TIME)
BLUE JEAN BOP
—GENE VINCENT/HAL LEVY
INTRO
G G6 C G6/9
Blue-jean ba-by, with your big blue eyes,
don't want you look-in' at oth-er guys.
Got to make you give me one more chance.
FAST ROCK
N.C.
I can't keep still so, ba-by, let's dance. Well, the
VERSE
blue-jean bop is the bop for me. Well, it's the
blue-jean ba-by, when I bop with you, well, my
bop that's done in dun-ga-ree. You dip your hip,
heart starts a hop-pin' like a, a kan-ga-roo. My feet do things they've nev-er
free your knee, swing in on your heel, ba-by, one, two, three.
done be-fore. Well, a blue-jean ba-by, give me more, more, more.
Well, the
CHORUS
blue-jean bop, blue-jean bop, oh, ba-by, blue-jean bop. Blue-jean bop, oh, ba-by,

D
G
3rd x, To
blue - jean bop. Ba - by, won't you bop with Gene?
GUITAR SOLO
G
C
G
D
G
1.
2.
D.S. AL
Well,
Well, the
GUITAR SOLO
G
D
G
D
OUTRO
G
G
Well, it's a blue - jean, a blue - jean bop.
A blue - jean, a, blue - jean bop, oh, ba - by.
C
A blue - jean, a
G
D
blue - jean bop. A blue - jean, a blue - jean bop. A blue - jean, oh,
G
(GTR.)
G6/9
ba - by, won't you bop with Gene?

MED. FAST
THE BOYS ARE BACK IN TOWN
—PHILIP PARRIS LYNOTT
INTRO
A5
B5
D5
A5
* PLAY 4x
P.M.
(GUITAR)
* TIE INTO BEAT 1 ON REPEAT
VERSE
A5
C#-7
D
F#7sus4
C#-7
1. Guess who just got back___ to-day.___ Them wild-eyed_ boys___ that had been a-way.___
2.,3. See additional lyrics
F#7sus4
B-7
E9sus4
A5
Have-n't changed,_ had-n't much to say, but man, I still think them_ cats are cra-zy.
C#-7
D
F
C#-7
They were ask-in' if you were a-round,___ how you was,___ where you could___ be found.___
F#7sus4
B-7
E9sus4
Told them you were liv-in' down-town, driv-in' all the old men cra - zy. The
CHORUS
A5
B5
D5
A5
boys_ are back in town.___ The boys_ are back in town.___
Spoken: I said the
B5
D5
To Coda A5
boys___ are back in town.___ The boys___ are back in town.___ The
B5
D5
boys_ are back in town.___ The boys_ are back in town.___ The boys___ are back in { town.___ * The } boys___
* Sung at once
INTERLUDE
N.C. (A)
(A/B)
(Aadd9/C#)
(GTRS.)
___ are back in town.___

Additional Lyrics

2. You know that chick that used to dance a lot?
Every night she'd be on the floor shakin' what she got.
Man, when I tell you she was cool, she was red hot.
I mean she was steamin'.
And that time over at Johnny's place,
Well, this chick got up and she slapped Johnny's face.
Man, we just fell about the place.
If that chick don't want to know, forget her.

3. Friday night they'll be dressed to kill
Down at Dino's Bar and Grill.
The drink will flow and blood will spill,
And if the boys wanna fight, you better let 'em.
That jukebox in the corner blasting out my favorite song.
The nights are getting warmer, it won't be long.
Won't be long till summer comes,
Now that the boys are here again.

42
(FAST)
BRISTOL STOMP
—KAL MANN/DAVE APPELL
INTRO
G E- C 1. D 2. D
(The
CHORUS
G E- C D
kids in Bris-tol are sharp as a pis - tol when they do the Bris-tol Stomp.
G E- C D
Real-ly some-thin' when the joint is jump-in' when they do the Bris - tol Stomp.) Whoa._
VERSE
G E- C D
1.,3. The sounds are spin - nin' ev - 'ry Fri - day night.
2.,4. It start-ed in Bris - tol at a D. J. hop;
G E- C D
They dance the great - est, and they do it right.
they hol-ler and whis - tle, nev - er wan - na stop.
G E- C D
But here's the lat - est; it's a cra - zy sight to
We po-ny and twist - ed and we rocked with Dad - dy
(The
CHORUS
G E- C
see.
G.
Whoa,
kids in Bris-tol are sharp as a pis - tol when they do the

D
G
E-
C
4th x, To
whoa.
Ha,
Bris - tol Stomp.
Real - ly some - thin' when the joint is jump - in' when they do the
1.
D
2.
D
BRIDGE
C
oh.
Whoa.
ah.
It's got that groov - y beat
Bris - tol Stomp.)
Bris - tol Stomp.)
G
that makes you stomp your feet.
Come on get in line,
C
gon - na feel fine.
And once you dance with me,
you'll fall in
D.S. AL
(TAKE REPEAT)
D
C#-
D
C#-
D
love, you'll see, the Bris - tol Stomp will make you mine all mine.
OUTRO - CHORUS
W/ LEAD VOC. AD LIB.
D
G
E-
Bris - tol Stomp.)
(The kids in Bris - tol are sharp as a pis - tol
C
D
G
when they do the Bris - tol Stomp.
Real - ly some - thin' when the
E-
C
D
REPEAT AND FADE
joint is jump - in' when they do the Bris - tol Stomp.)
(The

44
(MED. ROCK)
BROWN EYED GIRL
—VAN MORRISON
INTRO
G C G D
(GUITAR)
VERSE
G C G
Hey where did we go? Days when the rains
Now, what-ev - er hap - pened to Tues - day and so
So hard to find my way now that I'm all
D7 G C
came? Down in the hol - low,
slow? Go - in' down the old mine with a
on my own. I saw you just the oth - er day;
G D7 G
play-in' a new game. Laugh-in' and a -
tran - sis - tor ra - di-o. Stand-in' in the
My, how you have grown. Cast my mem-'ry back
C G D7
run-nin', hey, hey, skip-pin' and a - jump-in',
sun-light laugh - in', hid-in' 'hind a rain-bow's wall.
there, Lord. Some - times I'm o - ver-come think-in' 'bout
G C G
in the mist - y morn - in' fog with our
Slip-pin' and a slid - in' all a-long the
mak-in' love in the green grass be - hind the
D7 C D7
hearts a thump - in' and you,
wa - ter - fall with you,
sta - di - um with you,
my brown - eyed girl.

G
(GTR.)
E-
C
You, my
D7
G
1.
D7
brown - eyed girl.
2.,3.
D7
TO
Do you re - mem - ber when
we used to sing?
CHORUS
G
C
G
Sha, la, la, la, la, la, la, la, la, la, la, te, da.
D7
G
C
Sha, la, la, la, la, la, la, la,
INTERLUDE
G
D7
G
la, la, la, te, da,
la, te, da.
(GUITAR)
N.C.(G)
(BASS)
BASS INTERLUDE
N.C.(G)
(C)
(G)
(D)
D.S. AL
OUTRO-CHORUS
REPEAT AND FADE
(W/ LEAD VOC. AD LIB.)
G
C
G
D7
Sha, la la, la, la, la, la, la, la, la, la, te, da.

(MED.)
CALIFORNIA GIRLS
-BRIAN WILSON/MIKE LOVE
INTRO
N.C.(E/B) (B)
(ORGAN & GUITARS)
(E/B) (B)
(ORGAN & GTRS. CONT. SIM.)
(HORNS)
(E/B) (B) (D/A) (A)
(ORGAN & GTRS.)
RIT.
(HORNS)
FASTER
B (ORGAN)
(BASS (8VB))
VERSE
B
(ORGAN & BASS CONT. SIM.)
Well, East Coast girls are hip, I real - ly dig
West Coast has the sun - shine, and the
A/B
those styles they wear. And the South - ern girls with the
girls all get so tan. I dig a French bi - ki - ni on Ha -
E
way they talk, they knock me out when I'm down there. The
wai - ian is - land dolls by a palm tree in the sand. I've
F#
B
Mid - west farm - er's daugh - ters real - ly
been all a - round this great big world, and I've

A/B
E
make you feel al - right. And the North - ern girls with the
seen all kinds of girls. Yeah, but I could-n't wait to get
F#
way they kiss, they keep their boy - friends warm at night.
back in the States, back to the cut-est girls in the world.
I
CHORUS
B
C#-
A
wish they all could be Cal - i - for - nia, I wish they all could be
B-
G
A-
Cal - i - for - nia, I wish they all could be Cal - i - for - nia girls.
1.
B
2.
B
The
OUTRO
N.C.
(KEYS)
B
I wish they all could be
C#-
REPEAT AND FADE
Cal - i - for - nia, I wish they all could be Cal - i - for - nia, I

(MED.)
CAN'T TAKE MY EYES OFF OF YOU
—BOB CREWE/ BOB GAUDIO
INTRO
F#7/E
F#-7b5/E
E
(GTR. & HORNS)
(HORNS)
You're just too
VERSE
E
Emaj7
good to be true, can't take my eyes off of you.
way that I stare, there's noth-ing else to com-pare.
E7
You'd be like heav-en to touch, I wan-na
The sight of you leaves me weak, there are no
A
A-6
hold you so much. At long last love has ar-rived, and I thank
words left to speak. But if you feel like I feel, please let me
God I'm a-live.
know that it's real.
You're just too good to be true, can't take my
1.
2.
eyes off of you. Par-don the eyes off of you.
INTERLUDE
F#-7
B7
(HORNS)

2.
CHORUS
C#7#9 F#-9 B13 B13(b9)
I love you, ba - by, and if it's quite all right, I need you,
G#-7 C#9sus4 C#7#9 F#-7 B9sus4 B7b9
ba - by, to warm the lone-ly night. I love you, ba - by, trust in me when I
Emaj7 C#7#9 F#-9 B13 B13(b9)
say: Oh, pret-ty ba - by, don't bring me down, I pray. Oh, pret-ty
G#-7 TO ⊕ C#9sus4 C#7#9 F#-7
ba - by, now that I've found you, stay, and let me love you, ba - by. Let me
D9
VERSE
G
love you. You're just too good to be true, can't take my
Gmaj7 G7
eyes off of you. You'd be like heav-en to touch, I wan-na
C C-6 G
hold you so much. At long last love has ar-rived, and I thank God I'm a-live.
A7/G A-7b5/G G
D.S. AL ⊕
(TAKE 2nd ENDING)
You're just too good to be true, can't take my eyes off of you.
C#9sus4 C#7#9 F#-7 B9sus4 B7(b9) Emaj7 C#7#9
FADE OUT
found you, stay, oh, pret-ty ba - by, trust in me when I say: Oh, pret-ty

(MED.)

CELEBRATE

—Alan Gordon/Garry Bonner

VERSE
A
A/G
Slip-pin' a - way,
sit-tin' on a pil - low,
Sat - in and lace,
is - n't it a pi - ty,

F#-
F
wait-in' for night
to fall.
did - n't find time
to call.

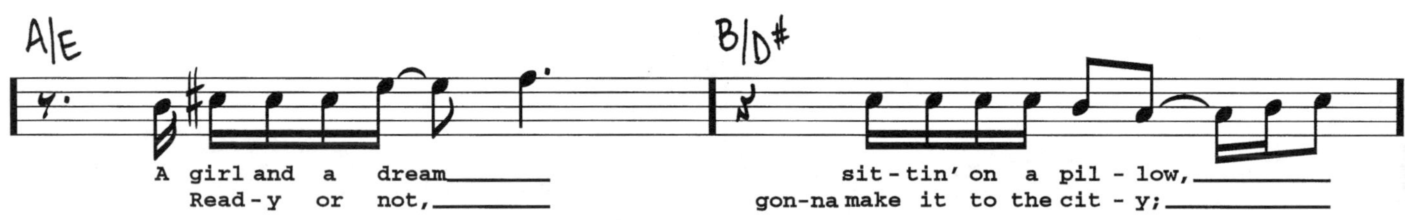
A/E
B/D#
A girl and a dream
sit-tin' on a pil - low,
Read - y or not,
gon-na make it to the cit - y;

D
A
this is the night to go to the ce - leb - ri - ty ball.
This is the night to go to the ce - leb - ri - ty ball.

BRIDGE

A
G
Dress up to - night; why be lone - ly?

A
G
You'll stay at home and you'll be a - lone, so why be lone - ly?

VERSE
A
A/G
Sit-tin' a-lone,
sit-tin' on a pil-low,
F#-
F
wait-in' to climb the walls.
A/E
B/D#
May-be to-night,
de-pend-ing how your dream goes,
D
A
she'll o-pen her eyes when she goes to the cel-e-bri-ty ball.
BRIDGE
A
G
Dress up to-night; why be lone-ly?
A
G
You'll stay at home and you'll be a-lone, so why be lone-ly?
OUTRO-CHORUS
A
G
(Cel-e-brate, cel-e-brate, dance to the mu-sic!)
A
G
REPEAT AND FADE
Cel-e-brate, cel-e-brate, dance to the mu-sic!

CHANGE THE WORLD
(MED.)
–WAYNE KIRKPATRICK/GORDON KENNEDY/TOMMY SIMS
INTRO
E F#-7 G F#-7 E
(GUITAR 1)
E F#-7 G F#-7 B7sus4
(GUITAR 2)
(GTR. 1 CONT. SIM.)
VERSE
E A/E E7(NO 3rd) A/E E
If I could reach the stars, pull one down for you,
If I could be king, even for a day,
A/E E7(NO 3rd) A/E E
shine it on my heart so you could see the truth,
I'd take you as my queen, I'd have it no other way.
A D/A A7(NO 3rd)
then this love I have inside
And our love would rule in this
D/A A E A/E E(NO 3rd)
is ev'rything it seems. But for now I find
kingdom we have made. 'Til then I'd be a fool
A/E G#7
it's only in my dreams
wishing for the day
that I can
CHORUS
F#-7 G#7 C#-7 D#-7b5 G#7
change the world. I will / would / would be the sunlight in your

C#-7 D#-7b5 G#7 C#-7 C-7 B-7
u - ni - verse. You would think my love was real - ly some - thing good, ba - by,
A E/G# TO 1. G07 F#-11
if I could change the world.
INTERLUDE
E F#-7 G F#-7 E
(GTR. 2)
2. G07 F#-11 E A7sus4 E/G# G07 F#-11
change the world, ba - by, if I could change
GUITAR SOLO
E F#-7 G F#-7 E
the world.
F#-7 G F#-7 G#7 D.S. AL
I could
G07 F#-11 A E/G#
change the world, ba - by, if I could
G07 F#-11 A E/G# G07
change the world, ba - by, if I could change
G6/9 E F#-7 G
the world.
(GTR.)
F#-7 E

(MED. FAST)
CHINA GROVE
—TOM JOHNSTON
INTRO
E
1., 2., 3.
D C#– A E
4.
D C#– (GUITAR) A
VERSE
E
When the sun comes up on a
preach-er and the teach-er, Lord,
D C#– A E
sleep-y lit-tle town down a-round San An-tone and the
they're a cau-tion, they are the talk of the town. When the
D C#– A
folks are ris-ing for an-oth-er day 'round a-bout their homes.
gos-sip gets to fly-in' and they ain't ly-in' when the sun go fall-in' down.
E
PRE-CHORUS
C#– B E/B B
The peo-ple of the town are strange and they're
They say that the father's in-sane and
3rd time, gtr. solo continues
A7 A#7 B7 C7 N.C.
proud of where they came. Well, you're
dear Mis-ses Per-kin's a game. We're talk-
Solo ends
CHORUS
E D A/C# E
talk-ing
-ing
Talk-ing
'bout Chi-na Grove, whoa, ho, ho.
D A/C# E D5 A/C# E5
(Whoa, ho.) Chi-na Grove.
TO

55
BRIDGE
1.
N.C.
2.
N.C.
G#-
B
C#-
Well, the
But ev - 'ry day___ there's a
(Oo,
new thing_ com-in', the ways of an or-i-en-tal view._ The
oo, oo.
F#-7
C#-
F#
F#sus4
sher-iff and his bud-dies with their sam-ur-ai swords,_ you can e-ven hear the mu -
Oo.
- sic at___ night.____ And
though it's a part of the Lone Star State,_ peo-ple don't seem_ to care._
Oo, oo,
A
D/A
They just keep on look - ing to the East._
oo.)
C
D
E
(GTR.)
INTERLUDE
(GTR. W/ INTRO RIFF)
8
PLAY 4X, THEN D.S. AL
GUITAR SOLO
G/E
D
C#-
N.C.

(MED.)
COME ON EILEEN
—KEVIN ROWLAND/JAMES PATTERSON/KEVIN ADAMS
INTRO
N.C. (C)
(STRINGS)
F C F7 Bb Bb6 F
(BS. CONT. RHY. SIM.)
8VB (BASS)
1. Csus4 C Csus2 C
2. Csus4 C Csus2 C
C E- F
(Come on_ Ei-leen.)
C G
VERSE
C E-
Poor old John-ny Ray___ sound-ed
These peo-ple 'round here___ wear beat-en-
F C G
sad up-on___ the ra-di-o,___ moved a mil-lion hearts in mon-o.
down eyes sunk in smoke-dried face, so re-signed to what their fate is, but
1st X ONLY
C E- F C G
Our moth-ers cried,___ sang a-long; who'd blame_them?
C E- F
You're grown, (You've grown up.) so grown.____ (So grown up.) Now I must say more than ev-er:
not us, (No, nev-er.) no, not us. (No, nev-er.) We are far too young and clev-er.
C G C E- F
(Come on___ Ei-leen.) Too ra, loo ra, too ra, loo rye_ aye. And we can
(Re-mem-ber.) Too ra, loo ra, too ra, loo rye_ aye. Ei-leen, I'll

CHORUS
C G D
sing just like our fa - thers.
hum this tune for-ev - er.
Come on Ei - leen, oh, I
Come on Ei - leen, oh, I
A E- G A
swear (Well he means...) at this mo - ment you mean ev - 'ry - thing. With
swear, (Well he means...) ah, come on, let's take off ev - 'ry - thing. That
D A E- TO
you in that dress, my thoughts I con - fess verge on dirt - y, ah, come on
pret - ty red dress, Ei - leen, (Tell him yes.) ah, come on, let's, ah, come on
G A N.C. (A) D.S. AL (NO REPEAT)
Ei - leen.
(BANJO)
G A D A E-
Ei - leen. That pret - ty red dress, Ei - leen, (Tell him yes.) ah, come on, let's, ah, come on,
G A RIT. D D F#-
1st X, SLOWLY
2nd & 3rd XS, GRAD. ACCEL.
W/ LEAD VOC. AD LIB.
Ei - leen.
Come on Ei - leen, too loo rye aye, come on Ei -
G D A PLAY 3X
- leen, too loo rye aye, too ra. Too ra, too loo ra.
OUTRO - CHORUS
TEMPO I
D A E- G A
Come on Ei - leen, oh, I swear (Well he means...) at this mo - ment you mean ev - 'ry - thing. With
REPEAT AND FADE
D A E- G A
you in that dress, my thoughts I con - fess verge on dirt - y, ah, come on Ei - leen.

(MED.)

COME TOGETHER

-JOHN LENNON/PAUL McCARTNEY

INTRO
D-7
(BASS)
VERSE
D-7
Here come old flat-top, he come

groov - ing up slow-ly, he got
Joo Joo eye-ball, he one
ho - ly roll-er, he got

A7
G7 N.C.
hair down to his knee._
Got to be a jok - er, he just

INTERLUDE
D-7
do what he please._
(BASS)

VERSE
D-7
He wear no shoe-shine, he got toe - jam foot-ball, he got
He bag pro - duc - tion, he got wal - rus gum-boot, he got
He roll - er coast - er, he got ear - ly warn-ing, he got

mon - key fin - ger, he shoot Co - ca Co - la, he say,
O - no side-board, he one spi - nal crack - er, he got
mud - dy wa - ter, he one Mo - jo fil - ter, he say,

A7
"I know you, you know me."
feet down be - low his knee.
"One and one and one is three."
G7 N.C.
One thing I can tell you is you got to be free.
Hold you in his arm - chair, you can feel his dis - ease.
Got to be good - look - ing 'cause he's so hard to see.
Come to-geth -
CHORUS
B5
B5/A
G5
A5
N.C.
- er, right now, o - ver me.
INTERLUDE
D-7
1.
To
2.
KEYBOARD SOLO
D-7
PLAY 4 X
(KEYS)
GUITAR SOLO
A7
8VA
(GUITARS)
8VA
D-7
D.S. AL
(TAKE 1st ENDING)
BASS W/ INTRO RIFF
OUTRO-GUITAR SOLO
D-7
GTR. CONT. SIM.
REPEAT AND FADE
Come to-geth - er, Yeah!

(MED. SHUFFLE)

CRAZY LITTLE THING CALLED LOVE

-FREDDIE MERCURY

E
A
N.C.
3. I've got-ta be cool,
VERSE
2nd x, A CAPELLA
D
G
C
G
re-lax, get hip, get on my tracks. Take a
D
G
C
G
back seat, hitch-hike, take a long ride on my mo-tor bike un-til I'm
D
Bb
C
D
TO 1
N.C.
read-y. Cra-zy lit-tle thing called love.
GUITAR SOLO
Bb
D
Bb
E
A
F
N.C.
E
A
N.C.
D.S. AL 1
(GTR.)
4. I've got-ta be cool,
1
D.SS. AL 2
5. This thing
2
Bb
C
D
REPEAT AND FADE
Cra-zy lit-tle thing called love.

62
DA DOO RON RON
(WHEN HE WALKED ME HOME)
(MED.)
-ELLIE GREENWICH/JEFF BARRY/PHIL SPECTOR
INTRO
(PIANO)
(PNO. CONT.)
VERSE
I met him on a Mon-day and my heart stood still. Da doo ron ron ron, da doo ron ron. Some-bod-y told me that his name was Bill. Da doo ron ron ron, da doo ron ron.
Knew what he was do-in' when he caught my eye. Da doo ron ron ron, da doo ron ron. He looked so qui-et but my, oh my. Da doo ron ron ron, da doo ron ron.
Picked me up at sev-en and he looked so fine. Da doo ron ron ron, da doo ron ron. Some-day soon I'm gon-na make him mine. Da doo ron ron ron, da doo ron ron.
CHORUS
Yes, my heart stood still. Yes, his name was Bill.
Yes, he caught my eye. Yes, my, oh my.
Yes, he looked so fine. Yes, I'll make him mine.
And when he walked me home, da doo ron ron ron, da doo ron ron.
TO ⊕
SAX SOLO
2nd X, D.S. AL ⊕
OUTRO
REPEAT AND FADE
Yeah, yeah, yeah, yeah. Yeah, yeah.
Yeah, yeah, yeah, yeah.

ELEANOR RIGBY
(MED.)
-JOHN LENNON/PAUL McCARTNEY
INTRO-CHORUS
C
E-
(STRINGS)
Ah, look at all the lone-ly peo - ple.
VERSE
E-
El - ea-nor Rig - by picks up the rice in the church where a wed - ding has been
Fa-ther Mc - Ken - zie, writ-ing the words of a ser - mon that no one will hear
El - ea-nor Rig - by died in the church and was bur - ied a - long with her name
C
E-
Lives in a dream. Waits at the win - dow,
No one comes near. Look at him work - ing,
No-bod - y came. Fa-ther Mc - Ken - zie,
E-/D
C
wear-ing a face that she keeps in a jar by the door.
darn-ing his socks in the night when there's no - bod - y there.
wip-ing the dirt from his hands as he walks from the grave.
E-
CHORUS
E-7
E-6
Who is it for?
What does he care?
No one was saved.
All the lone - ly peo - ple, where do
Cmaj7/E
E-
E-7
E-6
they all come from?
All the lone - ly peo - ple, where do
Cmaj7/E
TO
1.
E-
2.
E-
D.C. AL
(TAKE REPEAT
they all be - long?
E-

(MED.)
DANCING QUEEN
– BENNY ANDERSSON/BJORN ULVAEUS/STIG ANDERSON
A D/A A E/A D/A
(Oh.)
A E/G# D/F# A/E
Oo, oo.
CHORUS
E
You can dance,
C#/E# F#– B/D#
you can jive, having the time of your life. Oo,
Dadd9 B–11 D/E A
see that girl, watch that scene, dig-gin' the danc-ing queen.
D/A A D/A A D/A
(PIANO)
(Oh.)
VERSE
A D/A
Fri-day night and the lights are low.
An-y-bod-y can be that guy.
You're a teas-er, you turn 'em on,
A F#–
Look-ing out for a place to go
Night is young and the mu-sic's high.
leave 'em burn-ing and then you're gone.
E7 A/E E7 A/E
where they play the right mu-sic. Get-ting in the swing, you come to
With a bit of rock mu-sic, ev-'ry-thing is fine.
Look-ing out for an-oth-er; an-y-one will do. You're in the

E F#-
1. E F#-
2. E F#-
look for a king.
mood for a dance.
CHORUS
And when you
B-
E
A
get the chance,
you are the dancing queen,
D/A
A
E/A D/A
young and sweet, only seventeen.
(PIANO)
A
D/A
A
E/G# D/F# A/E
Dancing queen, feel the beat from the tambourine, oh, yeah.
E
C#/E#
F#-
B/D#
You can dance you can jive, having the time of your life.
Oo,
D
B-11
A
D/A
TO ⊕
see that girl, watch that scene, diggin' the dancing queen.
(Oh.)
A
D/A
A
(PIANO)
D/A
A
D/A
D.S. AL ⊕
(TAKE 2nd ENDING)
⊕ A
D/A
A
Diggin' the dancing queen.
(Oh.)
D/A
A
D/A
D
See that girl,
B-11
D/E
A
watch that scene, diggin' the dancing queen.

DANIEL
(MED.)
–ELTON JOHN / BERNIE TAUPIN
INTRO
HALF-TIME FEEL
C
F
(FLUTE)
G
C F/C C F/C
VERSE
C
D-7
1.,4.Dan - iel is trav - 'ling to - night on a plane.
2. They say Spain is pret - ty, 'though I've nev - er been.
3. Instrumental
G
I can see the red tail - lights
Well, Dan - iel says it's the best place he's
E7
A-
G
F
head-in' for Spain. Oh, and I can see Dan -
ev - er seen. Oh, and he should know;
G
A-
G
- iel wav - ing good - bye. God, it looks
he's been there e - nough. Lord, I
F
G
F/G
4th X, TO
like Dan - iel. Must be the clouds in my eyes.
miss Dan - iel. Oh, I miss him so
1. INTERLUDE
C
G
(FLUTE)

2., 3.

CHORUS

C F

much. Oh,____ Dan - iel,__ my broth - er, you are

Instrumental ends

C F

old-er__ than me.___ Do you__ still feel the pain__ of the scars__

C G/B A-

____ that__ won't heal?__ Your eyes__ have died,____ but

G F Ab C

you see more__ than I.____ Dan - iel, you're a star

A7 D-7 1. G D.S. 2. G D.S. AL ⊕

in the face__ of the sky.____ ___

⊕

C F

___ Oh God,____ it looks like Dan - iel.

G F/G

Must be___ the clouds____ in__ my eyes.__

OUTRO

C F

(FLUTE)

G C F/C C

DAYDREAM

–JOHN SEBASTIAN

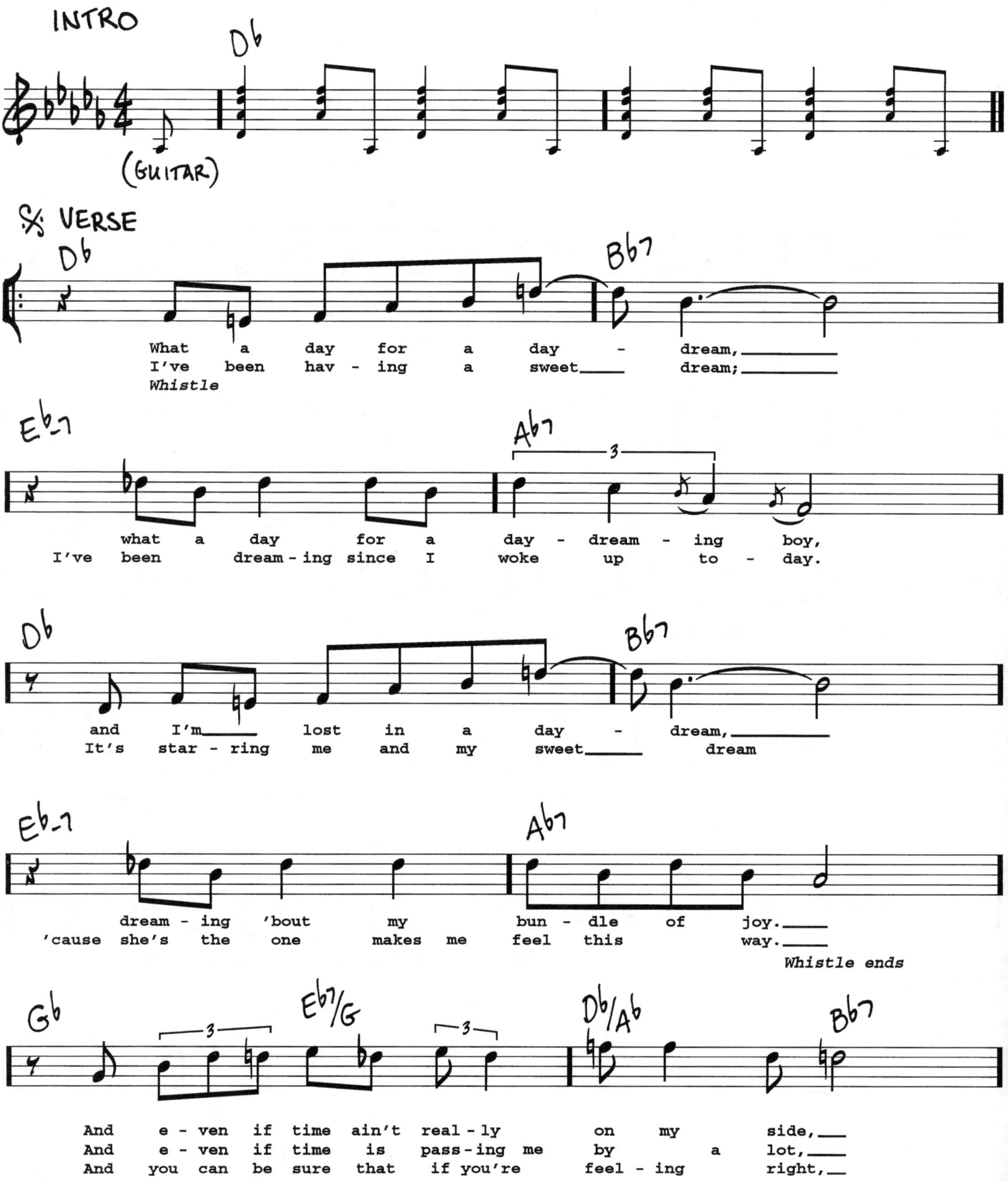

INTRO

D♭

(GUITAR)

𝄋 VERSE

D♭ B♭7

What a day for a day - dream,
I've been hav - ing a sweet dream;
Whistle

E♭-7 A♭7

what a day for a day - dream - ing boy,
I've been dream - ing since I woke up to - day.

D♭ B♭7

and I'm lost in a day - dream,
It's star - ring me and my sweet dream

E♭-7 A♭7

dream - ing 'bout my bun - dle of joy.
'cause she's the one makes me feel this way.
Whistle ends

G♭ E♭7/G D♭/A♭ B♭7

And e - ven if time ain't real - ly on my side,
And e - ven if time is pass - ing me by a lot,
And you can be sure that if you're feel - ing right,

Gb
Eb7/G
Db
Bb7
it's one of those days for tak-ing a walk out - side.
I could-n't care less a-bout the dues you say I got.
a day-dream will last till long in-to the night.
Gb
Eb7/G
Db
Bb7
To
I'm blow-ing the day to take a walk in the sun
To-mor-row I'll pay the dues for drop-ping my load,
To-mor-row at break-fast you may pick up your ears,
Ab
Db/Ab
1. Ab7
Db/Ab
Ab
and fall on my face on some-bod-y's new-mowed lawn.
a pie in the face for be-ing a
2. Ab7
Db/Ab
D.S. AL
Ab
Ab
Db/Ab
sleep-y bull toad.
VERSE
or you may be day-dream-ing for a
Ab7
Db/Ab
Ab
Db
Bb7
thou-sand years.
What a day for a day - dream,
Eb-7
Ab7
Db
cus-tom-made for a day-dream-ing boy,
and I'm lost in a day -
Bb7
Eb-7
Ab7
- dream,
dream-ing 'bout my bun-dle of joy.
OUTRO
REPEAT AND FADE
Gb
Eb7/G
Db
Bb7
Gb
Eb7/G
Db
Bb7
(WHISTLE)

DON'T BE CRUEL
(TO A HEART THAT'S TRUE)

—OTIS BLACKWELL/ELVIS PRESLEY

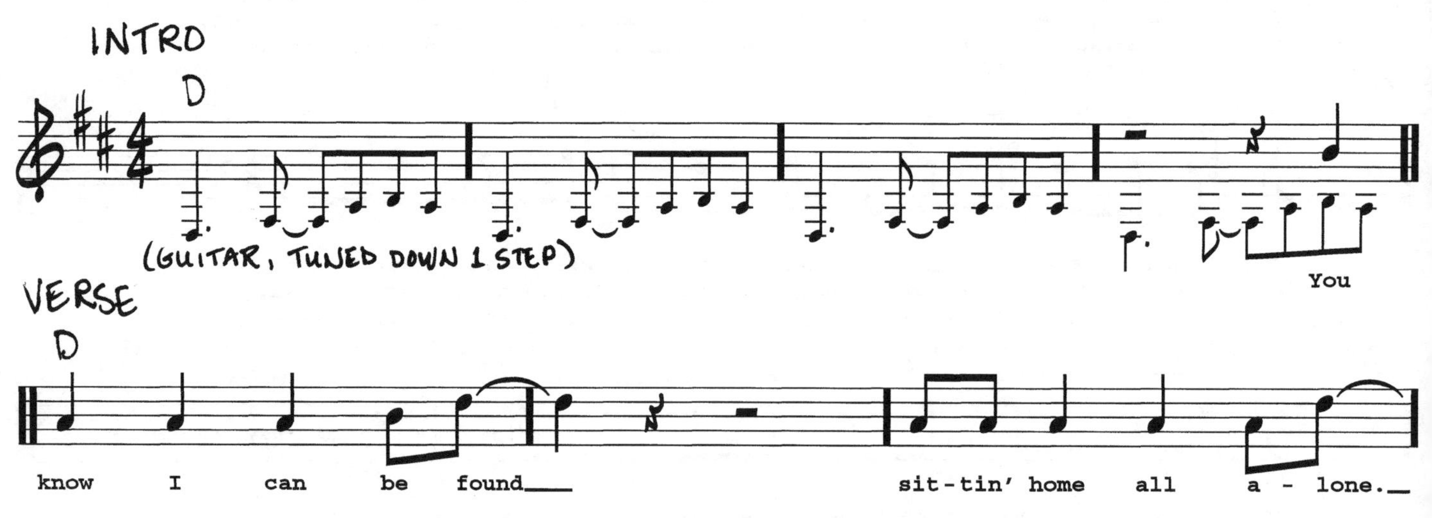

G
let's for - get my past. The
on o - ver here and love me. You
Then you'll know you'll have me, and I'll
D
fu - ture looks bright a - head.
know what I want you to say. Don't be
know that I'll have you.
CHORUS
E-
A
D
cruel to a heart that's true. 1.,3.I don't
2.Why
BRIDGE
G
A
G
want no oth - er love. Ba - by, it's just
should we be a - part? I real - ly love you, ba -
A
D
1.,2.
3.
N.C.
you I'm think-in' of. Don't Don't be
- by, cross my heart. A, let's a
CHORUS
E-
A
D
1.
cruel to a heart that's true. Don't be
2.
OUTRO
G
A
I don't want no oth - er love.
G
A
D
D 6 9
(PNO & BASS)
Ba - by, it's just you I'm think-ing of.
(GTR.)

(MED. SLOW EVEN 8THS)
DON'T KNOW WHY
–JESSE HARRIS
INTRO
Bbmaj7 Bb7 Ebmaj7 D7#5 G-7 C7 F7sus4
(MELODY)
I
A
Bbmaj7 Bb7 Ebmaj7 D7#5 G-7 C7
wait-ed till I saw the sun. I don't know why I
When I saw the break of day, I wished that I could
F7sus4 Bb Bbmaj7 Bb7 Ebmaj7 D7#5
did-n't come. I left you by the house of fun.
fly a - way 'stead of kneel - ing in the sand
1. G-7 C7 F7sus4 Bb G-7 C7
I don't know why I did-n't come, I don't know why I did -
F7sus4 Bb 2. G-7 C7 F7sus4 Bb
n't come. catch-ing tear - drops in my hand. My
B
G-7 C7 F7
heart is drenched in wine,
G-7 C7
but you'll be on my mind

F7 F7/Eb Bb/D F7/C
A Bbmaj7 Bb7
for - ev - er.
Out a - cross the end - less sea, I would die in ec - sta - sy.
Some-thing had to make you run. I don't know why I did - n't come. I
Ebmaj7 D7#5 G-7 C7 F7sus4 Bb
Bbmaj7 Bb7 Ebmaj7 D7#5 G-7 C7 F7sus4 Bb
But I'll be a bag of bones driv-ing down the road a-lone. My
feel as emp - ty as a drum.
AFTER SOLOS, D.S. AL
(TAKE REPEAT)
G-7 C7 F7sus4 Bb G-7 C7
I don't know why I did-n't come, I don't know why I
F7sus4 Bb G-7 C7 F7sus4 Bb
did-n't come. I don't know why I did-n't come.

DREAM WEAVER

— GARY WRIGHT

INTRO

𝄋 VERSE

C#-7(#4) C#- B A

I've just closed my eyes a-gain,
Fly me high through the star-ry skies
Though the dawn may be com-ing soon,

C#- B A

climbed a-board the dream weav-er train.
or may-be to an as-tral plane.
there still may be some time.

E B A

Driv-er, take a-way my wor-ries of to-day
Cross the high-ways of fan-ta-sy,
Fly me a-way to the bright side of the moon

E B TO ⊕ A B/A A B/A

and leave to-mor-row be-hind.
help me to for-get to-day's pain.
and meet me on the oth-er
Ooh,

CHORUS

E E7/G# A E E7/G# A

dream weav-er, I be-lieve you can get me through the night.

E E7/G# A E E7/G# A E E7/G# A

Ooh, dream weav-er,

D.S. AL ⊕
E E7/G# A
1. E E7/G# A B
2. E E7/G# A B
I be - lieve_ we can reach_the morn - ing light._____
A B/A A B/A A B/A A B/A
side._____
Ooh,_
CHORUS
E E7/G# A E E7/G# A
dream_____ weav - er,_
I be - lieve_ you can get_ me through_ the night._
E E7/G# A E E7/G# A E E7/G# A
Ooh,_ dream_____ weav - er,_
E E7/G# A E E7/G# A
I be - lieve_ we can reach_ the morn - ing light._____
E E7/G# A E E7/G# A E E7/G# A
Dream___ weav - er,__
E E7/G# A E E7/G# A E E7/G# A A/B
dream_____ weav - er._
OUTRO
A B/A A B/A
1. A B/A A B/A
2. RIT.
C#-7(#4)

(FAST)

DREAMING

–DEBORAH HARRY / CHRIS STEIN

INTRO
D
G
(GUITAR)

D
G

VERSE

D
G
When I met you in the res - tau - rant,
I don't want to live on char - i - ty;
I sit by and watch the riv - er flow.

D
G
you could tell I was no deb - u - tante.
pleas - ure's real or is it fan - ta - sy?
I sit by and watch the traf - fic go.
I -

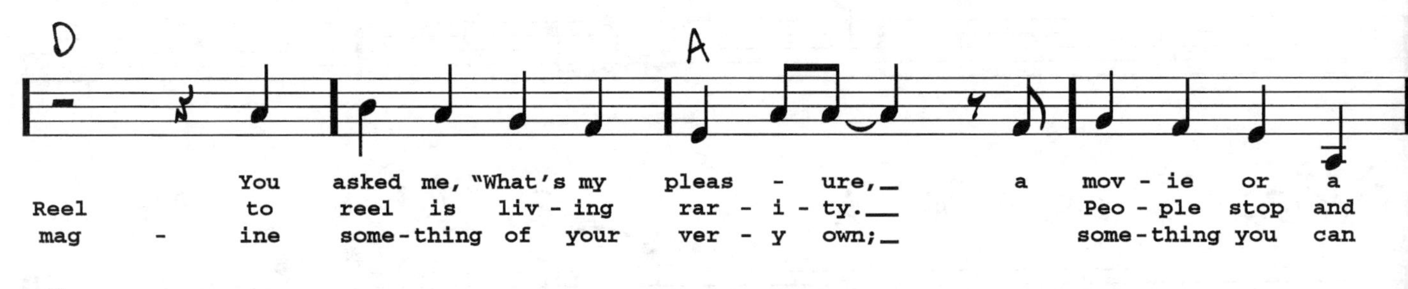
D
A
You asked me, "What's my pleas - ure, a mov - ie or a
Reel to reel is liv - ing rar - i - ty. Peo - ple stop and
mag - ine some-thing of your ver - y own; some-thing you can

E-
G
A
meas - ure?". I'll have a cup of tea and tell you of my
stare at me, we just walk on by; we just keep on
have and hold. I'll build a road of gold just to have some

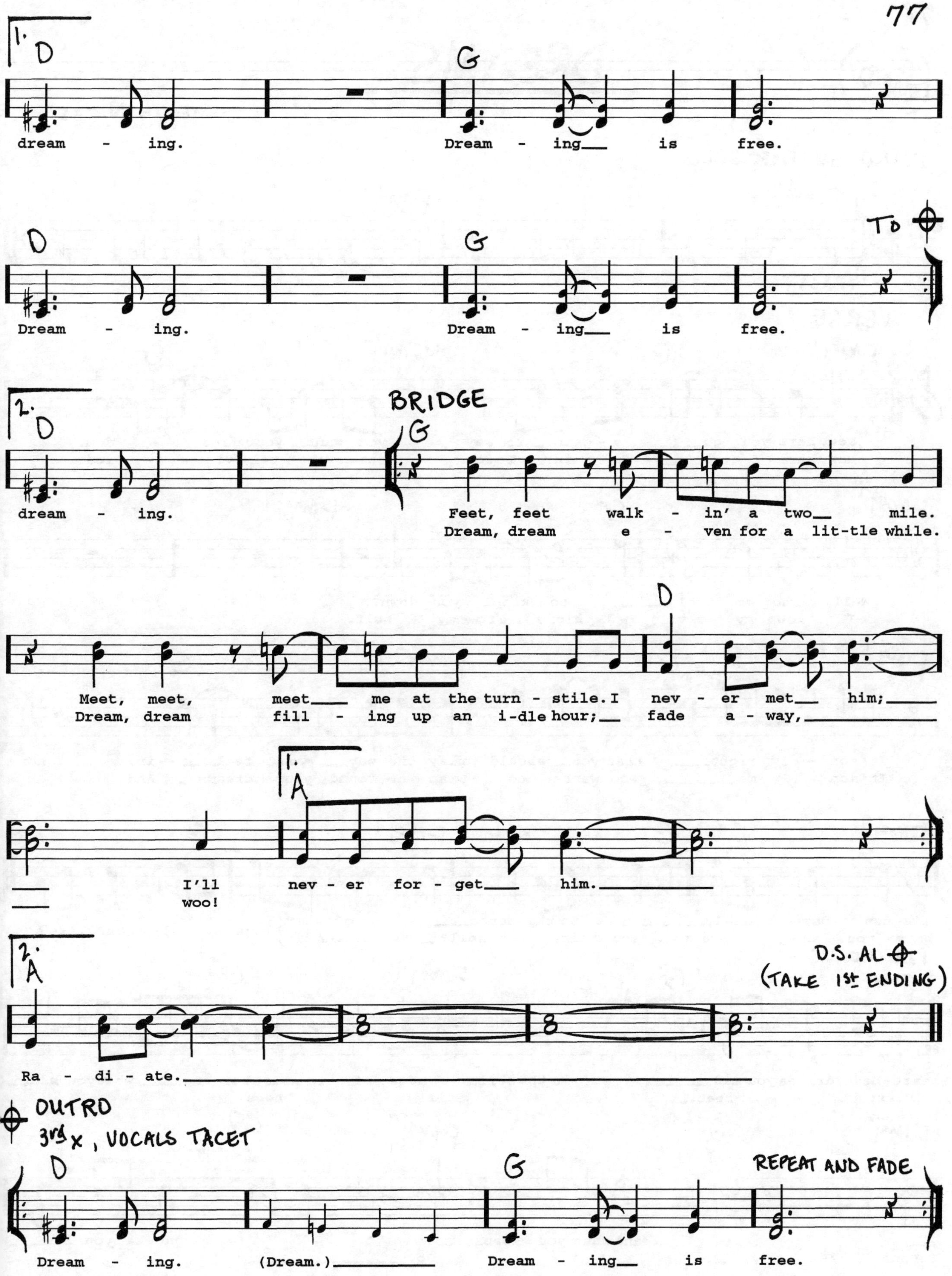

1. D G

dream - ing. Dream - ing is free.

D G TO ⊕

Dream - ing. Dream - ing is free.

2. D BRIDGE G

dream - ing. Feet, feet walk - in' a two mile.
Dream, dream e - ven for a lit-tle while.

D

Meet, meet, meet me at the turn - stile. I nev - er met him;
Dream, dream fill - ing up an i-dle hour; fade a - way,

1. A

I'll nev - er for - get him.
woo!

(MED.)
DREAMS
— STEVIE NICKS
INTRO-GUITAR SOLO
Fmaj7 G Fmaj7 G
(BASS)
VERSE
Fmaj7 G Fmaj7 G
Now, here you go___ a - gain._ You say you want_ your free - dom.
Now, here I go___ a - gain._ I see the crys - tal vi - sions.
Fmaj7 G Fmaj7 G
Well, who am I___ to keep_ you down?
I keep my vi - sions to my - self.
Fmaj7 G Fmaj7 G
It's on - ly right___ that you_ should play the way_ you feel___ it. But
It's on - ly me___ who wants to wrap a - round_ your dreams._ And
Fmaj7 G Fmaj7 G
lis-ten care - ful-ly___ to the sound___ of your
have you an-y dreams_ you'd like to sell?_ Dreams of
lone - li-ness, like a
PRE-CHORUS
Fmaj7 G7 Fmaj9 G7
heart-beat, drives you mad___ in the still - ness of re-mem-ber-ing___ what you had__
(Heart - beat.__ Still - ness.__
Fmaj7 G7 Fmaj9 G7
and what you lost___ and what you had__
Lone - ly.__ Oo.___ Oo._

Fmaj7
G7
Fmaj9
G7
and what you lost.
Ah.)
Oh,
CHORUS
Fmaj7
G6sus2/4
thun - der on - ly hap - pens when it's rain - ing.
Play - ers on - ly love you when they're play - ing.
Say,
wom - en, they will come and they will go.
When the rain wash - es you clean, you'll know.
TO
1.
You'll
GUITAR SOLO
G
know.
A-
2.
D.S. AL
Oh,
You'll know.
You will
know.
Oh,
you'll know.
Fmaj#11

(MED.)
DUST IN THE WIND
-KERRY LIVGREN
INTRO
(GUITAR)
C CMaj7 Cadd9 C Asus2 Asus4
A- Asus2 Cadd9 C CMaj7 Cadd9
A- Asus2 Asus4 A- G/B
VERSE
C G/B A-
I close my eyes,
Same old song,
don't hang on,
G D-7 A- G/B C G/B
on - ly for a mo - ment, and the mo - ment's gone. All my
just a drop of wa - ter in an end - less sea. All we
noth - ing lasts for - ev - er but the earth and sky. It slips a -
A- G D-7 A-
dreams pass be - fore my eyes, a cu - ri - os - i - ty.
do crum - bles to the ground though we re - fuse to see.
way and all your mon - ey won't an - oth - er min - ute buy.
CHORUS
D/F# G A- A-/G TO D/F# G
Dust in the wind. All they we are is dust in the
1. A- G/B 2. A-(add9) G/A
wind. wind.

INSTRUMENTAL BRIDGE
F(#11)/A
F6(#11)/A
A-(add9)
G/A
(STRINGS)
Oh, ho, ho.
1.
2.
C
(GTR. W/ INTRO RIFF)
A-
* CHORD SYMBOLS REFLECT BASIC HARMONY, NEXT 8 MEAS.
D.S. AL
G/B
Now
D/F#
G
A-/G
All we are_ is dust in_ the wind._
(All we are_ is dust in_ the wind._
Dust_ in_ the
wind.
Ev - 'ry-thing_ is dust in_ the wind.)
Ev - 'ry-thing_ is dust in the
OUTRO
REPEAT AND FADE
(W/ LEAD VOC. AD LIB.)
Asus2
Asus4
wind.
The_ wind._

(MED.)
EASY LOVER
—PHIL COLLINS/PHILIP BAILEY/NATHAN EAST
INTRO
(KEYS)
(GUITAR)
CHORUS
(GTR. CONT. SIM.)
Eas - y lov - er, she'll get a hold on you, be - lieve ___ it.
Like no oth - er. Be-fore you know it, you'll be on your knees. ___
She's an eas-y lov - er. She'll take your heart, but you won't feel ___ it.
3rd x, To ⊕1
4th x, To ⊕2
She's like no oth - er, and I'm just try'n' to make __ you see. _
VERSE
1. She's the kind of girl you dream of, dream ___ of keep-ing hold of.
2. You're the one ___ that wants to hold her, hold ___ her and con-trol her.
Bet-ter for-get ___ it. You'll _ nev-er get it. _
Bet-ter for-get ___ it. You'll _ nev-er get it. _

C- Db C- Db C- Db C- Db
She will play a - round and leave you, leave you and de-ceive you.
'Cause she'll say that there's no oth - er till she finds an-oth - er.
Eb F-7 Eb F-7 C- F-7
Bet-ter for-get it. Oh, you'll re - gret it.
Bet-ter for-get it. Oh, you'll re - gret it.
Bb-7 PRE-CHORUS C-7 F-7 Bb-7
1. No, you'll nev - er change her, so leave her, leave her.
2. And (3.) don't try to change her. Just leave her, leave her.
C-7 F-7 Bb-7
Get out quick 'cause see-ing is be-liev-ing.
You're not the on-ly one, and see-ing is be-liev-ing.
It's the on - ly way
C-7 F-7 Gbmaj13#11 1. Db
you'll ev - er know.
(2nd X, KEYS W/ INTRO RIFF SIM.)
She's
Eb F-7 2. F-11
an eas - y lov-
Ah.
Gbmaj13#11 F-11 Db Eb F-7
GUITAR SOLO
Bb-7 C-7 F-7 Db 1.-3. Eb F-7 4. Eb Bb-7
D.S. AL ⊕1 (TAKE REPEAT)
3. Now,
⊕1 Db Eb F-7
D.S.S. AL ⊕2
She's an eas-y lov-
⊕2 Db Eb F-7 N.C.
She's an eas-y lov - er.

EVERY BREATH YOU TAKE
(MED. ROCK)
—STING
INTRO
Abadd9
F-(add9)
(GUITAR)
SIM.
Dbsus2
Ebsus2
Abadd9
CONT. SIM.
VERSE
1. Ev-'ry breath you take,
3. Solo
ev-'ry move you make,
ev-'ry bond_ you break,
ev-'ry step_ you take,
I'll be watch - ing you.
VERSE
2. Ev-'ry sin-gle day,
4. Solo
ev-'ry word you say,
ev-'ry game_ you play,
ev-'ry night_ you stay,
I'll be watch - ing you.
SOLO ENDS
CHORUS
Oh, can't you_____ see,_____
Dbsus2/B
you be-long to____ me?_____
Bbadd9
How my poor heart__ aches___

Ebsus2
with ev - 'ry step you take. Ev - 'ry move you
Abadd9
F-(add9)
make, ev-'ry vow you break, ev - 'ry smile you fake,
Dbsus2
Ebsus2
TO ⊕ F-(add9)
ev-'ry claim you stake, I'll be watch - ing you.
BRIDGE
E
F#
Since you've gone, I've been lost with-out a trace. I dream at night, I can on -
E
F#
- ly see your face. I look a-round, but it's you I can't re-place. I feel so cold and I
E
D.S. AL ⊕
long for your em - brace. I keep cry - ing, ba - by, ba - by, please.
* HOLD TIE NEXT 4 MEAS.
⊕
F-(add9)
Dbsus2
Ev - 'ry move you make, ev - 'ry step you take,
Ebsus2
F-(add9)
I'll be watch - ing you. I'll be watch-ing
OUTRO
W/ INTRO RIFF
Abadd9
F-(add9)
Dbsus2
REPEAT AND FADE
you. I'll be watch - ing

(MED.) EVERY LITTLE THING SHE DOES IS MAGIC
—STING
INTRO
(KEYBOARD)
VERSE
Though I've tried be-fore to tell her of the feel-ings I have for her in my heart, ev-'ry time that I come near her, I just lose my nerve as I've done from the start.
have to tell a sto-ry of a thou-sand rain-y days since we first met? It's a big e-nough um-brel-la, but it's al-ways me that ends up get-ting wet.
CHORUS
Ev-'ry lit-tle thing she does is mag-ic; ev-'ry-thing she do just turns me on. E-ven though my life be-fore was trag-ic, now I know my love for her goes on.
Do I

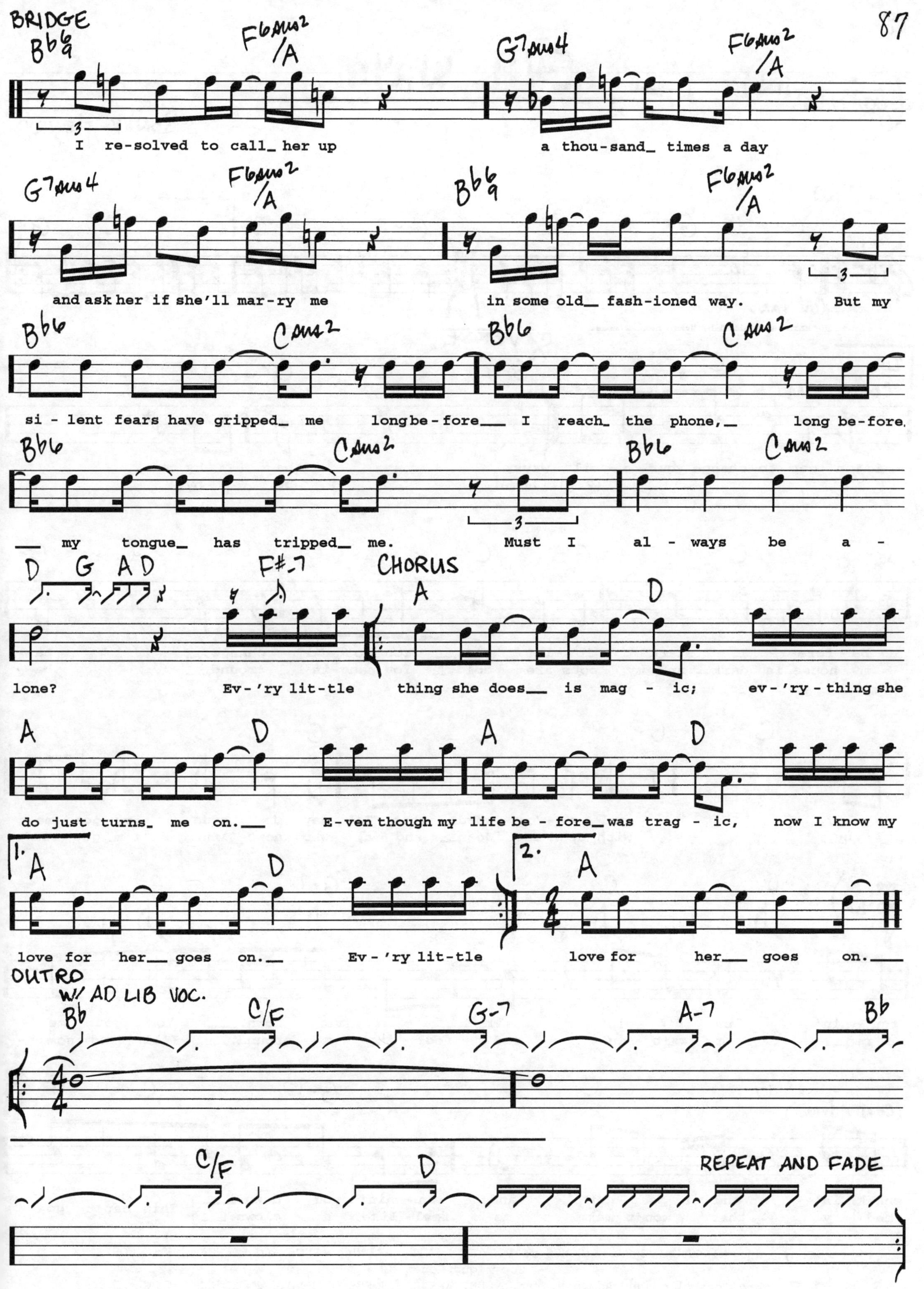
BRIDGE
Bb6/9
F6sus2/A
G7sus4
F6sus2/A
I re-solved to call_ her up
a thou-sand_ times a day
G7sus4
F6sus2/A
Bb6/9
F6sus2/A
and ask her if she'll mar-ry me
in some old_ fash-ioned way.
But my
Bb6
Csus2
Bb6
Csus2
si - lent fears have gripped_ me
long be-fore__ I reach_ the phone,_
long be-fore
Bb6
Csus2
Bb6
Csus2
__ my tongue_ has tripped_ me.
Must I al - ways be a -
D G A D
F#-7
CHORUS
A
D
lone?
Ev-'ry lit-tle
thing she does__ is mag - ic;
ev-'ry-thing she
A
D
A
D
do just turns_ me on.__
E-ven though my life be - fore_was trag - ic,
now I know my
1.
A
D
2.
A
love for her__ goes on.__
Ev - 'ry lit-tle
love for her__ goes on.__
OUTRO
W/ AD LIB VOC.
Bb
C/F
G-7
A-7
Bb
C/F
D
REPEAT AND FADE

EVIL WAYS
(MED. LATIN)
–SONNY HENRY
INTRO
*G- C G- C G- C G- 1. C G-
(GUITAR)
*Harmony implied by bass, next 2 meas.
2. C
CONT. SIM.
𝄋 VERSE
G- C G- C
1. You got to change your e - vil ways, ba - by,
(2.,3.) home, ba - by,
G- C G- C G- C G-
be - fore I start lov - in' you. You got to change, ba -
my house is dark and my pots are cold. You hang - in' 'round, ba -
C G- C G- C
- by, and ev - 'ry word that I say is true. You got me
- by, with Jean and Joan and a, who knows who. I'm get - tin'
(GTR. & ORGAN)
G- C G-7 C
run - nin' and hid - in' all o - ver town. You got me
tired of wait - in' and fool - ing a - round. I'll find some -
(CONT. SIM.)
G- C G-7 C To 𝄌
sneak - in' and a, peep - in' and run - nin' you down.
bod - y that won't make me feel like a clown.
This can't go

1.
INTERLUDE
D7
N.C.
G-
C
G-
on.
Lord__ knows, you got to change, ba -
C
G-
C
G-
C
- by,
ba - by.
2.When I come
2.
ORGAN SOLO
G-
C
G-
C
G-
C
G-
C
G-
PLAY 12 x
change.
INTERLUDE
D.S. AL
*G-
C
G-
C
G-
C
G-
C
G-
(GTR.)
*HARMONY IMPIED BY BASS, NEXT 4 MEAS.
3.When I come
D7
N.C.
G-7
C7
G-7
C7
(GTR.)
CONT. SIM.
(GTR.)
on,
yeah, yeah, yeah!
G-7
C7
G-7
C7
OUTRO-GUITAR SOLO
REPEAT AND FADE
G-
C
G-
C
Hey, hey, hey,__ now come on.

(MED.)
FIELDS OF GOLD
—STING
INTRO
B-7
1.-3.
4.
(BASS)
(BASS CONT. SIM.)
VERSE
Bsus2
You'll re - mem - ber me when the
stay with me, will you
G
D
west wind moves up - on the fields of bar - ley. You'll for-
be my love a - mong the fields of bar - ley? We'll for-
Bsus2
G
D
G/B
A
get the sun in his jeal - ous sky as we walk in fields of gold.
get the sun in his jeal - ous sky as we lie in fields of gold.
INTERLUDE
B-7
G
D
(NORTHUMBRIAN SMALLPIPES)
So she
See the
VERSE
Bsus2
G
took her love for to gaze a - while up - on the fields of bar -
west wind move like a lov - er so up - on the fields of bar -
Instrumental
D
Bsus2
G
D
- ley. In his arms she fell as her hair came down a - mong
- ley. Feel her bod - y rise when you kiss her mouth a - mong
G/B
A
TO
1.
D
2.
D
BRIDGE
G
the fields of gold.
the fields of gold.
Will you
I nev - er made

D G D
prom-is-es light-ly, and there have been some that I've bro-ken,
G D G/B A
but I swear in the days still left we'll walk in fields of gold.
D G/B A D D.S. AL ⊕
We'll walk in fields of gold.
⊕ D VERSE BAR 2 G
Man-y years have passed since those sum-mer days a-
mem-ber me when the west wind moves up-
D BAR 2
mong the fields of bar-ley. See the chil-dren run as the
on the fields of bar-ley. You can tell the sun in his
G D G/B A 1. D
sun goes down a-mong the fields of gold. You'll re-
jeal-ous sky when we walked in fields of gold,
2. D G/B A D
when we walked in fields of gold, when we
G/B A OUTRO D G/D D (PLAY 7X) D
walked in fields of gold.

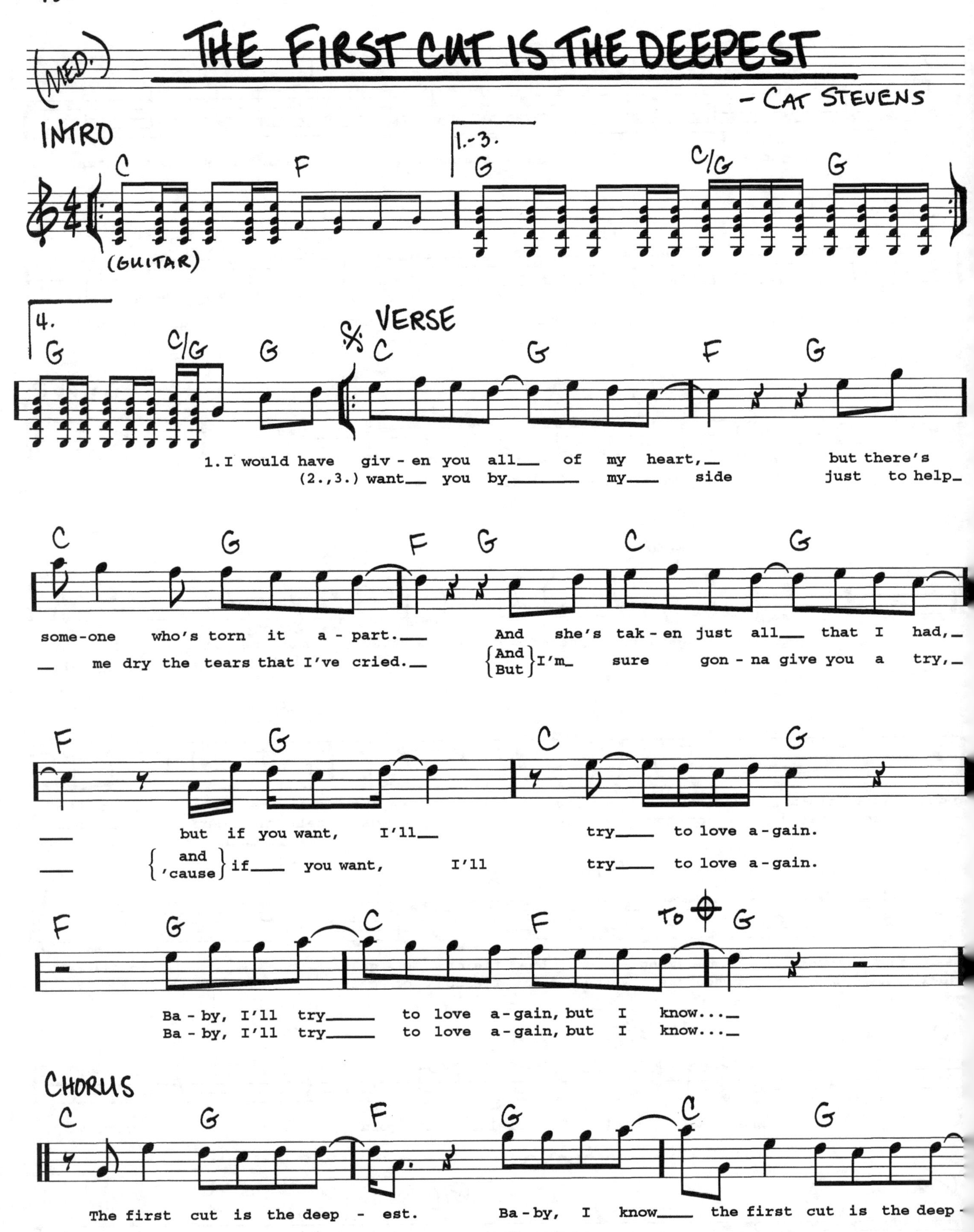
(MED.)
THE FIRST CUT IS THE DEEPEST
- CAT STEVENS
INTRO
(GUITAR)
1.-3.
4.
VERSE
1. I would have giv - en you all of my heart, but there's some-one who's torn it a - part. And she's tak - en just all that I had, but if you want, I'll try to love a - gain.
(2., 3.) want you by my side just to help me dry the tears that I've cried. {And But} I'm sure gon - na give you a try, {and 'cause} if you want, I'll try to love a - gain.
Ba - by, I'll try to love a - gain, but I know...
Ba - by, I'll try to love a - gain, but I know...
To
CHORUS
The first cut is the deep - est. Ba - by, I know the first cut is the deep -

F G C G F G
- est. And when it come to be-in' luck-y, she's cursed;_ when it come_
C F 1. G 2. G
__ to lov-in' me, she's worst._ 2.I still __
(GTR.)
GUITAR SOLO
C F 1.-3. G 4. G D.S. AL ⊕
3.I still__
⊕ G
(GTR.)
woo!
CHORUS
C G F G C G
The first cut is the deep - est. Ba-by, I know__ the first cut is the deep -
F G C G
- est. And when it come to be - in' luck - y, she's cursed;_
F G C G F G
when it come__ to lov-in' me, she's worst._
OUTRO
REPEAT AND FADE
C F G C F G
(STRINGS)

(FAST)
FOOTLOOSE
—DEAN PITCHFORD/KENNY LOGGINS
INTRO
N.C.(A)
PLAY 3X
(GUITAR)
D/A
VERSE
A
1. I've been work - in' so hard.
2. You're play - in' so cool,
I'm punch - in' my card. Eight hours, for what?
o - bey - ing ev - er - y rule. Dig way down in your heart;
Oh, tell me what I got. I've got this feel - in'
you're burn - in', yearn - in' for some, some - bod - y to tell you
that time's just hold - in' me down.
that life ain't a pass - in' you by.
(GUITAR FILL)
1st X ONLY
D
D#-7b5
E
F#7sus4
I'll hit the ceil - in', or else I'll tear up this town.
I'm try - in' to tell you it will if you don't e - ven try.
G6add#9
E/G# N.C.
CHORUS
To - night I got - ta cut (1.,3.,4.) loose, foot - loose; kick off your Sun - day
You can fly if you'd on - ly cut (2.) loose, foot - loose; kick off your Sun - day
shoes. Please, Lou - ise, pull me up from my
shoes. Oo, wee, Ma - rie, shake it, shake it for
knees. Jack, get back; come on be - fore we
me. Whoa, Mi - lo, come on, come on, let's

TO 𝄌 1
INTERLUDE
A
D/A
A
TO 𝄌 2
1.
G
D
A
(GTR.)
crack. Lose your blues, ev-'ry-bod-y cut foot - loose.
go. Lose your blues,
2.
G
D
ev-'ry-bod-y cut foot -
BRIDGE
A N.C.
PLAY 3X
loose. (Oh.) Cut foot - loose. (Oh.)
A N.C.
A N.C.
(First.) You've got to turn me a - round (Sec-ond!) and put your feet
A N.C.
E7
on the ground. (Third!) Now, take a hold of your soul. (Ah.)
N.C.
D.S. AL 𝄌 1
I'm turn-in' it
𝄌 1
G
D
D.S. AL 𝄌 2
ev-'ry-bod-y cut foot -
𝄌 2 OUTRO
N.C.
G
D/F#
N.C.
ev-'ry-bod-y cut, ev-'ry - bod-y cut, ev-'ry-bod-y cut, ev-'ry
G
D/F#
N.C.
D
N.C.
bod-y cut, ev-'ry bod-y cut, ev-'ry - bod-y cut, (Ev-'ry-bod-y!)
A
(GTR.)
ev-'ry-bod-y cut foot - loose.

96
(MED.)
FOREVER YOUNG
-ROD STEWART/KEVIN SAVIGAR/JIM CREGAN/BOB DYLAN
INTRO
E A E
1. 2.
(GUITAR)
May the
VERSE
E A E
good Lord be with you down ev-er-y road you roam.
And may
A
sun - shine and hap - pi - ness sur - round you when you're far from home.
E
VERSE
E
And may you
grow to be proud,
for - tune be with you, may your
fi - n'lly fly a - way, I'll be
A E
dig - ni - fied and true.
guid - ing light be strong.
hop - ing that I served you well.
And
Build a
For all the
3
A E
do un - to oth - ers as you'd have done to you.
stair - way to heav - en with a prince or a vag - a - bond.
wis - dom of a life - time, no one can ev - er tell.

F#-
A
Be cou - ra - geous and be brave, and in my
And may you nev - er love in vain. And in my
But what - ev - er road you choose, I'm right be -
C#-
A
CHORUS
E
heart you'll al - ways stay
heart you will re - main
hind you, win or lose,
for - ev - er young. (For - ev - er
A/E
E
1.
2., 3.
young.) For-ev-er young. (For-ev-er young.) May good young.)
F#-7
A
E
F#-
For - ev - er young. For -
A
E
To
GUITAR SOLO
B
ev - er young.
A
1.
E
2.
B
E
D.S. AL
And when you
F#-
A
E
For, for - ev - er young.
F#-
A
E
For - ev - er young.

FREE FALLIN'
(MED.)
—TOM PETTY/JEFF LYNNE
INTRO
*F Bbsus2 F Csus4 F Bbsus2 F Csus4
She's a
*MUSIC REFLECTS SOUNDING KEY (GUITAR CAPO I IN E.)
VERSE
F Bbsus2 F Csus4 F Bbsus2
good girl,_ loves her ma - ma, loves Je - sus,_ and A-
F Csus4 F Bbsus2 F Csus4
mer-i-ca,_ too._ She's a good girl,_ cra-zy 'bout_ El - vis, loves
F Bbsus2 F Csus4 F Bbsus2
hors - es___ and her boy-friend, too._
𝄋 VERSE
F Csus4 F Bbsus2 F Csus4
And it's a long day___ liv-in' in Re - se - da. There's a
vam - pires_ walk-in' through the val - ley move
glide down___ o - ver Mul-hol - land. I wan - na
F Bbsus2 F Csus4 F Bbsus2
free - way__ run-nin' through the yard.__ And I'm a bad boy__ 'cause I
west down_ Ven - tu - ra Bou-le - vard. And all the bad boys_ are
write her__ name in the sky.___ I'm gon-na free fall_
F Csus4 F Bbsus2 F Csus4 To ⊕
don't e-ven miss__ her. I'm a bad boy__ for break - in' her__ heart.___
stand-in' in the shad - ows. And the good girls_ are home with bro - ken hearts._
out in-to noth - in', gon-na leave this_ world for a while.___
Now I'm

CHORUS
F Bbsus2 F Csus4 F Bbsus2
free, free fall - in'.
F Csus4 F Bbsus2 F Csus4
Yeah, I'm free,
free
F Bbsus2 1. F Csus4 2. F Csus4 INTERLUDE F Bbsus2
fall - in'.
Now all the
F Csus4 F Bbsus2 1. F Csus4
(GUITAR)
(Free fall - in', I'm a free fall - in'. I'm a...)
2. F Csus4 D.S. AL ⊕ ⊕ CHORUS F Bbsus2 F Csus4
free fall - in'. I'm...) I wan - na
free,
free
(Fall - in', I'm a free fall - in'. I'm a
F Bbsus2 1. F Csus4 2. F Csus4
fall - in'.
Yeah, I'm
free fall - in', I'm a free fall - in'. I'm a...) free fall - in'. I'm a...)
INTERLUDE
F5 Bb5 F5 C5 F5 Bb5 F5 C5
GTR.
Yeah, I'm
OUTRO-CHORUS
F Bbsus2 F Csus4 F Bbsus2 F Csus4
free,
free fall-in'.
Oh!
REPEAT AND FADE (W/ LEAD VOC. AD LIB)
F Bbsus2 F Csus4 F Bbsus2 F Csus4
Free fall-in'.
And I'm
(Free fall - in', I'm a free fall - in'. I'm a free fall - in', I'm a free fall - in'. I'm a...)

100
FREEZE FRAME
FAST
-SETH JUSTMAN/PETER WOLF
INTRO
C N.C.
Bb N.C.
F N.C.
(ORGAN)
Spoken: Freeze frame.
C
Bb
F
(HORNS)
C
Bb
F
VERSE
*C
Bb
I can see it was a roughed-up Tues-day. Slow mo-tion week-
Thurs-day morn-ing was a hot flash fac-tor, her face still
Now, I'm look-in' at a flash-back Sun-day. Zoom lens feel-in'
Instrumental
* Horns 1st x only
F
C
-days stare me down.
fo-cused in my mind.
just won't dis-ap-pear.
Bb
F
C
Her lip-stick re-flex got me wound.
Test strip, proof-sheet love is hard to find.
Close up, dark-room sweet talk in my ear.
Bb
F
C
There were no de-fects to be found.
Fri-day night we'll dance the spot-light grind.
Her hot spot love for me is strong.

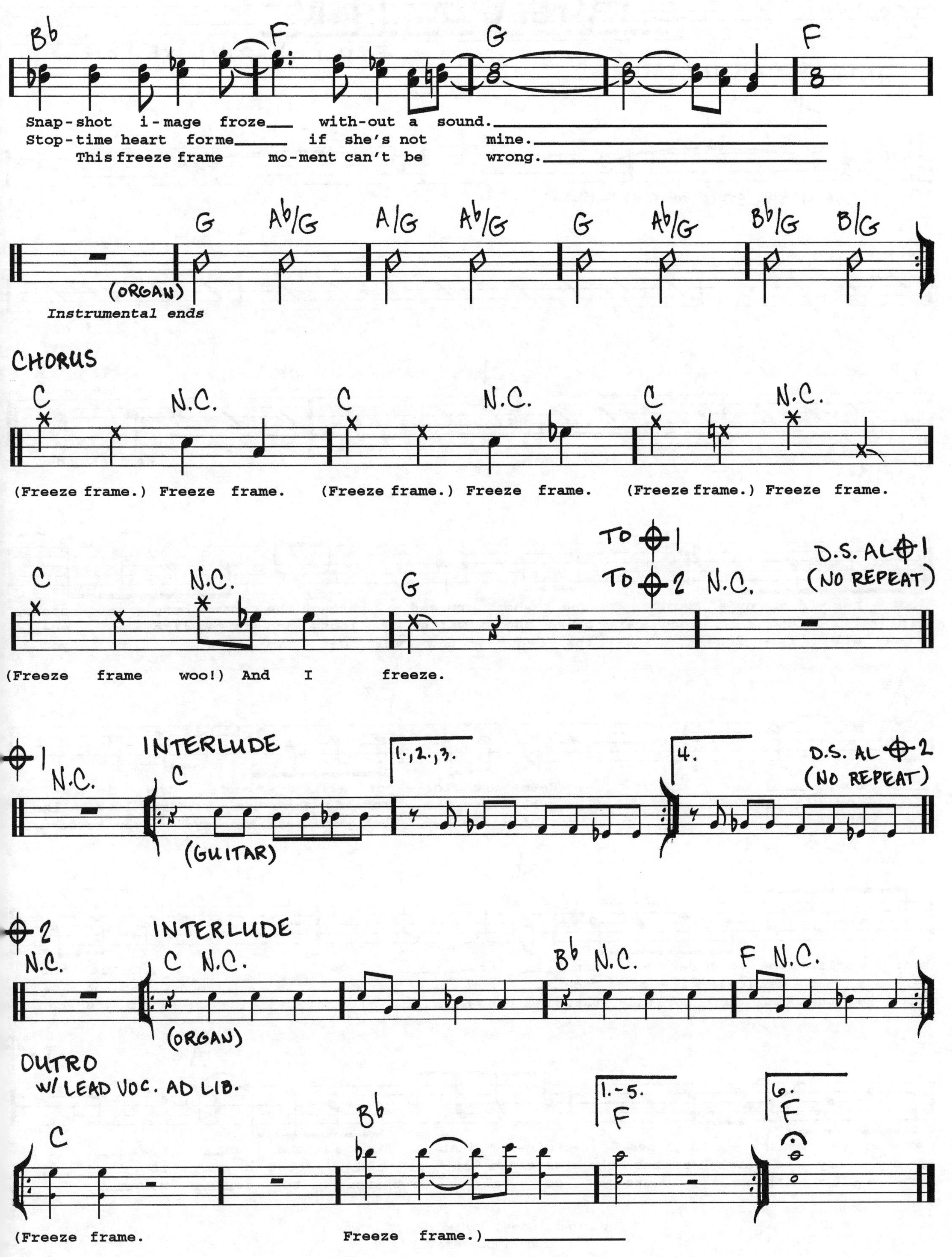
Bb F G F
Snap-shot i-mage froze___ with-out a sound.
Stop-time heart forme_____ if she's not mine.
This freeze frame mo-ment can't be wrong.
G Ab/G A/G Ab/G G Ab/G Bb/G B/G
(ORGAN)
Instrumental ends
CHORUS
C N.C. C N.C. C N.C.
(Freeze frame.) Freeze frame. (Freeze frame.) Freeze frame. (Freeze frame.) Freeze frame.
C N.C. G
TO ⊕1
TO ⊕2 N.C.
D.S. AL ⊕1 (NO REPEAT)
(Freeze frame woo!) And I freeze.
⊕1
INTERLUDE
N.C. C
1.,2.,3.
4.
D.S. AL ⊕2 (NO REPEAT)
(GUITAR)
⊕2
INTERLUDE
N.C. C N.C. Bb N.C. F N.C.
(ORGAN)
OUTRO
W/ LEAD VOC. AD LIB.
C Bb
1.-5. F
6. F
(Freeze frame. Freeze frame.)

(FAST)
FUN, FUN, FUN
-BRIAN WILSON/MIKE LOVE
INTRO - * GUITAR SOLO
Eb
*IN THE STYLE OF CHUCK BERRY
Ab
Eb
Bb
Ab
Eb
Bb
Well, she
VERSE
Eb
got her dad - dy's car and she cruised through the ham - burg - er stand
girls can't stand her 'cause she walks, looks and drives like an ace
knew all a - long that your dad was get - tin' wise to you
Ab
Eb
now. Seems she for - got all a - bout the li -
now. She makes the In - dy Five Hun - dred look like
now. And since he took your set of keys you've been
Bb
brar - y like she told her old man now. And with her
a Ro - man char - i - ot race now. A lot - ta
think-ing that your fun is all through now. But you can
Eb
Ab
To
ra - di - o blast - in', goes cruis-in' just as fast as she can now.
guys try to catch her, but she leads 'em on a wild goose chase now.
come a - long with me, 'cause we got - ta lot - ta things to do now.

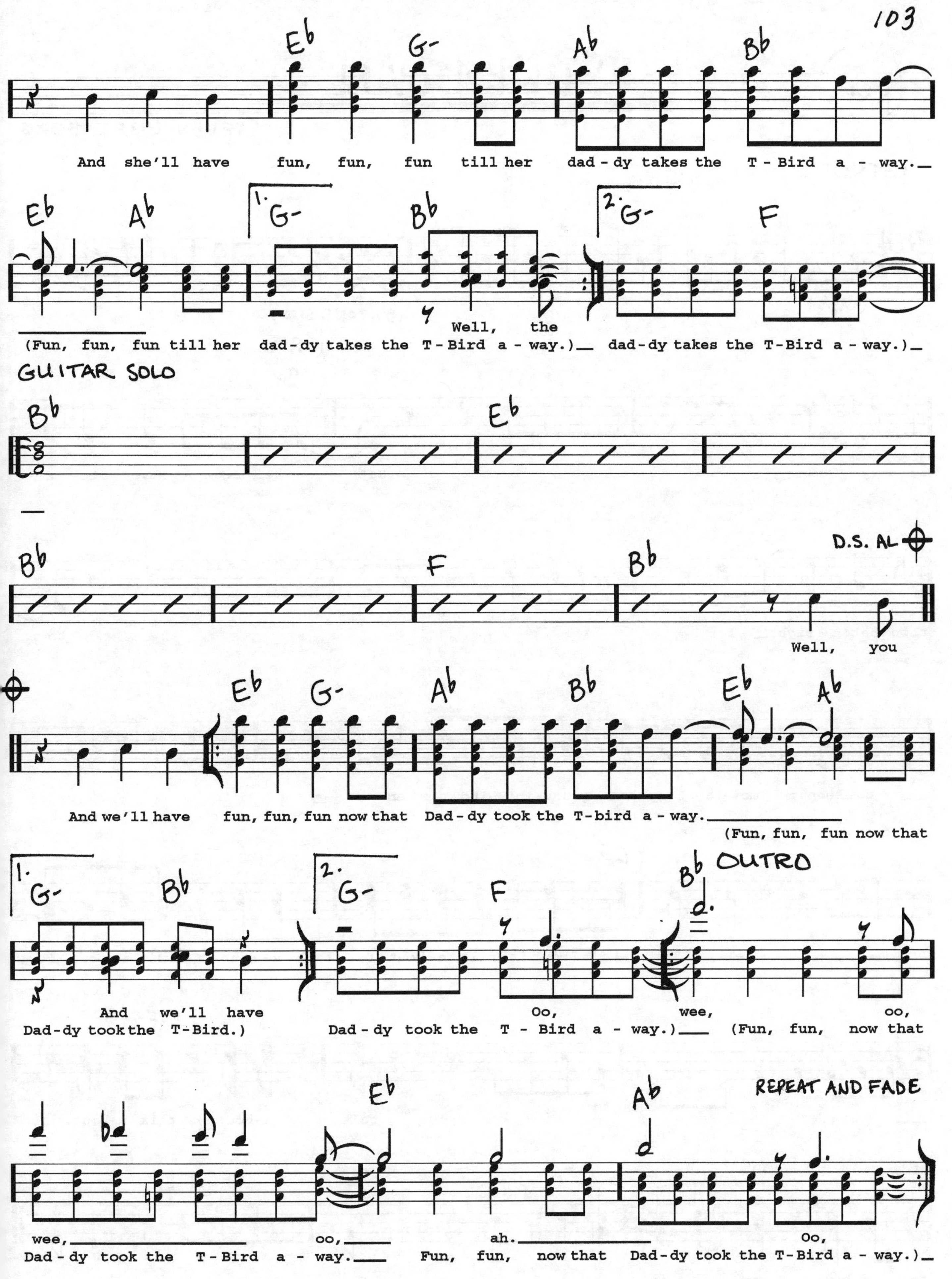
Eb G- Ab Bb
And she'll have fun, fun, fun till her dad - dy takes the T - Bird a - way.
Eb Ab 1. G- Bb 2. G- F
Well, the
(Fun, fun, fun till her dad-dy takes the T-Bird a - way.) dad-dy takes the T-Bird a - way.)
GUITAR SOLO
Bb Eb
Bb F Bb
D.S. AL
Well, you
Eb G- Ab Bb Eb Ab
And we'll have fun, fun, fun now that Dad-dy took the T-bird a - way.
(Fun, fun, fun now that
1. G- Bb 2. G- F Bb OUTRO
And we'll have
Oo, wee, oo,
Dad-dy took the T-Bird.) Dad - dy took the T - Bird a - way.) (Fun, fun, now that
Eb Ab REPEAT AND FADE
wee, oo, ah. Oo,
Dad - dy took the T - Bird a - way. Fun, fun, now that Dad-dy took the T-Bird a - way.)

104
(MED.)
FUNKYTOWN
-STEVEN GREENBERG
INTRO
C5
(BASS)
(KEYS)
(BS. CONT. SIM.)
VERSE
C5
Got - to make a move to a
town that's right_ for me,
town_
_ to keep me mov-in', keep me groov-in' with some en - er - gy.
G5
Well, I talk a-bout it, talk a-bout it, talk a-bout it, talk a-bout it,_
_
F5
talk a-bout, talk a-bout,
E5
D5
C5
talk a-bout mov - in'._

(KEYS CONT. SIM.)
PLAY 3X
G5
F5
E5
D5
Got-ta move on.
(BASS)
C5
N.C.
CHORUS
C-7
(GUITAR)
(BS. CONT. SIM.)
1. A won't
2.-4. Won't
you take me to
Funk-y-town?
Won't you take me to
INSTRUMENTAL CHORUS
C-7
Funk-y-town?
(STRINGS)
4th X TO ⊕
INTERLUDE
F
N.C.
(GTR.)
(SAX)
F
N.C.
CHORUS
C-7
(GTR.)
(SAX)
Won't you take me to
Funk-y-town?
1.
2.
D.C. AL ⊕
(TAKE REPEATS)
Won't you take me to
Funk-y-town?
Funk-y-town?
⊕ OUTRO-CHORUS
C-7
REPEAT AND FADE
Won't you take me down
to Funk-y-town?
Won't you take me down

(MED.)
GAMES PEOPLE PLAY
–JOE SOUTH
INTRO
A E
La, n, da, da, da, da, da, da. La, n, da, da, da, da, da, dee.
D E A
La, da, da, da, da. La, da, da, da, da, da. Oh, the games peo-ple
VERSE
A E
play now, ev-'ry night and ev-'ry day, now,
oth - er cry, break a heart then we say good-bye,
to ya, sing-in', "Glo-ry, hal-le-lu-jah!"
what you see. What's a hap-pen-in' to you and me?
D E
nev-er mean-in' what they say, now, nev-er say-in' what they
cross our hearts and we hope to die that the oth-er was to
and they're try'n' to sock it to ya in the name of the
God, grant me the se-ren-i-ty to just re-mem-ber who I
A
mean. While they while a-way the ho-urs
blame, whoa, ah. But nei-ther one will ev-er give in.
Lord. They gon-na teach you how to med-i-tate,
am, whoa, ah. 'Cause you're giv-in' up your san-i-ty
E
in their i-vo-ry tow-ers, 'til they're cov-ered up with
So, we gaze at an eight by ten think-in' 'bout the things that
read your hor-o-scope, cheat your fate, and fur-ther-more, to
for your pride and your van-i-ty Turn your back on hu-
D E A
flow-ers in the back of a black lim-ou-sine, whoa, ah.
might have been, and it's a dirt rot-ten shame, whoa, ah.
hell with hate. Come on get on board, whoa, ah.
man-i-ty, oh, and you don't give a da, n, da, n, da.
La, n, da, da, da,

CHORUS
A
E
D
da, da, da.
La, n, da, da, da, da, da, dee.
Talk - in''bout you and me,
E
A
1.
2.
and the games peo-ple play, now.
Oh, we make one an -
BRIDGE
W/ LEAD VOC. AD LIB.
D
E
D
(STRINGS)
E
INTERLUDE
W/ LEAD VOC. AD LIB.
A
E
(STRINGS)
(SITAR W/ INTRO MELODY SIM.)
D
E
A
D.S. AL 1
Peo-ple walk-in' up
1
D.S. AL 2
Look a - round, tell me
2
OUTRO - CHORUS
W/ LEAD VOC. AD LIB.
A
La, n, da, da, da, da, da, da.
E
D
La, da, da, da, da, da, da, dee.
Talk-in' 'bout you and me,
E
A
REPEAT AND FADE
and the games peo-ple play, now.
La, da, da, da, da,

(MED.)
GET BACK
—JOHN LENNON/PAUL McCARTNEY
INTRO
PLAY 3x
(GUITAR)
VERSE
Jo - Jo was a man who thought he was a lon - er, but he knew it could - n't last.
Sweet Lor - et - ta Mar - tin thought she was a wom - an, but she was an - oth - er man.
Jo - Jo left his home in Tuc - son, Ar - i - zo - na for some Ca - li - for - nia grass.
All the girls a - round her say she's got it com - ing, but she gets it while she can.
CHORUS
Get back,
Oh, get back,
get back, get back to where you once be - longed.
Get back, get back, get back to where you once be - longed.
To ⊕
Get back Jo - Jo.
GUITAR SOLO
2nd time: Go home!
Get back,
CHORUS
get back, back to where you once be - longed.

A7 G D
2.
D7
Get back, to where you once be - longed. Here.
PIANO SOLO
2nd x, D.S. AL ⊕
A7 D7 A7 G D
Uh, get back Jo!
GUITAR SOLO
A7 D7
1.
A7 G D
Get back, Lor-et-ta!
CHORUS
2.
A7 G D A7
Go home. Oh, get back, you get back, get back, get back
D7
1.
A7 G D
2.
to where you once be - longed. Yeah, get back,
OUTRO
A7
Oo. Get back Lor - et - ta.
D7 A7 G D A7
Your mom - my's wait - in' for ya. Wear - in' her high - heel shoes
D7 A7 G D
and her low - necked sweat - er. Get back home Lor - et - ta.
W/ LEAD VOC. AD LIB.
REPEAT AND FADE
A7 D7 A7 G D
(GUITAR)

(MED. FAST)
GIMME SOME LOVIN'
—STEVE WINWOOD/MUFF WINWOOD/SPENCER DAVIS
INTRO
N.C.
PLAY 4x
G7
C/G G7 C/G
(BASS)
(ORGAN)
(BS. CONT. SIM.)
G
1.
2.
C/G G
Hey!
Well, my tem -
VERSE
G C/G G
- p'ra-ture's ris - ing and my feet on the floor.
— so good,— ev - 'ry - thing is kind - a high. You
— so good,— ev - 'ry - thing is get - tin' high. You
C/G G
Cra - zy peo - ple knock - in' 'cause they want it some more.—
bet - ter take it eas - y 'cause the place is on fire.—
bet - ter take it eas - y 'cause the place is on fire.—
C/G G
Let me in, ba - by, I don't know what you've got. But you'd
Been a hard day— and I had so much to do.
Been a hard day,— noth - in' went too good. Now I'm
C/G G
bet - ter take it eas - y. This— place is hot.
We made it, ba - by, and it hap - pened to you.
gon - na re - lax like ev - 'ry - bod - y should.
And I'm
PRE-CHORUS
G Bb C
so glad— we made— it, so glad— we made—

CHORUS
Eb
G
C/G
it. You got-ta
gim-me some a lov-in'. (Gim-me, gim-me some
G
C/G
To
lov-in'.) Gim-me some a lov-in'. (Gim-me, gim-me some
G
C/G
lov-in'.) Gim-me some a lov-in' ev-'ry-day.
INTERLUDE
N.C.
1st X ONLY
(BASS)
G7
C/G G7 C/G G
(ORGAN)
(BS. CONT. SIM.)
3
G7
C/G G7 C/G G
3
Hey!
C/G G
1.
C/G
2.
C/G
D.S. AL
Well, I feel
Well, I feel
OUTRO
LEAD VOC. AD. LIB.
G
C/G
REPEAT AND FADE
lov-in'.)
(Gim-me, gim-me some

(MED.)
GLORIA
—VAN MORRISON
INTRO
PLAY 3X
(GUITAR)
(CONT. SIM.)
VERSE
Like to tell you 'bout my ba - by.
You know she comes a - round.
Just 'bout five feet four,
a, from her head to the ground.
You know she comes a - round here,
a, just a - bout mid - night.
She make me feel so good, Lord.
She make me feel al - right.
And her name is G, L, O, R, I,
G, L, O, R, I, A.
CHORUS
(Glo - ri - a.) G, L, O, R, I, A. (Glo - ri - a.)
I'm gon - na shout it all night. (Glo - ri - a.) I'm gon - na shout it ev - 'ry day.

To
Yeah, yeah, yeah, yeah, yeah, yeah, yeah.
(Glo - ri - a.)
INTERLUDE
PLAY 6x
PLAY 4x
(GUITAR)
(ORGAN)
(ORGAN CONT.)
She comes a-round
VERSE
here
just a-bout mid-night.
She make me feel so
good, Lord.
I wan-na say she make me feel al - right.
Comes walk-in' down my street.
Watch her come to my house.
She knock up-on my door
and then she come to my room.
D.S. AL
Then, she make me feel al-right.
G, L, O, R, I, A.
yeah, yeah, yeah, so good.
Al-right.
Feels so good.
Oh, al-right.
(Glo - ri - a.
Glo - ri - a.)
PLAY 3x
Yeah.
(GUITAR)

114
GOOD THING
MED. FAST
-ROLAND GIFT/DAVID STEELE
INTRO
A9
D F A- G
PLAY 4X
VERSE
D F A- G D F A- G
The one good thing in my life
Peo - ple say I should for - get,
D F A- G D F A- G
has gone a - way; I don't know why.
there's plen - ty more, don't get up - set.
D F A- G D F A- G
She's gone a - way I don't know where.
Peo - ple say she's do - ing fine;
D F A- G D F A- G
Some - where I can't fol - low her.
mu - tu'l friends I see some - times.
PRE-CHORUS
E- A
The one good thing did - n't stay here too long.
That's not what I want to hear.
(Hey, hey, hey, hoo, hoo, hoo,
F#- B N.C.
My back was turned and she was gone.
I wan - na hear she wants me near.
hoo, hey, hey, hey.)

CHORUS
115
D F A- G D F A- G
Good thing, where have you gone? My
(Good thing. Doo, doo, be, doo.
D F A- G D F
good thing, you've been gone too long.
Good thing. Good thing.
PIANO SOLO
A- G D F A- G
PLAY 8X
Doo, doo, doo, be, doo. *(Good thing.)
*Sung 1st time only
D F A- G D F A- G
Then one day, she came back.
D F A- G D F A- G
I was so hap - py that I did - n't act.
PRE-CHORUS
E- A
Morn - ing came in - to my room,
(Hey, hey, hey, hoo, hoo, hoo,
F♯- B N.C.
caught me dream - in' like a fool
hoo, hey, hey, hey.)
OUTRO-CHORUS
D W/VOC. AD LIB. F A- G D F A- G
(Good thing. Doo, doo, be doo.
D F A- G D F A- G
REPEAT AND FADE
Good thing. Good thing. Doo, doo, doo, be, doo.)

116
SLOW
GOODBYE YELLOW BRICK ROAD
—ELTON JOHN/BERNIE TAUPIN
INTRO
F C/E D- D-/C Bb F/C C F
(PIANO)
8VB
VERSE
G- Bb C C/E
When are you gon - na come down?
What do you think you'll do then? I
F F/A Bb Bb/F
When are you go - ing to land? I
bet they'll shoot down the plane. It - 'll
Eb C
should have stayed on the farm. I should have
take you a cou - ple of vod - ka and ton - ics to
F
lis - tened to my old man. You
set you on your feet a - gain.
G- Bb C C/E
know you can't hold me for - ev - er. I
May - be you'll get a re - place - ment. There's

did-n't sign up with you. I'm not a pres - ent for your friends to o - pen. This
plen-ty like me to be found, mon-grels who ain't got a pen - ny
boy's too young to be sing-ing the blues.
sniff-ing for tid - bits like you on the ground.
Ah. Ah. So
CHORUS
good-bye yel-low brick road, where the dogs of so-ci-e-ty howl. You
can't plant me in your pent-house. I'm go-ing back to my plow, back
to the howl-ing old owl in the woods, hunt-ing the horn - y backed toad.
Oh, I've fin - 'ly de-cid - ed my fu-ture lies be - yond the yel-low brick
road. Ah. Ah.

(MED.)
GOT MY MIND SET ON YOU
– RUDY CLARK
CHORUS
I got my mind set on you. I got my mind set on you.
(Set on you, set on you.
I got my mind set on you. Got my mind set on you.
Set on you, set on you.)
VERSE
But it's gon-na take mon-ey, a whole lot-ta spend-ing mon-ey,
it's gon-na take plen-ty of mon-ey to do it right, child.
It's gon-na take time, a whole lot-ta pre-cious time,
it's gon-na take pa-tience and time, mm, to do it, to do it, to
do it, to do it, to do it, to do it
1. right, child.
2., 3. right.
2nd X, TO ⊕ 1
3rd X, TO ⊕ 3

N.C.
2.
N.C.
BRIDGE
E
I got my mind
And this time I know it's real,
A
E
A
the feel - ing that I feel.
I
E
A
E
know if I put my mind to it, I know that I real-ly can do
B
3
2nd x, to ⊕2
N.C.
D.S. AL ⊕1
(TAKE 1st ENDING)
it.
I got my mind
⊕1
N.C.
HORN SOLO
C#-
G#
C#-
E
B
E
1.
2.
D.S. AL ⊕2
(TAKE 2nd ENDING)
I got my mind
⊕2
D.S.S. AL ⊕3
But it's gon - na take a mon -
⊕3
N.C.
OUTRO - SAX SOLO
C#-
G#
C#-
N.C.
E
B
E
N.C.
REPEAT AND FADE
(Set on you, set on you.)

(MED. FAST)
GREAT BALLS OF FIRE
–JACK HAMMER/OTIS BLACKWELL
VERSE
C N.C. C
(PIANO & BASS)
You shake my nerves and you rat-tle my brain._
F N.C. F
Too much love drives a man in - sane.__
G N.C. G F N.C. F
You broke my will,_ but what a thrill.
C N.C. C
Good - ness gra - cious, great____ balls of fire!___
VERSE
C
I laughed at love 'cause I thought it was fun - ny.
F7 G7
You came a - long and moved___ me, hon-ey. I changed my mind;
F7 C N.C. F7
this love is fine. Good - ness gra - cious, great___ balls of fire!_
BRIDGE
F7 C
Kiss me, ba - by. Mm,_________ feels__ good.
kiss

F7
G7 N.C.
Hold me, ba - by. Well, I want to love you like a
G7 N.C. G7 N.C. G7
lov - er should. You're fine, so kind.
N.C. G7
Got to tell this world that you're mine, mine, mine, mine.
VERSE
C
I chew my nails and then I twid - dle my thumb.
F7 G7
I'm real nerv - ous but it sure is fun. Come on, ba - by,
F7 To ⊕ C N.C. C
ou're driv - ing me cra - zy. Good - ness gra - cious, great balls of fire!
PIANO SOLO
C F7 G7
F7 1. C 2. C D.S. AL ⊕
Well,
⊕ C N.C. C
Good - ness gra - cious, great balls of fire!

(MED.)
THE GREAT PRETENDER
—BUCK RAM
INTRO
G C D7 Eb7 D7
(SAX)
VERSE
G C
Oh, yes, I'm the great pre-
yes, I'm the great pre-
G G7 C G G7
ten - der, pre - tend - ing that I'm do - ing well. My
ten - der, a - drift in a world of my own. I
C D7 G C G D7
need is such, I pre - tend too much. I'm lone - ly, but no one can
play the game, but to my real shame you've left me to dream all a -
1. G D7 2. G G7
tell. Oh, lone, Too
BRIDGE
C
real is this feel - ing of
G G7 C G D7
make be-lieve, too real when I feel what my heart can't con - ceal. Oh,
VERSE
G C G G7 C G G7
yes, I'm the great pre-ten-der, just laugh - in' and gay, like a clown. I
C D7 G C G D7 1. B7
seem to be what I'm not, you see. I'm wear-ing my heart like a crown, pre -
G D7 G G7 2. B7 N.C.
tend - ing that you're still a - round. Too crown, pre -
FREELY
G D7 N.C. C G
tend - ing that you're still a - round (Still a - round.)

MED.
GREEN ONIONS
– AL JACKSON, JR./LEWIS STEINBERG/BOOKER T. JONES/STEVE CROPPER
INTRO
F- Ab Bb F- Ab Bb F- Ab Bb F- Ab Bb
(ORGAN)
HEAD
F- Ab Bb F- Ab Bb F- Ab Bb F- Ab Bb
Db Eb Bb Db Eb F- Ab Bb F- Ab Bb
C Eb F Bb Db Eb F- Ab Bb F- Ab Bb
SOLOS
F- Ab Bb F- Ab Bb F- Ab Bb F- Ab Bb Db Eb Bb Db Eb
(BASS)
F- Ab Bb F- Ab Bb C Eb F Bb Db Eb F- Ab Bb
OPEN
F- Ab Bb
LAST X
F- Ab Bb
OUTRO - SOLO
F- Ab Bb F- Ab Bb F- Ab Bb F- Ab Bb
REPEAT AND FADE
(ORGAN W/ INTRO PATTERN)

GROOVIN'
(MED.)
-FELIX CAVALIERE/EDWARD BRIGATI, JR.
INTRO
Eb6 F-7 F-7/Bb Eb6 F-7 F-7/Bb
(VIBES)
VERSE
Eb6
Groov - in'_
- in'_
- in'_
F-7 F-7/Bb Eb6 F-7 F-7/Bb
on a Sun-day af-ter - noon.__ Real -
down a crowd-ed av - e - nue,__ do -
on a Sun-day af-ter - noon.__ Real -
Eb6 F-7 F-7/Bb
1.,2. Eb6
- ly___ could-n't get a-way too soon.__
- in'___ an - y-thing we'd like to do.____
- ly___ could-n't get a-way too
F-7 F-7/Bb
BRIDGE
G-7 F-7
I can't i-mag-ine an - y - thing that's bet - ter.
There's al-ways lots of things that we can see.____
G-7 F-7
The world is ours when-ev - er___ we're to - geth - er.
We can be an - y - one we___ like to be.____
G-7 F-7 Ab Bb
There ain't a place I'd like to be in - stead__ of... Groov -
And all those hap - py peo - ple we could meet___ just... Groov -
3. Eb6 F-7 F-7/Bb
INTERLUDE
Eb6 F-7 F-7/Bb
soon, no, no, no,____ no. (Ah, ha, ha.

Eb6 F-7 F-7/Bb Eb6 F-7 F-7/Bb

Ah, ha, ha. Ah, ha, ha.)

BRIDGE

G-7 F-7

We'll keep on spend - in' sun - ny days this way.___

G-7 F-7

We're gon - na talk and laugh our_____ time a - way_____

G-7 F-7

I feel it com - in' clos - er_____ day by day._____

Ab G- F- Bb

Life would be ec - sta - sy, you and me end - less - ly... Groov -

VERSE

Eb6 F-7 F-7/Bb Eb6 F-7/Bb

- in'___ on a Sun-day af-ter - noon.__

Eb6 F-7/Bb

Real - ly___ could-n't get a - way too

Eb6 F-7/Bb

soon, no, no, no,_____ no. Groov -

OUTRO

Eb6 F-7/Bb REPEAT AND FADE

- in',___ ah, ha,_____ ah, ha. Groov -

(MED.)
A HARD DAY'S NIGHT
INTRO
—JOHN LENNON / PAUL McCARTNEY
G7add4
VERSE
G
C
G
1.,3.,4. It's been a hard day's night, and I've been
work all day to get you
F
G
C
G
work-in' like a dog. It's been a hard day's night,
mon-ey to buy your things. And it's worth it just to hear you say
F
G
I should be sleep-in' like a log. But when I
you're gon-na give me ev-'ry-thing. So why on
C
D
get home to you, I find the things that you do will make me
earth should I moan, 'cause when I get you a-lone, you know I
TO
G
C
G
1.
2.
BRIDGE
B-
feel al-right. 2. You know I When I'm home,
feel o-kay.
E-
B-
G
ev-'ry-thing seems to be right. When I'm home,
E-
C7
D7
feel-ing you hold-ing me tight, tight, yeah. 3. It's been a

3.

GUITAR SOLO

G C G

Ow!

F 1. G 2. G

So why on

C D G C G

earth should I moan, 'cause when I get you a - lone, you know I feel o - kay.

BRIDGE

B- E-

When I'm home, ev - 'ry-thing seems to be

B- G

right. When I'm home,

D.S. AL

E- C7 D7

feel-ing you hold - ing me tight, tight, yeah. 4. It's been a

OUTRO

C G C G C G C

You know I feel al - right. You know I feel al - right.

Fadd9 F Fadd9 F Fadd9 F Fadd9 F FADE

(MED. SLOW)
HARD TO SAY I'M SORRY
– PETER CETERA / DAVID FOSTER
INTRO
E A/C# B/D# B/C# G#/B#
(PIANO)
C#– C#–/B F#/A# Bsus4 B E
VERSE
E G#–7 A B
Ev-'ry-bod-y needs a lit-tle time a-way, I heard her say, from each
Could-n't stand to be kept a-way, just for the day, from your
C#– B E G#–7
oth - er. E-ven lov-ers need a hol-i-day,
bod - y. Would-n't wan-na be swept a-way,
A B C#– B C#– F#–7
far a-way from each oth - er. Hold me now. It's
far a-way from the one that I love. Hold me now. It's
Bsus4 B E C#– F#–7 Bsus4 B To Coda 1
hard for me to say I'm sor-ry. I just want you to stay.
hard for me to say I'm sor-ry. I just want you to know.
CHORUS
E A/C# B/D# B/C# G#/B# C#– C#–/B F#/A#
Af-ter all that we've been through, I will make it up to you. I prom-

Bsus4 B F#7sus4/C# B/D# E A/C# B/D# B/C# G#/B# To ⊕2
- ise to. And af - ter all that been said___ and done, you're just__
C#- C#-/B F#/A# Bsus4 B Bsus4 B D.S. AL ⊕1
___ the part__ of me__ I can't___ let go.
⊕1 C#- F#-7 Bsus4 B E B/D#
Hold________ me now___ I real-ly want to tell you I'm sor - ry.
C#- F#-7 Bsus4 B D.S.S. AL ⊕2
I could nev - er let you go.
⊕2 C#- C#-/B F#/A# B B/A
CHORUS
G C/E
___ the part_ of me__ I can't_let go. Af - ter all that we've_been
D/F# D/E B/D# E- E-/D A/C# D E-7 D/F#
through, I will make it up____ to you. I prom - ise to.
OUTRO - GUITAR SOLO
G C/E D/F# D/E B/D# E- E-/D A/C# D E-7 D/F#
G C/E D/F# D/E B/D#
(STRINGS)
You're gon-na be___ the luck -
E- E-/D A/C# C-6 Bsus4 B E
RIT.
- y one.
(PIANO)

(MED.)
HEART OF GLASS
—DEBORAH HARRY/CHRIS STEIN
INTRO
E
(GUITAR)
VERSE
E
C#–
Once I had a love__ and it was a gas.__
Soon turned out, had a heart of glass._
E
C#
Seemed__ like the real thing,_ on-ly to find____
C#–
E
(GTR: W/ INTRO RIFF)
mu-cho mis-trust, love's gone be-hind.__
VERSE
E
C#–
Once I had a love_ and it was di-vine.__
Once I had a love_ and it was a gas.__
Once I had a love_ and it was a gas.__
Soon found out, I was los-in' my
Soon turned out, had a heart_ of glass
Soon turned out to be a pain in the
E
C#
3
mind.
ass.
Seemed__ like the real thing,_ but I__ was so____ blind.__
Seemed__ like the real thing,_ on-ly to find____
Seemed__ like the real thing,_ on-ly to find____
C#–
E
TO
Mu-cho mis-trust, love's gone be-hind.__
mu-cho mis-trust, love's gone be-hind.__
mu-cho mis-trust, love's gone be-hind.__
(GTR.)

BRIDGE
A
E
In be - tween, what I find is pleas - ing and I'm feel - ing fine.
Lost in - side a - dor - a - ble il - lu - sion and I can - not hide.
A
Love is so con - fus - ing; there's no peace of mind,
I'm the one you're us - ing; please don't push me a - side. We
1.
F#
B
yet I fear I'm los - ing you. It's just no good, you teas - ing like you do.
could - 've made it cruis - ing, yeah.
INTERLUDE
E
(GUITAR)
2.
E
INTERLUDE
A
(KEYS)
1.
E
2.
E
A
E
La, da, da, do, da, do, da, do, da, da, do, do la, do, da, do,
A
da, do, da, do, da, da, do, do. La, da, da, do, da, do, da, do, da, do. Yeah,
F#
B
E
PLAY 4x, THEN D.S. AL ⊕
rid - ing high on love's true blu - ish light. Ooh, whoa.
⊕ OUTRO
E
PLAY 4x
REPEAT AND FADE
Ooh, whoa.
(GTR.)

(FAST)
HELLO MARY LOU
-GENE PITNEY/C. MANGIARACINA
INTRO
A
(BASS)
(BASS CONT.)
Hel -
CHORUS
A
D
lo Mar - y Lou, good - bye
Guitar Solo
A
heart. Sweet Mar - y Lou, I'm so in love with you.
E7
A
I knew, Mar - y Lou,
C#7
F#-
we'd nev - er part, so hel - lo
B7
E7
A D A
Mar - y Lou, good - bye heart.
Guitar Solo ends I
VERSE
A
Passed me by one sun - ny day,
saw your lips, I heard your voice. Be -
D
A
flashed those big brown eyes my way, and ooh, I want - ed you
lieve me, I just had no choice; wild hors - es could - n't make

E7 A
for-ev - er-more. Now I'm not one that
me stay a - way. I thought a - bout a
D A
gets a-round, swear my feet stuck to the ground, and though I nev - er did
moon-lit night, my arms a-round you good an' tight; that's all I had to see
E7 A D A
CHORUS
A
meet you be-fore, I said,
for me to say, hey, hey,
hel - lo Mar - y Lou,
D A
good-bye heart. Sweet Mar - y Lou, I'm
E7 A
so in love with you. I knew, Mar - y Lou,
C#7 F#- B7
we'd nev - er part, so hel - lo Mar - y Lou,
1. 2.
E7 A D A A
good-bye heart. So, hel - lo
OUTRO
B7 E7 A D A
Mar - y Lou, good-bye heart. Yes, hel -
B7 E7 A D A E7 A
lo Mar - y Lou, good-bye heart.

MED. SLOW
HI-DE-HO
(THAT OLD SWEET ROLL)
- GERRY GOFFIN / CAROLE KING
INTRO
C/E
F
C/E
F
C/E
F
C/B
A-
F
D-7
(HORNS)
(ORGAN)
(HORNS)
(ORGAN)
CHORUS
C
F7
Hi - de - ho,
hi - de - hi,
gon - na get me a piece of the sky,
gon - na get me some o' that old sweet roll, I'm sing-in' hi - de - hi - de - hi - de - hi - de -
ho.
VERSE
G6
F6
I been down so low,
bot - tom looked like up.
Once I met the dev - il;
he was might - y slick.
E-/B
F/A
Once I thought that sec - ond saves was e - nough to fill my cup.
Now I
Tempt - ed me with world - ly goods and said, "You can have your pick."
But when he
of - fered all I got,
and that ain't no way to live,
be - in'
laid that pa - per on me and he showed me where to sign,
I said,
N.C.
F/G
tak - en by the ones who got the least a - mount to give.
"Thank you ver - y kind - ly, but I'm in too great a need of mine."
Hi - de - ho,

C F7 C F7 C F7 C F7 TO ⊕
hi - de - hi, I'm gon-na get me a piece of the sky, gon-na get me some o' that
C F7 C F7 C F7
old sweet roll, I'm sing-in' hi - de - hi - de - hi - de - hi - de - ho.
INTERLUDE
C N.C. F7 C N.C. G7 C E-/B
(HARMONICA)
(HORNS)
D.S. AL ⊕
F/A C F C F C F7 C7 F7 C7 F7
C E/B A- A-/G F7 F/G C F7
old sweet roll, I'm sing-in' hi-de-hi-de-hi - de-hi - de - ho.
OUTRO-CHORUS
W/ LEAD VOC. AD LIB.
C F7 C F7 C F7 C F7
(Hi - de - ho, hi - de - hi, gon - na get me a piece of the sky,
C F7 1. C E/B A- A-/G F7 F/G C F7
gon-na get me some o' that old sweet roll, sing-in' hi-de-hi-de-hi-de-hi-de - ho. Sing - in'...)
2. C E/B A- FREE TIME N.C. F7 C
old sweet roll.) Sing-in' hi-de-hi-de-hi - de-hi - de - ho.

(MED. FAST)

(YOUR LOVE HAS LIFTED ME)

HIGHER AND HIGHER

-GARY JACKSON/ CARL SMITH / RAYNARD MINER

INTRO

*D PLAY 3x G/D

(BASS) * CHORDS ENTER 3rd x

E-/D D

VERSE

D G/D

1. Your love keeps lift - ing me high - er
I was down - heart - ed;
glad I fi - n'lly found you;

(BASS CONT. SIM.)

E-/D D

than I've ev - er been lift - ed be - fore.
dis - ap - point - ment was my clos - est friend.
yes, that one in a mil - lion girls.

G/D

So keep it up, quench my de - si - re,
But then you came and he soon de-part - ed.
And now with my lov-in' arms a - round you, hon-

E-/D D

and I'll be at your side for - ev - er-more.
And you know, he nev - er showed his face a - gain.
ey, I can stand up and face the world.

CHORUS

D VOC. FIG. 1 G/D

You know your love
That's why your love
Let me tell you, your love
keep on lift - ing me
(Your love keeps lift - ing me, love keeps

E/D
D
high - er,
lift-ing me. Lift - ing me
high - er and high - er.
higher and high - er, high -
END VOC. FIG. 1
LD. VOC. 8VA
G/D
I said your love keep on
- er. (Your love keeps lift-ing me, love keeps
E/D
D
To ⊕
lift - ing me high - er and high - er
lift-ing me. Lift - ing me high-er and high - er, high -
1.
2.
INSTRUMENTAL
D
2. Now once er.)
- er.)
(HORNS)
G/D
E/D
D
1.
2.
D.S. AL ⊕
OUTRO-CHORUS
W/ LEAD VOC. AD LIB
BKGD. VOC.: W/ VOC. FIG. 1
3. I'm so
D
G/D
- er.)
E/D
D
REPEAT AND FADE

(MED.)
HIGHER LOVE
—WILL JENNINGS/STEVE WINWOOD
VERSE
Bb F Eb F
Think a-bout___ it, there must be___ high-er love, down-
-ing and we're just___ hang-ing on, fac-
Eb Bb G- F Bb F
___ in the heart or hid-den in the stars a-bove._ With-out___ it, life is wast-
- ing our fear_ and stand-ing out there a - lone.___ A yearn - ing, and it's real_
Eb F Eb Bb F C
- ed time. Look___ in-side your_heart, I'll look in-side mine.
___ to me. There__ must be some - one who's feel-ing for me.
PRE-CHORUS
C D- C
Things look so bad ev - 'ry-where.___ In this whole_ world,_
A- Bb C Bb F
what is fair? We walk blind_ and we try___ to see,,___
CHORUS
C A- D- Bb F C D-
fall-ing be-hind_ in what could be. Bring me a high-er___love, (SYNTH.)
Bb F C D- Bb F
bring me a high - er___ love, whoa._ Bring me a high - er___ love.
C D- Bb F 1. D- C
Where's that high-er love___ I keep think - ing of? Worlds are turn-
I could rise a - bove___ on a

BRIDGE
high - er love._ I___will wait for it.
I'm not__ too late for_ it.________ Un-til then, I'll
sing my song to cheer__ the night__ a-long._ Bring.
INTERLUDE
(SYNTH)
*TIE INTO BEAT 1
PRE-CHORUS
I could light_ the night_ up with_ my soul__ on fire.______
I could make_ the sun-shine from pure__ de-sire.____ Let me feel that love__
__ come o - ver me. Let me feel how strong it could be.__
OUTRO-CHORUS
W/ LEAD VOC. AD LIB.
N.C. (C)
PLAY 3X
(SYNTH)
Oh.__________
(2nd x till fade, synth w/chorus riffs)
(Bring me a high - er__ love,
bring___ me a high - er__ love, whoa.
REPEAT AND FADE
Bring me a high-er__ love, bring me a high-er__ love.)__

HOLDING BACK THE YEARS
(MED.)
-MICK HUCKNALL/NEIL MOSS
INTRO
Eb-9
Ab13
VERSE
Hold-ing back the
Hold-ing back the
years, thinking-ing of the fear I've had so long.
years, chance for me es - cape from all I've known.
tight. Instrumental solo
When some-bod - y hears, lis-ten to the
Hold-ing back the tears 'cause noth-ing here has
*3rd X, SUBSTITUTE Ab13
fear that's gone.
grown.
Instrumental ends
Stran-gled by the
I've wast - ed all my
wish-es of pa - ter, hop-ing for the arms of ma - ter,
tears, wast-ed all those years.
get to meet her soon-er or lat - er, oh.
Noth-ing had the
CHORUS
I'll keep hold - ing on. I'll keep

2., 3.
hold - ing on.
chance to be good.
Eb-9
Ab13
Noth-ing ev - er could, yeah, oh.
CHORUS
Eb-9
Ab13
I'll keep hold - ing on.
Eb-9
Ab13
I'll keep
hold - ing on.
Eb-9
Ab13
I'll keep hold - ing on.
Eb-9
To
Ab13
D.S. AL
I'll keep hold - ing on so
hold - ing on, hold - ing, hold - ing, hold - ing. Ah,
Eb-9
Ab13
Eb-9
Ab13
la, la, la, la, la, la. I said ooh, yeah.
Eb-9
Ab13
That's all I have to pay.
Eb-9
Ab13
OUTRO
Eb-9
Ab13
REPEAT AND FADE
It's all I have to say.

(MED. LATIN)
HOT HOT HOT
—ALPHONSUS CASSELL
INTRO
N.C.
O - lé, o - lé, o - lé, o - lé. O - lé, o - lé, o - lé, o - lé.
(PIANO)
(GUITAR)
(HORNS)
F Bb C Bb/C
VERSE
Me mind on fi - re, me soul on fi - re, feel-ing hot, hot, hot!
See peo-ple rock-ing, hear peo-ple chant-ing, feel-ing hot, hot, hot!
All the peo-ple all a-round me feel-ing hot, hot, hot!
Keep up the spir-it, come on let's hear it, feel-ing hot, hot, hot!
A what to do on a night like this? Is it sweet? I can't re -
It's in the air, cel-e-bra-tion time. Is it sweet? Cap-ti-vate your
sist! We need a par-ty sound, a fun - da-men-tal
mind. We have this par-ty sound, this fund - da-men-tal

Additional Lyrics

People in the party, hot, hot, hot.
People in the party, hot, hot, hot.
They come to the party know what they got.
They come to the party know what they got.
I'm hot, you're hot, he's hot, she's hot.
I'm hot, you're hot, he's hot, she's hot.

(MED. ♫ = ♩♪ triplet)

HOW SWEET IT IS
(TO BE LOVED BY YOU)

—EDWARD HOLLAND/LAMONT DOZIER/BRIAN HOLLAND

CHORUS

F6 C/G D-/G C/G D-/G C

How sweet it is___ to be loved by you,_ {yes, ba- / oh, ba- / oh, yes}

F6 C/G D-/G C/G D-/G

- by, oo.___ / - by.___ / it is, ba - by. } How sweet it is___ to be___ loved by

C

you,_ {yes, it is. / yes, it is, ba - by.} oo, ba - by.

VERSE

C

I need-ed the shel - ter / Close my eyes___ / *Instrumental*

A- G F TO ⊕

of some-one's_ arms, and there___ you___ were._ I / at night and won-der what would I be with-out you in my_ life. / *Instrumental ends*

C A- G

need - ed some-one to un-der-stand my ups and___ downs,_ and there_ you___ / Ev-'ry-thing was just a bore. All the things I did,_

C
F
deep - ly touch - ing my e - mo - tions.
with a love so sweet in so man - y ways.
I wan - na stop
PRE - CHORUS
C
F
and thank you, ba - by. I wan - na stop
C
1. F
2. F
D.C. AL ⊕
and thank you, ba - by, hey, now. ba - by, hey.
⊕
C
F
C
You were bet - ter to me than I've been to my - self. For me there's you
PRE - CHORUS
F
C
F
and no - bod - y else. Stop and thank you, ba - by. I wan - na stop
OUTRO - CHORUS
W/ VOCAL AD LIB.
C
F
F6
and thank you, ba - by, oh. How sweet it is
C/G D-/G C/G D-/G C
REPEAT AND FADE
to be loved by you.
Tell the truth, ba - by.
Well, it's like sug - ar to my soul.
Oh, yes it is, ba - by.

(MED.)
I CAN SEE FOR MILES
-PETER TOWNSHEND
INTRO
E G/E A/E E
G/E A/E
(GUITAR)
VERSE
E G/E A/E E-7 G/E A/E
I know you've de-ceived me. Now here's a sur-prise.
I
E G/E A/E E
know that you have 'cause there's mag - ic in my eyes.
I can see for
CHORUS
G/E A/E C/E D/E E
miles and miles and miles and miles and miles.
Oh, yeah.
TO
VERSE
E G/E A/E
If you think that I don't know a-bout the lit-tle
You took ad - van-tage of my trust in you when I was so
E G/E A/E E G/E A/E
tricks you play
and nev-er see you when de - lib-'rate-ly you put things
far a - way.
I saw you hold-ing lots of oth - er guys and now you got the
PRE-CHORUS
E A B
in my way,
well, here's a poke at you. You're gon-na choke on it, too. You're gon-na
nerve to say
that you still want me. Well, that's as may be, but you

A
B
lose that smile,
got - ta stand trial,
be - cause all the while,
I could see for
CHORUS
A B E A B E
miles and miles.
I could see for miles and miles.
I could see for
G/E A/E C/E D/E E
miles and miles and miles and miles and miles.
Oh, yeah.
GUITAR SOLO
E G/E A/E G/E E
PLAY 3X
D.S. AL
VERSE
A C/A D/A A C/A D/A
I
The Eif-fel Tow-er and the Taj Ma-hal are mine to see on clear days.
A C/A D/A A
You thought that I would need a crys-tal ball to see right through the haze.
Well, here's a
PRE-CHORUS
D E D E
poke at you. You're gon-na choke on it, too. You're gon-na lose that smile, be-cause all the while,
OUTRO-CHORUS
D E A D E
I could see for miles and miles.
I could see for miles and
A C/A D/A F/A G/A
PLAY 4X
miles. I could see for miles and miles and miles and miles and
A D E A
REPEAT AND FADE
miles.
I could see for miles and miles. I could see for

(MED.)

I FEEL THE EARTH MOVE

–CAROLE KING

INTRO

C-7 | 1. F/C | 2. F/C CONT. SIM.

I feel the

CHORUS (PIANO)

C-7 F/C C-7

earth move under my feet; I feel the sky tumblin' down, ah.

F7

I feel my heart start to tremblin' whenever

1. C-9 D-7/C Ab/Bb Ebmaj7 VERSE Ebmaj7 Abmaj7

you're around. Oo, baby, when I see

F-7 Ab/Bb

your face mellow as the month of May, oh, dar-

Ebmaj7 Abmaj7 F-7

-ling, I can't stand it when you look at me that a way.

Ab/Bb F/G 2. C-9 D-7/C C-7

Hey, I feel the you're around.

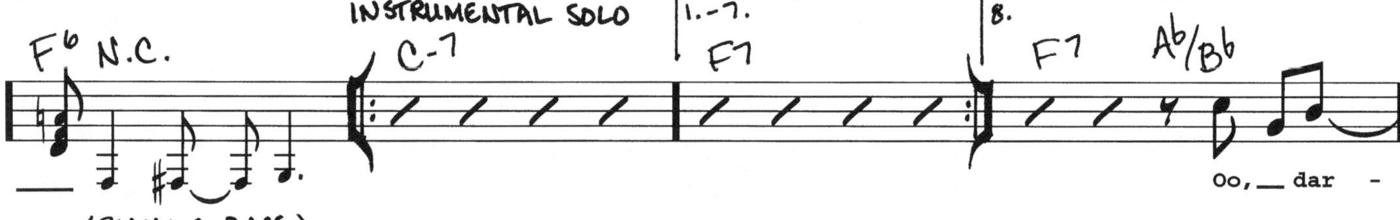

VERSE
Ebmaj7
Abmaj7
F-7
- lin', when you're near me and you ten - der-ly call my name.
Ab/Bb
I know that my e - mo - tions are some -
thing I just can't tame. I've just got to have ya, ba - by.
F/G
C-7
F/C
Ah, ah, ah, ah, ah, ah, yeah. I feel the
CHORUS
earth move un-der my feet; I feel the sky tum-bl-in'down, a tum-bl-in' down. I feel the
To
earth move un - der my feet. I feel the sky tum-bl-in' down, a tum-bl-in' down. I just a -
BRIDGE
F7
lose con-trol down to my ver - y soul. I get a -
D.S. AL
hot and cold all o - ver, all o - ver, all o - ver, all o-ver. I feel the
F6/C
RIT.
Bbmaj7/C
tum-bl-in' down, a tum-bl - in' down, a tum-bl-in' down, a tum - bl - in' down,
Abmaj7/C
tum - bl - in' down.

I GOT YOU
(I FEEL GOOD)
(MED. FUNK)
-JAMES BROWN
VERSE
N.C.
D7
Whoa! I feel good.
I knew that I would now.
like sug - ar and spice.
I feel good.
I feel nice,
G7
D7
I knew that I would now.
like sug - ar and spice.
So good, so good, I got you.
So nice, so nice, I got you.
A
G
3rd x, To
1. N.C. (D9)
(HORNS)
Whoa!
I feel good.
2. N.C. (D9)
(HORNS)
INTERLUDE
N.C. (D7)
(SAX)
BRIDGE
G
When I hold you in my arms, I

D
G
know that I can do no wrong.
And when I hold you in my arms,
my
my
A N.C.
VERSE
D7
love won't do you no harm.
love can't do me no harm.
And I feel nice,
like sug- ar and spice.
G7
I feel nice,
like sug-ar and spice.
D7
A
G
So nice,
so nice,
I got you.
1.
N.C. (D9)
(HORNS)
2.
N.C. (D9)
(HORNS)
Whoa!
D.S. AL
(1st LYRICS)
I feel good.
N.C. (D9)
(HORNS)
OUTRO
A
So good,
so good,
G
'cause I got you.
N.C. (D9)
(HORNS)
So good,
A
G
so good,
'cause I got you.
N.C. (D9)
(HORNS)
D9
Hey!

(MED.)

I HEARD IT THROUGH THE GRAPEVINE

—NORMAN J. WHITFIELD/BARRETT STRONG

INTRO

Eb- 1.,2. 3. (ORGAN) *TIE INTO BEAT 1 (GUITAR)

1. 2. (ORGAN CONT. SIM)

Oo, I bet

VERSE

Eb- Bb Ab7 Eb- Bb Ab7 C- Ab7 Eb7 Ab7

you won-der how I knew 'bout your plans to make me blue with some oth-er guy you knew be-fore. Be-tween the two of us guys, you know I love you more. It took me by sur-prise, I must say when I found out yes-ter-day. Don't you know that

ain't sup-posed to cry, but these tears I can't hold in-side. Los-in' a you would end my life you see, 'cause you mean that much to me. You could have told me your-self that you love some-one else. In-stead

of what you see, son, and none of what you hear." But I can't a help be-in' con-fused. If it's true, please tell me, dear. Do you plan to let me go for the oth-er guy you loved be-fore? Don't you know

I heard

CHORUS

Eb7 Ab7

it through the grape-vine, not much long-er would you be mine.

Eb7
Oh, I heard it through the grape - vine.
Ab7
Oh, I'm just a-bout to lose my mind, hon-ey, hon-ey, well.
(Well, I
Eb-
heard it through the grape-vine, not much long - er would you be mine, ba - by.
TO
1.
2.
Oo.)
Oo.
Yeah,
I know a man Oo.)
INTERLUDE
Eb-
(STRINGS)
(HORNS)
Peo - ple say, "Be - lieve half
OUTRO
Eb- W/ LEAD VOC. AD LIB TILL FADE
yeah, yeah, yeah.) (I heard it through the grape-vine, not much
REPEAT AND FADE
long-er would you be mine, ba - by. Yeah, yeah, yeah, yeah.)(I heard

(MED. FAST)
I SAW HER STANDING THERE
–JOHN LENNON/PAUL McCARTNEY
INTRO
N.C.
(GUITAR)
E7
1.
2.
Well, she was just
VERSE
One, two, three, four!
E7
A7
E7
sev - en - teen, and you know what I mean, and the
looked at me and I I could see that be -
way she looked was way be - yond com - pare. So,
fore too long I'd fall in love with her.
B7
E
E7/G#
A
C
how could I dance with an - oth - er, oh, when I
She would-n't dance with an - oth - er, oh,
E7
B7
E7
1.
saw her stand - ing there.
(GTR.)
Well, she
2.
BRIDGE
A7
Well, my heart went boom when I crossed that room,
and I held her hand in mine.
B7

VERSE

A7 E7

Whoa, we danced through the night
Oh, we danced through the night

A7 E7

and we held each oth - er tight, and be - fore too long I

B7 E

fell in love with her. Now I'll nev - er dance

E7/G# A C E7

with an - oth - er, woo, since I saw her

B7 E7 TO ⊕ GUITAR SOLO E7

stand - ing there. (GTR.)

B7 E7

A7 E7 B7 E7 D.S. AL ⊕

Well, my

⊕ E7 B7 E7

Oh, since I saw her stand - ing there. (GTR.)

B7 A7 E E9

Yeah, well, since I saw her stand - ing there. (BASS)

(MED. REGGAE)

I SHOT THE SHERIFF

—BOB MARLEY

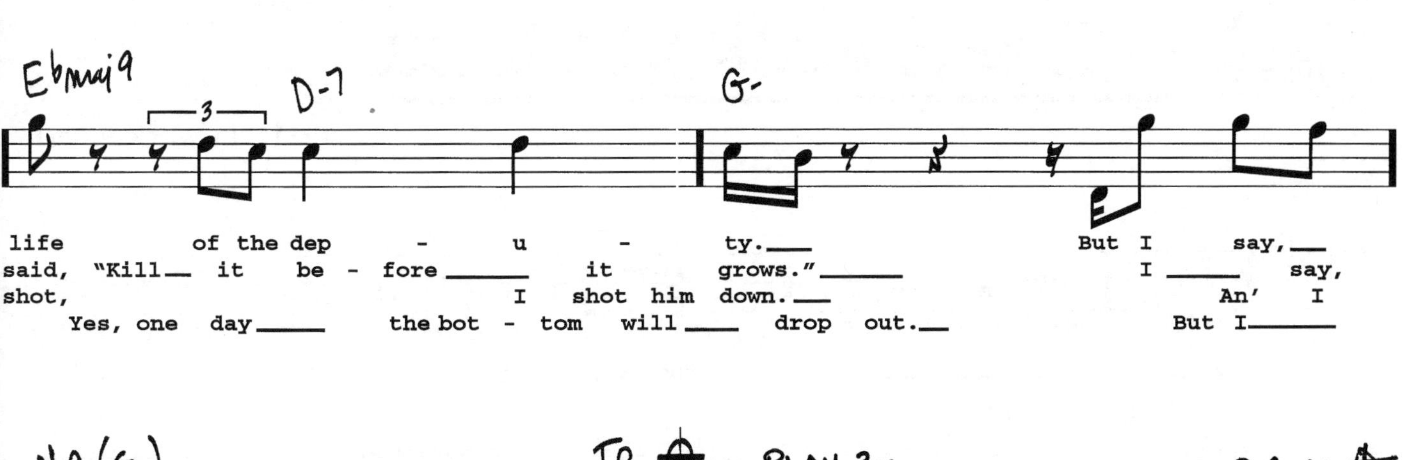
Ebmaj9
D-7
G-
life of the dep - u - ty. But I say,
said, "Kill it be - fore it grows." I say,
shot, I shot him down. An' I
Yes, one day the bot - tom will drop out. But I

N.C.(G-)
TO
PLAY 3x
D.C. AL
(GUITAR)
(ORGAN)
(3.) say,
(4.) say,

CHORUS
G-
C-7
I shot the sher - iff, but I did-n't shoot the

G-
dep - u - ty. Oh, no. I shot the sher - iff,

C-
G-
but I did not shoot no dep - u - ty. Oh, no.

OUTRO - GUITAR SOLO
Ebmaj9
D-7
G-
Ebmaj9
D-7
G-
REPEAT AND FADE

(FREELY)

I WILL ALWAYS LOVE YOU

-DOLLY PARTON

VERSE

N.C.

If_ I___ should_ stay,_ I_ would_

on - ly_ be_ in___ your way.___ So I'll___

go,___ but I___ know___ I'll think of

you ev-'ry step_ of the_ way.___ And

CHORUS SLOWLY

A F#- D E A F#- Dmaj7 E

I___ will_ al-ways love you.___ I will_ al-ways

___ will_ al-ways love_ you.___ I___ will_ al-ways love_

A 1. D

love you.___ You,___ my

you.___

A/C# B-7 A/B B-7 𝄋 VERSE A D/A

dar-ling, you._ Mm.___ Bit-ter - sweet mem - o -

hope life treats you_

A E/G# F#- C#-/E D E

ries, that is_ all___ I'm tak - ing___ with me.___ So, good-

___ kind. And I hope_ you have all you dreamed of.___ And I wish

A E/A A E/G# F#- C#-/E
bye. Please, don't cry. We both know I'm not what you, you
a you joy and hap-pi-ness. But a-bove all this, I wish you
Dmaj7 E To ⊕ 2. C#-/E C-/E B-/E
need. And I
love.
SAXOPHONE SOLO
A D/A A E/G# F#- C#-/E
D E A E/A A C#- F#- C#-/E Dmaj7 E
D.S. AL ⊕
I
CHORUS
B G#- Emaj7 F#
And I will always love
B G#- C#-7 F#
you. I will al - ways love you.
B G#-
I will al -
Emaj7 F# B G#- C#-7 F#
- ways love you. I will al - ways love
B G#- Emaj7 F# B G#-
you. I will al - ways love you.
FREELY
Emaj7 F# N.C.
I, I will al - ways love you.
E RIT. B/D#
You, dar-ling, I love you. Oo, I'll
E/F# F# Badd9
al - ways, I'll al - ways love you.

I'LL BE THERE

-BERRY GORDY/HAL DAVIS/WILLIE HUTCH/BOB WEST

INTRO

F Eb Bb F Fsus4

(HARPSICHORD)

VERSE

F C/E D-7 F/C

You and I must make a pact; we must bring sal-
Let me fill your heart with joy and laugh - ter. To-geth-er-ness, well, it's

A-7 Bb G-7 Bb/C

va - tion back. Where there is love, I'll
all I'm af - ter. When-ev - er you need me, I'll

F

be there. I'll reach out my
be there. I'll be there to pro-tect

C/E D-7 F/C A-7

hand to you; I'll have faith in all you do.
you with an un - self-ish love that re - spects you.

Bb G-7 Bb/C F

Just call my name and I'll be there.

BRIDGE
Ab
Eb
Bb
I'll be there to com - fort you, build my world of dreams a-round you; I'm so glad
F
Ab
Eb
that I found you. I'll be there with a love that's strong. I'll be your strength.
Bb
F
Fsus4
I'll keep hold - ing on.
VERSE
F
C/E
If you should ev - er find some - one new,
D-7
F/C
A-7
Bb
G-7
I know he'd bet-ter be good to you, 'cause if he
Bb/C
F
does - n't, I'll be there. Don't you know, ba - by,
OUTRO - CHORUS
F
C/E
D-7
F/C
A-7
I'll be there. I'll be there.
Bb
G-7
Bb/C
F
REPEAT AND FADE
(W/ VOC. AD LIB.)
Just call my name; I'll be there.

(MED. ROCK)
I'M A BELIEVER
-NEIL DIAMOND
INTRO
G7 C/G G N.C.
(ORGAN)
(GUITAR)
VERSE
G D G
I thought love was on - ly true__ in fair - y tales,
I thought love was more or less__ a giv-in' thing;
D G
meant for some-one else__ but not__ for me.
seems the more I gave__ the less I got
PRE-CHORUS
C G C G
1.,3.Love was out to get__ me. (Do, do, do, do, do.) That's the way it seemed.__ (Do, do, do, do,
2.What's the use in try - in'? (Do, do, do, do, do.) All you get is pain.__ (Do, do, do, do,
C G D N.C.
do.) Dis-ap-point-ment haunt-ed all my dreams.
do.) When I need - ed sun - shine I got rain.__
Then I saw her face;
CHORUS
G7 C G C G7 C G C G7 C
now I'm__ a be-liev - er! Not a trace__
G C G7 C G C G N.C.
of doubt__ in my mind. I'm in love,
(Mm,

C G F
I'm a be - liev - er! I could-n't leave her if I tried.
oh, yeah.)
D N.C. TO ⊕
INTERLUDE
G
(ORGAN)
(GUITAR)
D G
D G D.S. AL ⊕
OUTRO
G7 C G C G7 C
Yes, I saw her face; now I'm a be-liev - er.
G C G7 C G C
Well, not a trace of doubt in my
(Doubt in my
G7 C G C G7 C
mind. Said I'm a be - liev-er, yeah, yeah, yeah,
mind. I'm a be-liev - er.
G C G7 C G C
yeah, yeah, yeah. Said I'm a be -
I'm a be-liev - er.)
G7 C G C REPEAT AND FADE
liev - er, yeah. (I'm a be - liev - er.) Said I'm a be -

164
(MED.)
I'M STILL IN LOVE WITH YOU
—AL GREEN/WILLIE MITCHELL/AL JACKSON, JR.
INTRO
Gmaj7 Fmaj7 Gmaj7 D F G Bb
(HORNS)
(STRINGS)
VERSE
C C-9 A-9
Spend-ing my days think-in' 'bout you, girl;
Gmaj7 G7
be-ing here with you, be-ing near with you, I can't ex-
C C-9 A-9
plain my-self why I feel like I
Gmaj7 G7
do. Though it hurt me so to let you know. Oh, and I
VERSE
C C-9
look in your eyes, you ought to let me know
look in your eyes, for all, all the years,
A-9 Gmaj7 G7
how you feel, let me know that
I see me lov-ing you and

C-9
love is real-ly real.___ Well, it
you lov-ing me.___ It
seems to me___ that
A-9
C-9
I'm___ wrapped up in your love. Don't you know that I'm
CMaj7
B-7
TO
A-7
D7
INTERLUDE
E♭
still in love, sho - nuff in love with you, hey.___
(STRINGS)
F
G
Heav - en knows that I'm
CMaj7
B-7
A-7
D7
D-/G C/G G7 D-/G C/G G7
D.S. AL
still in love, sho - nuff in love with you, hey.___ Hey, hey._ When I
A-7
D7
OUTRO
C-9
3
A-9
nuff in love with you, hey. I,___
C-9
CMaj7
B-7
___ I,___ don't you know that I'm still in love, sho -
A-7
B-7
CMaj7
B-7
A-7
REPEAT AND FADE
D7
nuff in love with you. Yeah, I'll try if you want me to. I, I,___

(MED.)

IF YOU LEAVE ME NOW

—PETER CETERA

G#-7
C#-
D#-
E-
To
re - gret the things we said to - day.
GUITAR SOLO
Bmaj7
G#-7
D#-7
(GTR.)
G#-7
C#7
F#
B
G#-7
C#7
F#
B
F# B
D.S. AL
(TAKE REPEAT)
OUTRO-VERSE
Bmaj7
G#-7
D#-7
If you leave me now, you'll take a-way the big - gest part of me.
G#-7
C#7
F#
B
Oo, no, ba-by, please don't go.
(GTR.)
G#-7
C#7
F#
B
F#/B B
F#/B B
F#/B B
(HORNS)
G#-7
C#7
F#
B
Oo, girl, I just got to have you by my side.
Oo, ma - ma, I just got to have your lov-in'.
(GTR.)
G#-7
C#7
F#
B
F#/B B
F#/B B
F#/B B
REPEAT AND FADE
(HORNS)
Oo,

IN THE MIDNIGHT HOUR

1.
D
B
I just wan - na say right here.
I'm gon - na
2.
D
B
All right.
Play it for me one time, now.
INTERLUDE
E A E A E D
(HORNS)
B E A E A E A
3
OUTRO
B E A
I'm gon - na wait 'til the mid - night hour,
E A E A E A
that's when my love comes tum-bl-ing down.
I'm gon - na wait,
E A E A E A
wait in the mid-night hour.
That's when my love
be - gins to shine.
E A E A
3
REPEAT AND FADE
(W/ LEAD VOC. AD LIB.)
Just you and I.
Oh,
ba - by, ha!

IT'S ONLY MAKE BELIEVE

(MED. SLOW)

—CONWAY TWITTY / JACK NANCE

KANSAS CITY

—JERRY LIEBER/MIKE STOLLER

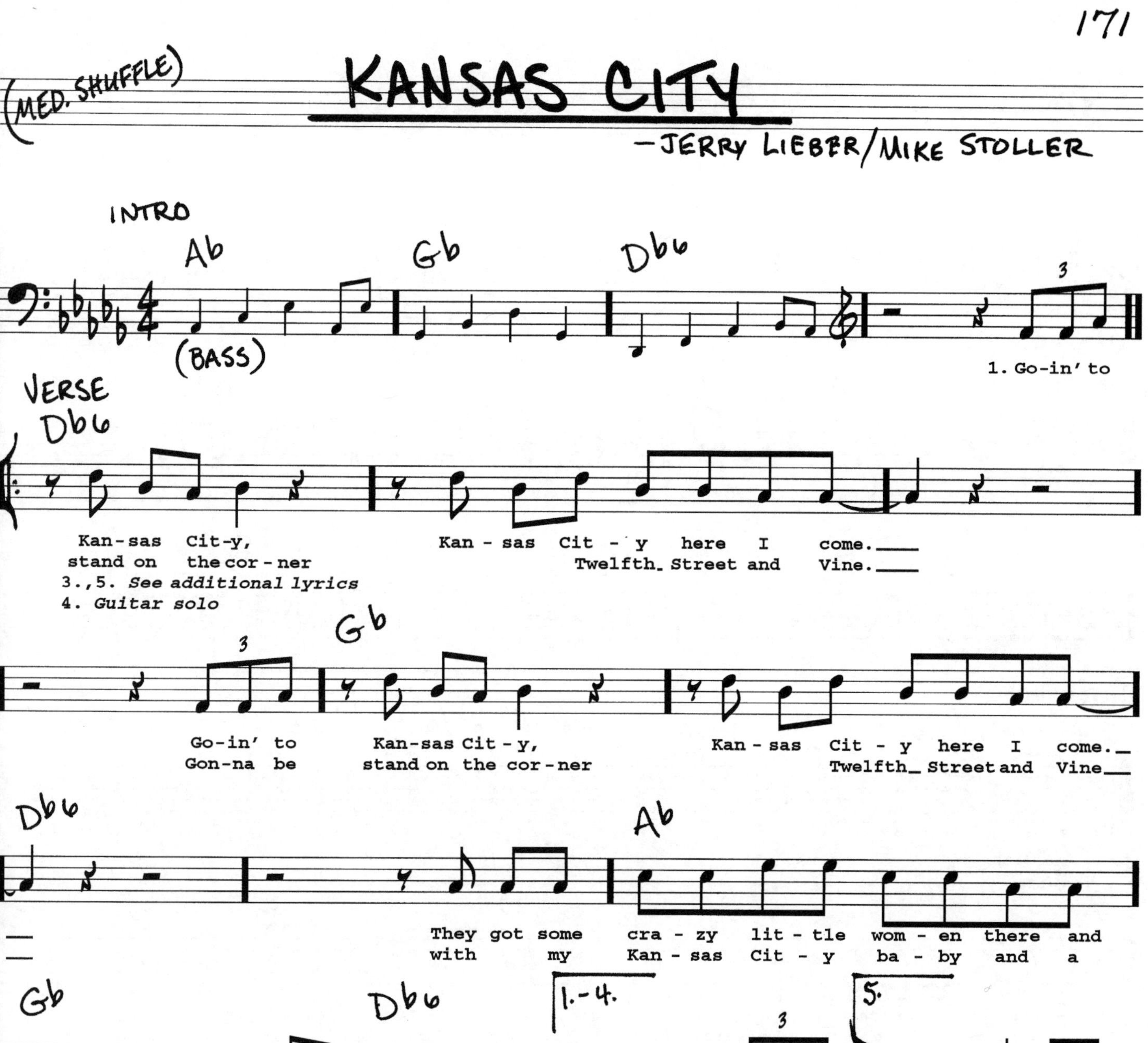
(MED. SHUFFLE)
INTRO
Ab
Gb
Db6
(BASS)
1. Go-in' to
VERSE
Db6
Kan-sas Cit-y, Kan - sas Cit - y here I come.
stand on the cor - ner Twelfth Street and Vine.
3.,5. See additional lyrics
4. Guitar solo
Gb
Go-in' to Kan-sas Cit - y, Kan - sas Cit - y here I come.
Gon-na be stand on the cor - ner Twelfth Street and Vine
Db6
Ab
They got some cra - zy lit - tle wom - en there and
with my Kan - sas Cit - y ba - by and a
Gb
Db6
1.-4.
5.
I'm gon - na get me one.
bot-tle of Kan-sas Cit-y wine.
2. I'm gon-na be
3. Well, I
They got some
OUTRO
Ab
Gb
Db6
REPEAT AND FADE
cra-zy lit-tle wom-en there and I'm gon-na get me one.
They got some

Additional Lyrics

3. Well, I might take a train,
I might take a plane, but if I have to walk
I'm goin' just the same.
Going to Kansas City, Kansas City here I come.
They got some crazy little women there and
I'm gonna get me one.

5. Now if I stay with that woman
I know I'm gonna die.
Gotta find a brand new baby,
That's the reason why
I'm going to Kansas City,
Kansas City here I come.
They got some crazy little women there
And I'm gonna get me one.

(MED.)
JACK AND DIANE
-JOHN MELLENCAMP
INTRO
A E/A A E/A D/A
PLAY 3X
(GUITAR)
VERSE
A E D E A E D E A
Lit-tle dit-ty 'bout Jack and Di - ane, two A-mer-i-can kids grow-in' up in the heart-land.
E D E A E D E A
Jack-ie gon-na be a foot-ball star. Di-ane's deb-u-tante back seat of Jack-ie's car.
INTERLUDE
A D/A A E/A D/A E/A C#/A E/A D/A A
(GTR.)
VERSE
A E D E
Suck-in' on a chil-i dog out - side the Tast - ee - Freez;
Jack-ie sits back, col-lects his thoughts for the mo - ment,
A E D E A
Di - ane sit-tin' on Jack-ie's lap, he's got his hands be - tween her knees.
scratch - es his head and does his best James Dean.
E D E
Jack - ie say, "Hey, Di - ane, let's run off be - hind the shad - y trees.
"Well, then there Di - ane, we ought - a run off to the cit - y."
A E D E A
Drib-ble off those Bob - by Brooks, let me do what I please." Say, uh,
Di - ane says, "Ba-by, you ain't miss - in' noth - ing." But Jack-ie say, ah,

CHORUS
A E D E A E D E
"Oh, yeah, life goes on long af-ter the thrill of liv-in' is gone." 1. They say, ah,
TO ⊕1
TO ⊕2
A E D E A E
"Oh, yeah, life
2.,3. "Oh, yeah," they say "life
goes on long af - ter the thrill of
INTERLUDE
D E A A E/A A E/A D/A
liv-in' is gone." They walk on.
(GTR.)
2nd x, D.S. AL ⊕1
⊕1
D E A
liv-in' is gone."
3
(DRUMS)
BRIDGE
N.C.(A) (D) (E)
So, let it rock, let it roll.
(A) (D) (G) (D) (A) (D) (G) (D) (Dsus2)
Let the Bi-ble belt come and save my soul. Hold on to six-teen as long as you can.
(A) (D) (E) (A)
Chang-es come a-round real soon, make us wom - en and men.
INTERLUDE
N.C.
4
(DRUMS)
A D/A A E/A 1. D/A E/A C#-/A E/A 2. D/A A
(GTR.)
D.S.S. AL ⊕2
⊕2
OUTRO
D E A A E D E A E
liv-in' is gone." A lit-tle dit-ty 'bout Jack and Di - ane, two A-mer-i-can kids do-in'
D A A E/A A E/A A E/A D/A
best they can.
(GTR.)
REPEAT AND FADE

174
(MED.)
JIMMY MACK
—BRIAN HOLLAND/LAMONT DOZIER/EDWARD HOLLAND
INTRO
Gb6 Eb-7 Dbmaj7
Jim-my Mack, Jim - my, oh, Jim-my Mack, when are you
1. Gb 2. Gb Ab
com-ing back? com-ing back?
VERSE
Db Gb
My arms are
He calls me
Db Gb Db Gb Ab
miss-ing you, my lips feel the same way too.
on the phone a-bout three times a day.
Db Gb Db Gb Db Gb
I tried so hard to be true like I
Now my heart's just lis-ten-ing to what he has to say.
Db Gb Db Gb
prom-ised I'd do; but this boy keeps
But this lone-li-ness I
Db Gb Db Gb Db Gb
com-ing a-round, he's try-ing to wear my re-sis-tance down.
have with-in keeps reach-ing out to be his friend.
Hey,
CHORUS
Gb6 Eb-7 Dbmaj7 Gb
Jim-my, Jim - my, oh, Jim-my Mack, when are you com-ing back?
(Ah, ah, ah, ah.

Gb6 Eb-7 Db maj7 TO ⊕ 1. Gb Ab
Jim-my, Jim - my, oh,__ Jim-my Mack, you bet-ter hur-ry back.
Ah, ah, ah, ah.)
2. Gb Ab Db Gb Db Gb
hur-ry back. Need your lov - ing, need your
ah. Jim-my Mack, won't you hur-ry back?
Db Gb Ab
INTERLUDE
Db Gb Db Gb Db Gb
lov - ing.
Jim-my Mack, you bet-ter hur-ry back.)
(HORNS)
Db Gb Eb-7 Ab7 Db Gb Ab
I wan-na say
VERSE
Db Gb Db Gb Db Gb Db Gb
I'm not get-ting an - y strong - er. I can't__ hold out ver-y much long - er.
D.S. AL ⊕
Db Gb Db Gb Db Gb Db Gb
Try-ing__ hard to be true, but, Jim-my, he__ talks just as sweet as__ you,_ hey._
⊕
Gb Ab Db Gb Db Gb Eb-7
hur-ry back. Need your lov - ing, need your lov - ing.
ah. Hur-ry back, Jim-my Mack. Hur - ry,____
OUTRO
Db Gb Db
REPEAT AND FADE
(W/ LEAD VOC. AD LIB.)
Gb
Hey,___ Jim - my Mack, you bet-ter hur-ry back. Hey,_
hur - ry.)_____ (Hur-ry back, Jim - my Mack.)

JUMP
(MED. ROCK)
-DAVID LEE ROTH/EDWARD VAN HALEN/ALEX VAN HALEN/MICHAEL ANTHONY
INTRO
C5 G/C C F/C G/C C F/C C/F Gsus4
PLAY 3X
(SYNTH)
C5 F/C C F/C C/F Gsus4
I get up,
VERSE
C5 G/C C F/C G/C C F/C C/F Gsus4 C5 G/C C
and noth-in' gets me down. You got it tough,
F/C G/C C F/C C/F Gsus4
I've seen the tough - est a - round. And I know,
C5 G/C C F/C G/C C F/C C/F Gsus4
ba-by, just how you feel. You got to
Hey you!" "Who said that?" Ba-by, how you been? You say you don't
C5 G/C C F/C G/C C F/C C/F Gsus4
roll with the punch-es and get to what's real.. Ah, can't ya
know, you won't know un-til you be - gin. So can't ya
PRE-CHORUS
A- F C D-
(GTR.)
see me stand-in' here, I got my back a-gainst the rec-ord ma - chine.

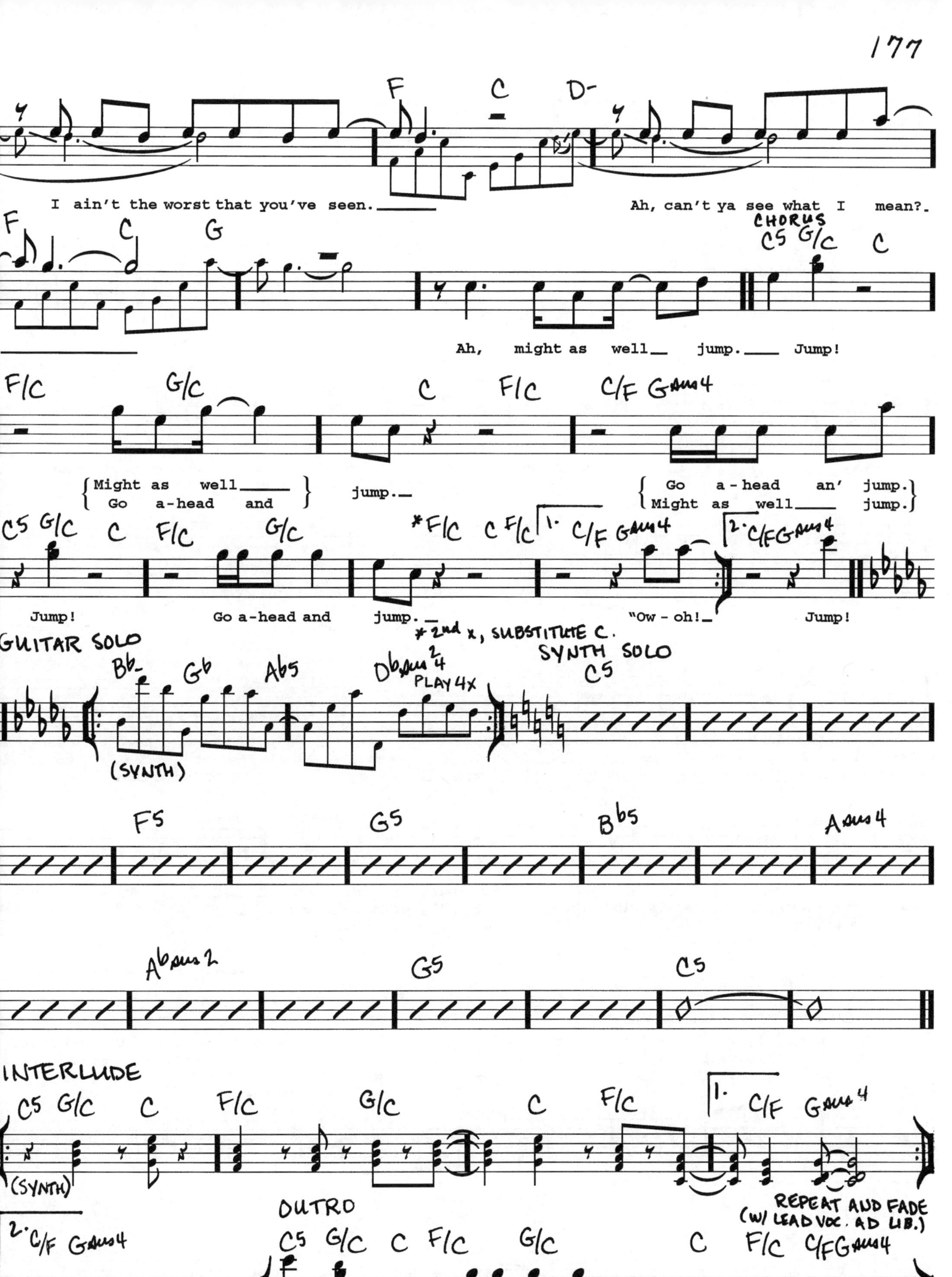
F C D-
I ain't the worst that you've seen.
Ah, can't ya see what I mean?
F C G
CHORUS
C5 G/C C
Ah, might as well jump. Jump!
F/C G/C C F/C C/F Gsus4
{Might as well / Go a-head and} jump. {Go a-head an' jump. / Might as well jump.}
C5 G/C C F/C G/C *F/C C F/C 1. C/F Gsus4 2. C/F Gsus4
Jump! Go a-head and jump. "Ow-oh! Jump!
GUITAR SOLO
Bb- Gb Ab5 Dbsus2/4
PLAY 4X
(SYNTH)
*2nd x, SUBSTITUTE C.
SYNTH SOLO
C5
F5 G5 Bb5 Asus4
Absus2 G5 C5
INTERLUDE
C5 G/C C F/C G/C C F/C 1. C/F Gsus4
(SYNTH)
2. C/F Gsus4
OUTRO
C5 G/C C F/C G/C C F/C C/F Gsus4
REPEAT AND FADE (W/ LEAD VOC. AD LIB.)
Might as well jump. Jump! Go a-head and jump. Get it in,

(MED. FUNK)

KISS

-PRINCE

INTRO E9 (GUITAR) A (KEYS)

N.C.* 𝄋 VERSE A7

U don't have 2 be beau - ti - ful 2 turn me on.
dirt - y, ba - by, if U wan - na im - press me.
girls, rule my world, I said they rule my world.

*sung one octave higher

I just need your bod - y, ba - by,
U can't be 2 flirt - y, ma - ma, I
Act your age, not your

from dusk till dawn.
know how 2 un - dress me, yeah.
shoe size. May - be we could do the twirl.

U don't need ex -
I want 2 be your
U don't have 2 watch

D

pe - ri - ence 2 turn me out.
fan - ta - sy. May - be U could be mine.
Dy - nas - ty 2 have an at - ti - tude.

A

U just leave it all up 2 me. I'm gon - na show U what it's all a - bout.
U just leave it all up 2 me. We could have a good time.
U just leave it all up 2 me. My love will be your food.

CHORUS E

U don't have 2 be rich 2 be my girl.

D

U don't have 2 be cool 2 rule my world.

E
Ain't no par - tic - u - lar sign I'm more com - pat - i - ble with.
D
To
I just want your ex - tra time and your
E9
(GUITAR)
kiss.
A
(KEYS)
1.
N.C.
U got to not talk
2.
N.C.
I think I wan-na dance.
INTERLUDE
A
(GUITAR)
GUITAR SOLO
D
A
N.C.
D.S. AL
Wom - en, not
E9
(GUITAR)
kiss.

(MED.)
LADY MADONNA
—JOHN LENNON/PAUL McCARTNEY
INTRO
A D A D
(PIANO)
A D E F G A
VERSE
A D A
La - dy Ma - don - na, chil - dren at your
La - dy Ma - don - na, ba - by at your
La - dy Ma - don - na, ly - ing on the bed,
La - dy Ma - don - na, chil - dren at your
D A D E
feet won - der how you man - age to make
breast won - ders how you man - age to feed
lis - ten to the mu - sic play - ing
feet won - der how you man - age to make
F G 4th x, TO A
ends meet. Who finds the mon -
the rest.
in your head.
ends meet.
2nd & 3rd times, Instrumental

D
A
D
A
- ey when you pay the rent?
Did you think that
D
E
F
G
A
mon - ey was heav - en sent?
Instrumental ends
BRIDGE
D-7
D-/G
Fri - day night arrives with-out a suit - case,
2nd time, Sax solo
Tues - day af - ter - noon is nev - er end - ing,
C
A-
Sun - day morn - ing, creep - ing like a nun.
Wednes - day morn - ing, pa - pers did - n't come.
D-7
D-/G
Mon - day's child has learned to tie his boot - lace.
Solo ends
Thurs - day night, your stock - ings need - ed mend - ing.
C
B-7
E7sus4
1.,2.
E7
3.
E7
D.S. AL
See how they run.
A
B-7
C-6
B-7
A
A
B-7
C-6
B-7
A
(PIANO)

LAY DOWN SALLY

-ERIC CLAPTON/MARCY LEVY/GEORGE TERRY

INTRO

A7

PLAY 8x

THUMB ON ⑥
(TWO GTRS. ARR FOR ONE)

𝄋 VERSE

A7

There is noth - ing that__ is wrong_ in
Sun ain't near - ly on____ the rise,_ and
long to see__ the morn - ing light_

D

want - ing you__ to stay____ here__ with me. I
we still got__ the moon____ and stars_ a - bove.
col - or - ing__ your face____ so dream - i - ly._____ So

A7

know you've got__ some - where____ to go____ but won't you make__ your - self_
Un - der - neath_ the vel - vet skies,_ love is all__ that mat -
don't you go____ and say_____ good - bye.__ You can lay__ your wor -

D E

__ at home__ and stay with me?__
- ters. Won't_ you stay with me?__ And don't you ev - er leave._
- ries down__ and stay with me.__

CHORUS

A D

Lay down Sal - ly, and rest here in__ my arms.__

E A

Don't you__ think__ you want____ some - one_ to talk____ to?

D
Lay down Sal - ly, no need to leave so soon.
E
A
To
I've been try - in' all night long just to talk to you.
1.
INTERLUDE
W/ INTRO RIFF
A7
8
2.
GUITAR SOLO
A7
1.-15.
16.
D.S. AL
I
D
Lay down Sal - ly and rest here in my arms.
E
A
Don't you think you want some - one to talk to?
D
Lay down Sal - ly, there's no need to leave so
E
soon. I've been try - ing all night long just to
A
OUTRO
A7 W/ INTRO RIFF
REPEAT AND FADE
talk to you.

(MED. SLOW)
LEAN ON ME
—BILL WITHERS
INTRO
C D-E-F E-D-C 1. D-E-G6 G9
2. D-C G7 C
VERSE
C D- E- F
Some - times in our lives
Please swal-low your pride
* 2nd X, SUNG 8VA, NEXT 7 MEAS.
E- D- C D- E- G6 G9
we all have pain, we all have sor - row,
if I have things you need to bor - row,
C D- E- F E- D- C D- C G7 To ⊕
but if we are wise we know that there's al-ways to-mor -
for no one can fill those of your needs that you won't let
C CHORUS C D- E- F E- D- C
- row. Lean on me when you're not strong, and I'll be your friend;
D- E- G6 G9 C D- E- F
I'll help you car - ry on, for it won't be long
E- D- C D- C G7 C D.S. AL ⊕
'til I'm gon-na need some-bod-y to lean on.
⊕ C BRIDGE N.C. (C)
show. You just call on me, broth-er, when you need a hand. We all

need some-bod-y to lean on. I just might have a prob-lem that
TO ⊕ 2
G9
C
you'llun-der-stand. We all need some-bod-y to lean on. Lean on me
CHORUS
C
D- E- F
E- D- C
D- E- G6
when you're not strong, and I'll be your friend; I'll help you car-
G9
C
D- E- F
E- D- C
- ry on, for it won't be long 'til I'm gon-na need
D- C G7
C
D.S.S. AL ⊕ 2
some - bod - y to lean on. You just
⊕ 2
VERSE
C
C
D- E- F
E- D- C
D- E- G6
on. If there is a load you have to bear that you can't
G9
C
D- E- F
car - ry, I'm right up the road,
E- D- C
D- E- G7
C
I'll share your load if you just call me.
OUTRO
W/ LEAD VOC. AD LIB.
D-
C
D-
C
REPEAT AND FADE
(Call me, call me.)

(MED. SLOW)
LEATHER AND LACE
-STEVIE NICKS
INTRO
Eb Eb/Db Ab/C Eb/Bb Ab Eb/G Bb7sus4
8VA
(ELECTRIC PIANO)
VERSE
Eb Eb/Db Ab/C Eb/Bb
Female: Is love so frag - ile and the hearts so hol - low,
Ab Eb/G Bb7sus4
shat - ter with words im - pos - si - ble to fol - low?
Eb Eb/Db Ab/C Eb/Bb
You're say - in' I'm frag - ile. I try not to be. I search
Male: You in the moon - light with your sleep - y eyes,
Ab Eb/G Bb7sus4
on - ly for some - thin' I can't see.
could you ev - er love a man like me?
Eb Eb/Db Ab/C Eb/Bb
I have my own life, and I am strong - er than you
And you were right: when I walked in - to your house,
Ab Eb/G Bb7sus4 Eb Eb/Db
know. But I car - ry this feel - in'
I knew I'd nev - er want to leave. Some - times I'm a strong man,

Ab/C
Eb/Bb
Ab
Eb/G
when you walked in - to my house___ that you won't be walk-in' out___ the door.___
some-times cold and scared,_and some - times_______ I cry.
Bb7sus4
Eb
Eb/Db
Ab/C
Eb/Bb
___ Still I car - ry this feel-in' when you walked_ in - to my house
But that time I saw___ you, I knew with you___ to light my nights,
Ab
Eb/G
Bb7sus4
that you won't be walk-in' out___ the door.______
some-how I'd___ get___ by.
CHORUS
Ab
Bb
Both: Lov - ers___ for - ev - er,_________ face to face,_
my cit - y or moun - tains.______ Stay with me, stay.___
Female: I need you to love_ me. I_________ need you to - day._
Both: Give to me your leath - er. Take from me_______ my_______
TO
1.
2.
Bb7sus4
___ lace. ___ lace.
D.S. AL
OUTRO
REPEAT AND FADE
___ lace. Female: Take from me___ my lace. Take

LET IT BE

–JOHN LENNON/PAUL McCARTNEY

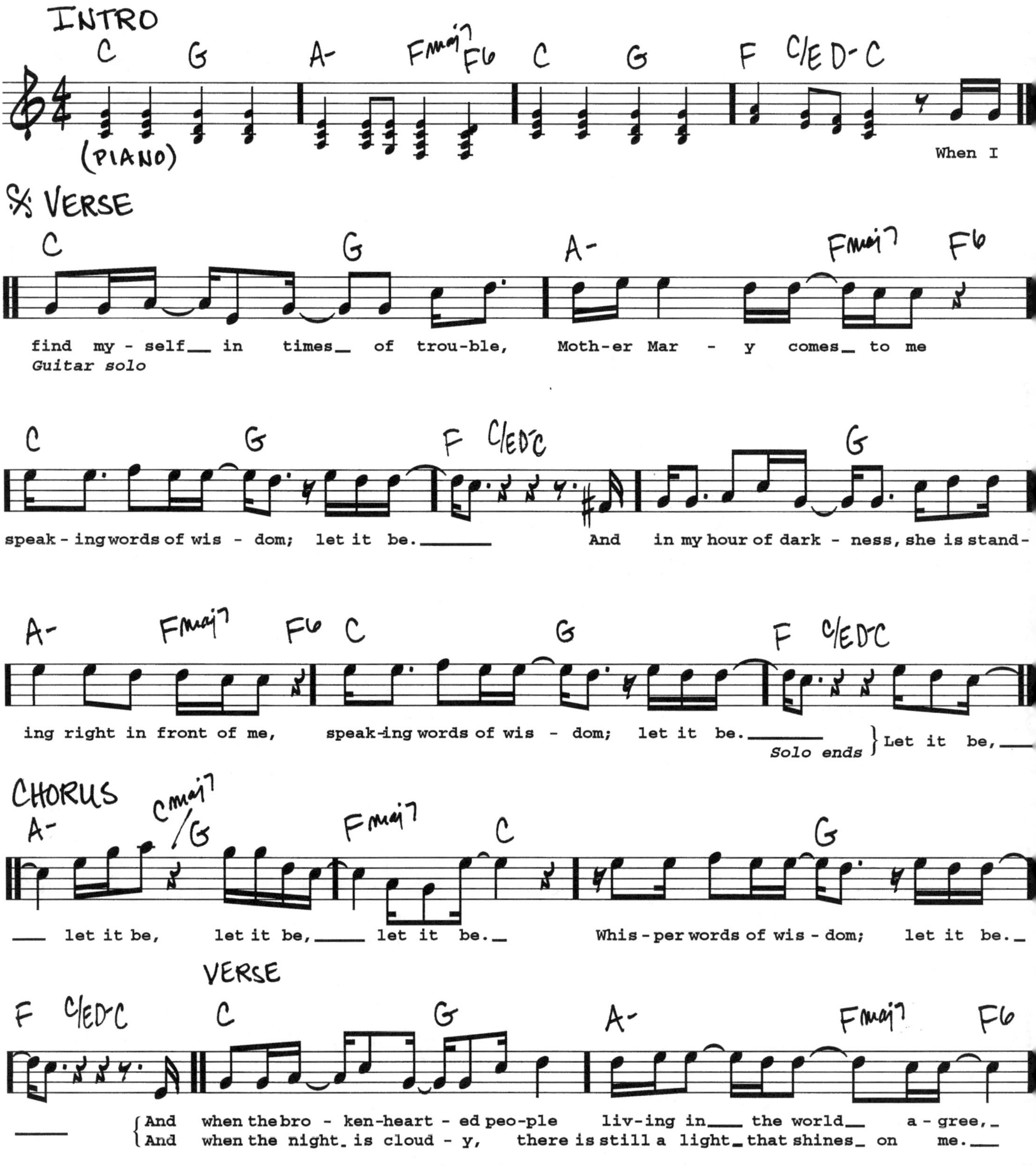

INTRO

C G A- Fmaj7 F6 C G F C/E D- C

(PIANO)

When I

𝄋 VERSE

C G A- Fmaj7 F6

find my - self__ in times__ of trou-ble, Moth-er Mar - y comes__ to me

Guitar solo

C G F C/E D-C G

speak - ing words of wis - dom; let it be.______ And in my hour of dark - ness, she is stand-

A- Fmaj7 F6 C G F C/E D-C

ing right in front of me, speak-ing words of wis - dom; let it be.______ *Solo ends* } Let it be,___

CHORUS

A- Cmaj7/G Fmaj7 C G

___ let it be, let it be,____ let it be._ Whis - per words of wis - dom; let it be._

VERSE

F C/E D-C C G A- Fmaj7 F6

______ { And when the bro - ken-heart - ed peo-ple liv-ing in___ the world__ a - gree,_
{ And when the night_ is cloud - y, there is still a light_ that shines_ on me.___

C G F C/E D- C
there will be an an - swer, let it be. For
Shine un - til to - mor - row; let it be. I
G A- Fmaj7 F6
though they may be part - ed, there is still a chance that they will see.
wake up to the sound of mu - sic, Moth - er Mar - y comes to me
C G F C/E D- C
There will be an an - swer; let it be.
speak - ing words of wis - dom; let it be.
Let it be,
CHORUS
A- Cmaj7/G Fmaj7 C G
let it be, let it be, let it be. Yeah, there will be an an - swer; let it be.
F C/E D- C A- Cmaj7/G Fmaj7 C
Let it be, let it be, let it be, let it be.
G To ⊕ F C/E D- C
Whis - per words of wis - dom; let it be.
D.S. AL ⊕
INTERLUDE
F C/E D- C Bb F/A G F C F C/G D-/G C Bb F/A G F C
(ELEC. PNO.)
(ORGAN)
⊕
F C/E D- C F C/E D- C Bb F/A G F C
(ELEC. PIANO)

(MED.)
LET'S HANG ON
–BOB CREWE/DENNY RANDELL/SANDY LINZER
INTRO
FREELY
There ain't no good in our good - bye - in'. True love takes a lot of try - in'. Oh, I'm cry - in'.
A TEMPO
(GUITAR)
(GTR. CONT. SIM.)
CHORUS
Let's hang on to what we've got. Don't let go, girl; we've got a lot. Got a lot of love be - tween us. Hang on, hang on, hang on to what we've got. (Doo, doo, doo, doo, doo, doo.)
VERSE
1. You say you're gon - na go and call it quits, gon - na chuck it all and break our love to bits. I wish you'd nev - er said it. No, no, we'll both re - gret it. That lit - tle chip of dia - mond on your hand ain't a for - tune, ba - by, but you
(Break it up. Break it up.
2. See additional lyrics

know it stands... ...for the love. A love to tie and bind ya. ...we just can't Such a love...)

PRE-CHORUS

leave be-hind us. Ba - by, ba - by, ba - by, (Don't you go, oh no no, think it o-ver and...

N.C.

stay - ay! Let's hang on

CHORUS

to what we've got. Don't let go, girl; we've got a lot. Got a lot of love be - tween us. Hang on, hang on, hang on to what we've got. (Doo, doo, doo, doo, doo, doo.)

TO ⊕

INTERLUDE

(HORNS)

D.S. AL ⊕

⊕ OUTRO

(HORNS)

REPEAT AND FADE

2. There isn't anything I wouldn't do.
I'd pay any price to get in good with you.
(Patch it up.) Give me a second turnin'.
(Patch it up.) Don't cool off while I'm burnin'.
You've got me cryin', dyin' at your door.
Don't shut me out, oh, let me in once more.
(Open up...) ...your arms, I need to hold you.
(Open up...) ...your heart, oh girl, I told you.

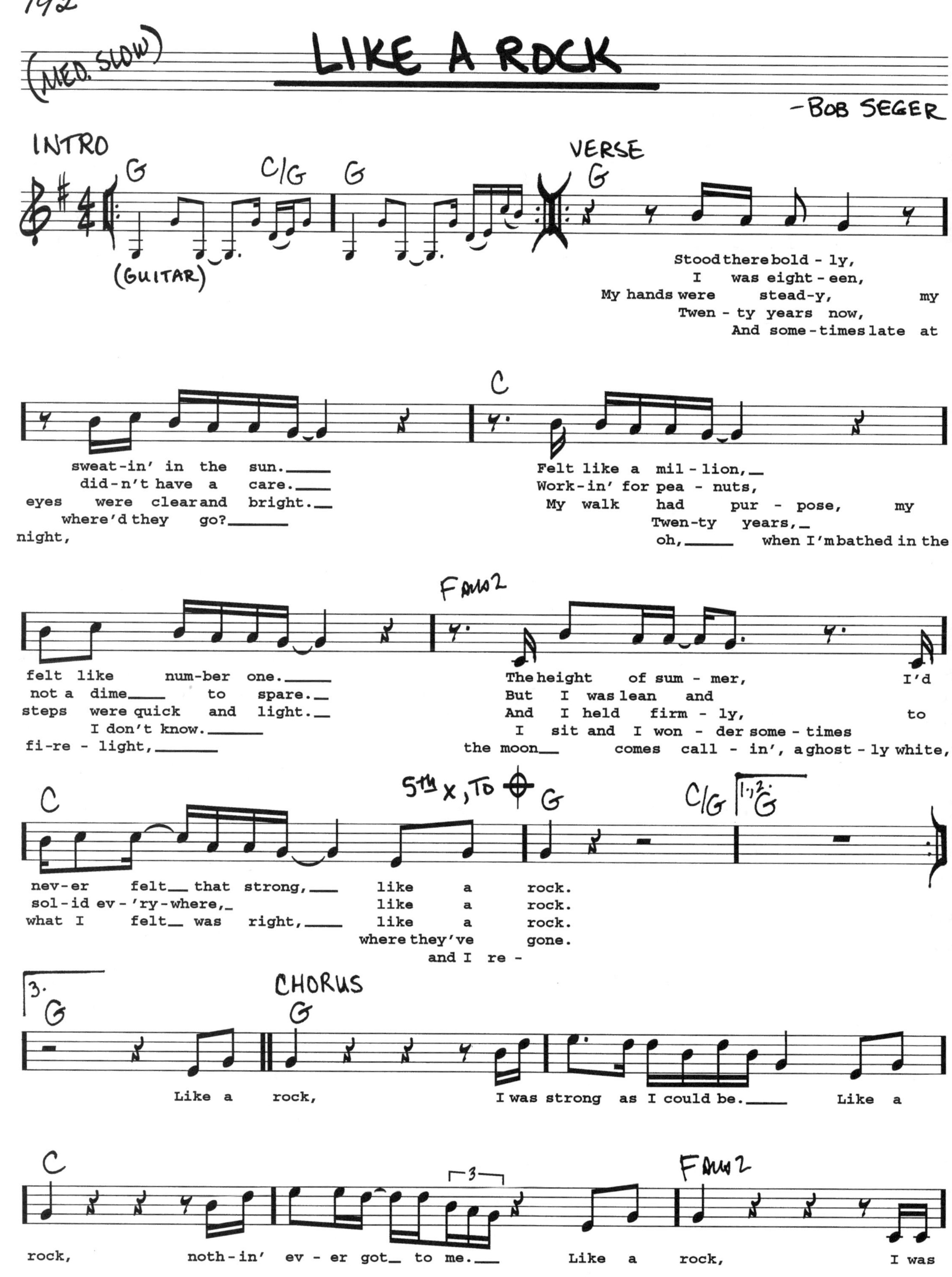
(MED. SLOW)
LIKE A ROCK
-BOB SEGER
INTRO
G
C/G
G
(GUITAR)
VERSE
G
Stood there bold - ly,
I was eight - een,
My hands were stead-y, my
Twen - ty years now,
And some-times late at
sweat-in' in the sun.
did-n't have a care.
eyes were clear and bright.
where'd they go?
night,
C
Felt like a mil - lion,
Work-in' for pea - nuts,
My walk had pur - pose, my
Twen-ty years,
oh, when I'm bathed in the
felt like num-ber one.
not a dime to spare.
steps were quick and light.
I don't know.
fi-re - light,
FADD2
The height of sum - mer, I'd
But I was lean and
And I held firm - ly, to
I sit and I won - der some - times
the moon comes call - in', a ghost - ly white,
C
5TH X, TO
G
C/G
1.,2.
G
nev-er felt that strong, like a rock.
sol-id ev-'ry-where, like a rock.
what I felt was right, like a rock.
where they've gone.
and I re -
3.
G
CHORUS
G
Like a rock,
I was strong as I could be. Like a
C
3
FADD2
rock,
noth-in' ev - er got to me. Like a rock, I was

C G C/G G

some-thin' to see. Like a rock. And I

BRIDGE

E♭- G

stood ar-row-straight, un-en-cum-bered by the weight of all these hus-tlers and their schemes.

C

I stood proud, I stood tall,

A♭- D

high a-bove it all; I still be-lieved in my dreams.

GUITAR SOLO

G C Fadd2 C G 2nd x, D.C. AL ⊕ (TAKE REPEATS)

⊕

G

call, I re-call. Like a

CHORUS

G

rock, / rock, the

C

stand-in' ar-row-straight. Like a rock, charg-in' from the gate. Like a
sun up on my skin. Like a rock, hard a-gainst the wind. Like a

Fadd2 C G

rock, car-ry-in' the weight. Like a rock. Oh, like a
rock, I see my-self a-gain. Like a rock, oh, like a rock.

OUTRO - GUITAR SOLO

G C Fadd2 C G REPEAT AND FADE

Fast
Little Bitty Pretty One
–Robert Byrd
INTRO
N.C.
Mm, mm, mm, mm, mm, mm,
mm, mm, mm, mm. mm, mm,
Mm, mm, mm,
mm, mm, mm, mm, mm, mm, mm, mm, mm. mm, mm.
Ab
1. Mm, mm, mm, mm, mm, mm,
2.-4. Whoa, whoa, whoa, whoa, whoa, whoa,
To Coda
mm, mm, mm, mm.
whoa, whoa, whoa, whoa.
1., 3. Lit - tle bit-ty
2. Tell you a
VERSE
Ab
pret-ty one, come on and talk to me. Lov - ey dov-ey
sto - ry, hap - pened long time a - go. Lit - tle bit-ty
1., 2.
3.
D.C. al Coda
lov-ey one, come sit down on my knee.
pret-ty one, I've been a watch-ing you grow.
OUTRO
Ab
Repeat and Fade
whoa, whoa, whoa.

LONESOME TOWN
MED. SLOW
- BAKER KNIGHT
INTRO
(GUITAR)
CONT. SIM.
(Oo.)
VERSE
There's a place where lov - ers go to cry their trou - bles a - way, and they call it Lone - some Town, where the bro - ken hearts stay. (Lone - some Town.)
You can buy a dream or two to last you all through the years, and the on - ly price you pay is a heart full of tears. (Full of tears.)
In the town of bro - ken dreams the streets are filled with re - gret; may - be down in Lone - some Town, I can learn to for - get. (To for - get.)
TO
BRIDGE
Go - in' down to Lone - some Town, where the bro - ken hearts stay;
go - in' down to Lone - some Town, to cry my trou - bles a - way.
D.S. AL (NO REPEAT)
May - be down in Lone - some Town I can learn to for - get.
N.C.
(Lone - some Town.)

196
(MED.)
LITTLE SISTER
-DOC POMUS/MORT SHUMAN
INTRO
E
(GUITAR)
Lit-tle sis - ter, don't you,
CHORUS
E
lit-tle sis - ter, don't you,
A
lit-tle sis - ter, don't you kiss me once or twice, then say it's ver - y nice and then you
E
B7
run._
Lit-tle sis - ter, don't you
C7
B7
TO
E
do what your big sis-ter done.
Well, I
Ev - 'ry
Well, I

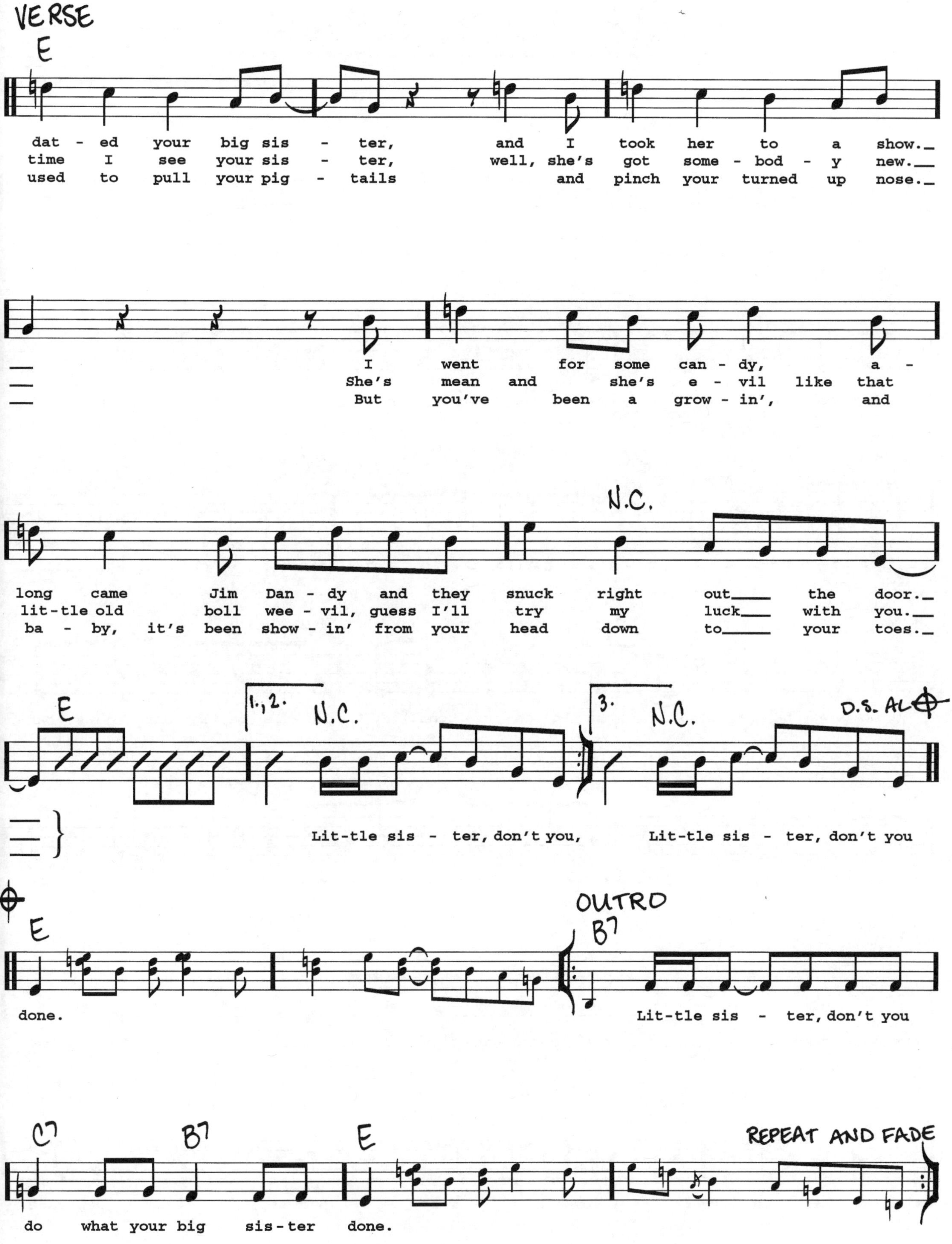

VERSE

E

dat - ed your big sis - ter, and I took her to a show.
time I see your sis - ter, well, she's got some - bod - y new.
used to pull your pig - tails and pinch your turned up nose.

I went for some can - dy, a -
She's mean and she's e - vil like that
But you've been a grow - in', and

N.C.

long came Jim Dan - dy and they snuck right out the door.
lit - tle old boll wee - vil, guess I'll try my luck with you.
ba - by, it's been show - in' from your head down to your toes.

E 1., 2. N.C. 3. N.C. D.S. AL ⊕

Lit - tle sis - ter, don't you, Lit - tle sis - ter, don't you

⊕ E OUTRO B7

done. Lit - tle sis - ter, don't you

C7
B7
E
REPEAT AND FADE
do what your big sis - ter done.

(MED.)
THE LOCO-MOTION
– GERRY GOFFIN/CAROLE KI
INTRO
Eb5
VERSE (HORNS)
Eb C- Eb
Ev-'ry-bod-y's do - in' a brand - new dance_ now._____ (Come on, ba-by, do_
C- Eb C-
___ the lo-co-mo-tion.) I know you'll get to like it if you give it a chance_ now._____
Eb C- Ab
(Come on, ba-by, do____ the lo-co-mo-tion.) My lit-tle ba-by sis - ter can
F- Ab F7
do it with ease;_ it's eas-i-er than learn - in' your A - B - C's._ So
Eb/Bb Bb BRIDGE Eb
come on, come on, do_____ the lo-co-mo-tion with me._____ You got-ta
Sax solo
Ab Eb
swing your hips now._ Come on,_ ba-by, jump up,____ jump back._

Bb
Oh, well, I think you got the knack. Whoa, whoa.
Sax solo ends Yeah, yeah, yeah, yeah.
VERSE
Eb C- Eb
Now that you can do it, let's make a chain now.
Move a-round the floor in a lo - co-mo - tion.
(Come on, ba-by, do
C- Eb C-
the lo-co-mo-tion.)
A chug-a chug-a mo-tion like a rail - road train now.
Do it hold-in' hands if a you get the no - tion.
Eb C- Ab
(Come on, ba-by, do the lo-co-mo-tion.)
Do it nice and eas-y now,
There's nev-er been a dance that's so
F- Ab F7
don't lose con-trol, a lit-tle bit of rhy-thm and a lot of soul.
eas-y to do. It e-ven makes you hap-py when you're feel-in' blue. So,
Eb/Bb Bb 1. 2.
Come on, come on, do the lo-co-mo-tion with me. the lo-co-mo-tion with me.
come on, come on, do
OUTRO
W/ LEAD VOC. AD LIB.
Eb Ab REPEAT AND FADE
(Come on, do the lo-co-mo-tion. Come on, do the lo-co-mo-tion.)

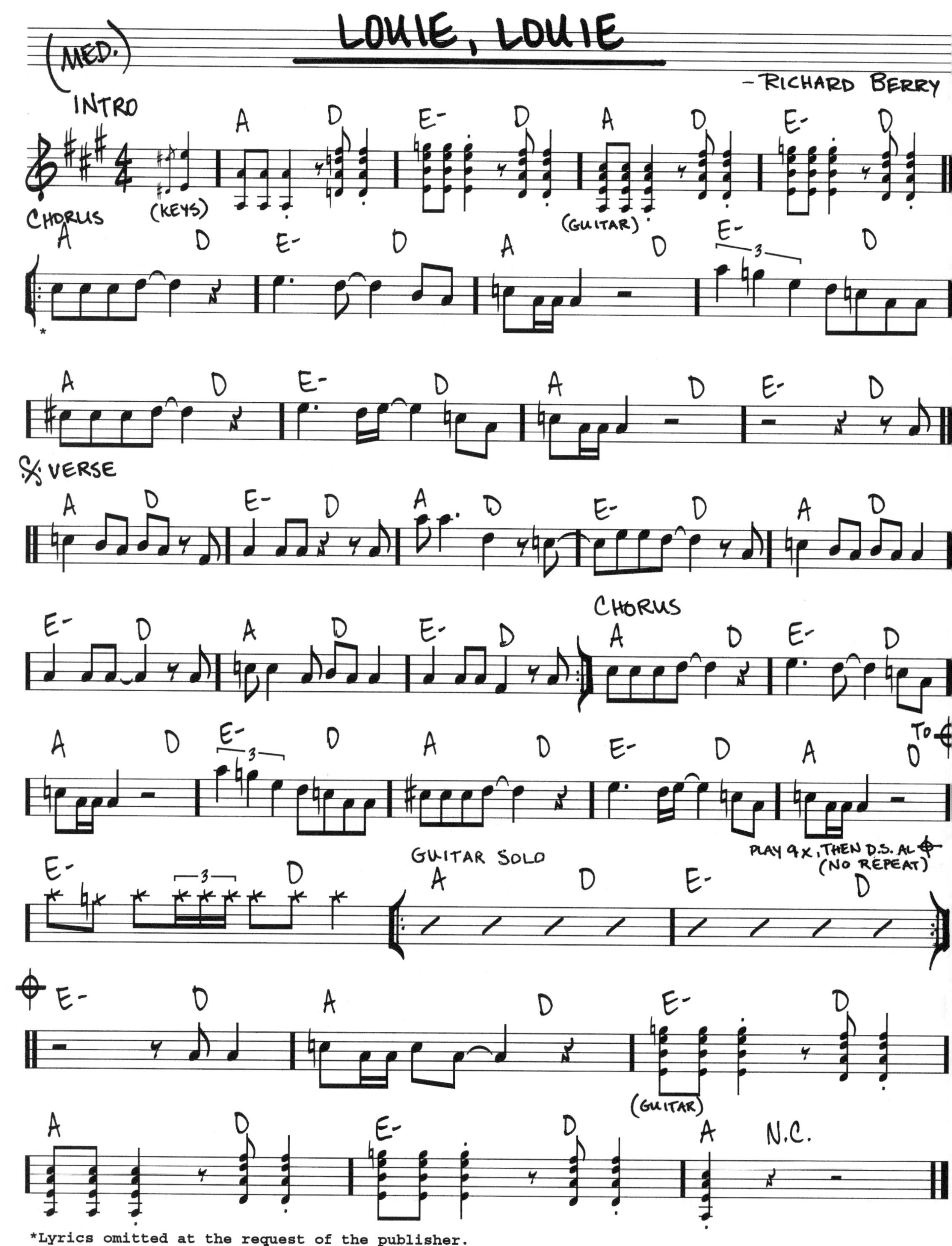

*Lyrics omitted at the request of the publisher.

MED.
LOVE ME DO
-JOHN LENNON/PAUL McCARTNEY
INTRO
G C G C G
(HARMONICA)
C G
CHORUS
G
Love, love me do,
C G C G
you know I love you. I'll al - ways be true,
C N.C. 4TH X TO 2 HARMONICA W/ INTRO RIFF SIM.
G
so please love me do.
C G 1. C 2., 3.
BRIDGE
D
Whoa, love me do.
(BASS)
Some - one to love,
Harmonica solo
C G D C TO 1 D.S. AL 1
G N.C.
some - bod-y new. Some-one to love, some-one like you.
1 G
D.S. AL 2
N.C.
(HARMONICA)
2 OUTRO
REPEAT AND FADE W/ LEAD VOC. AD LIB.
G HARMONICA W/ INTRO RIFF SIM. C G C
do. Whoa, love me do. Love me

202
LOW RIDER
(MED.)
–SYLVESTER ALLEN/HAROLD R. BROWN/MORRIS DICKERSON/JERRY GOLDSTEIN/LEROY JORDAN/LEE OSKAR/CHARLES W. MILLER/HOWARD SCOTT
INTRO
G7
(BASS)
VERSE
G7
All my friends know the low rid-er.
Low rid - er drives a lit-tle slow-er.
Low rid - er knows ev-'ry street, yeah.
Low rid - er don't use no gas now.
*Sung one octave lower.
The low rid - er is a lit-tle high - er.
Low rid - er, he's a real go - er.
Low rid - er is the one to meet, yeah.
Low rid - er don't drive too fast.
CHORUS
G7
(SAX & HARMONICA)
PLAY 4X

OUTRO
G7
Take a lit - tle trip, take a lit - tle trip,
take a lit - tle trip and see.
Take a lit - tle trip, take a lit - tle trip,
take a lit - tle trip with me.
(SAX & HARMONICA)
REPEAT AND FADE

(MED.)
LOWDOWN
-BOZ SCAGGS/DAVID PAICH
INTRO
E-9
A13
E-9
(FLUTE)
A13
E-9
A13
VERSE
E-9
A13
1. Ba - by's in - to run - nin' 'round, hang - in' with the crowd,
2.,3. See additional lyrics
E-9
A13
put - tin' your busi - ness in the street, talk - in' out loud,
E-9
A13
say - in' you bought her this and that, and how much you done spent.
E-9
A13
I swear, she must be - lieve, it's all heav - en sent.
E-9
A13
Hey, boy, you bet - ter bring the chick a - round
E-9
A13
to the sad, sad truth, the dirt - y low - down.

CHORUS
W/ LEAD VOC. AD LIB.

E-9 A13 E-9

(Oo, oo, I won-der, won-der, won-der, won-der,

A13 E-9 A13 E-9

oo. Oo, oo, I won-der, won-der, won-der, won-der,

A13 BRIDGE Dmaj7 C#+ A-/C B7

oo.) (HORNS)

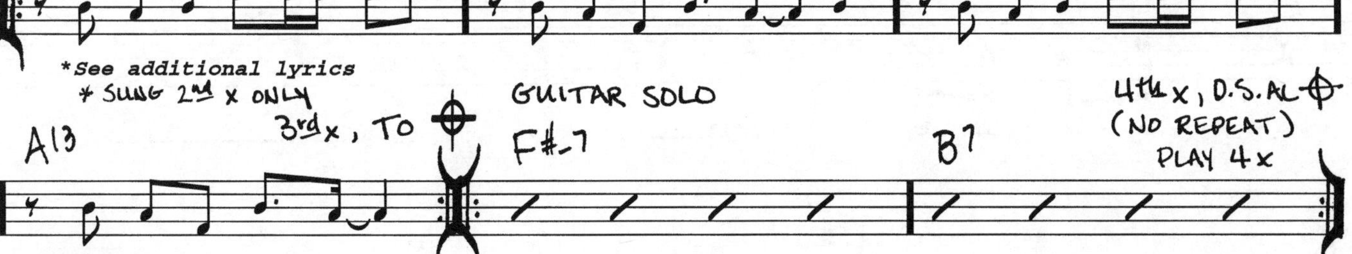

*See additional lyrics
* SUNG 2nd X ONLY

A13 3rd x, TO ⊕ GUITAR SOLO F#-7 B7 4th x, D.S. AL ⊕ (NO REPEAT) PLAY 4x

E-9 A13 REPEAT AND FADE

won-der, won-der, won-der, won-der, oo.

Additional Lyrics

2. Nothing you can't handle, nothing you ain't got.
Put your money on the table and drive it off the lot.
Turn on that ol' lovelight and turn a maybe to a yes.
Same old schoolboy game got you into this mess.
Hey son, better get on back to town,
Face the sad old truth, the dirty lowdown.

Bridge Come on back down earth, son.
Dig the low, low, low, low lowdown.

3. You ain't got to be so bad, got to be so cold.
This dog eat dog existence sure is getting old.
Got to have a Jones for this, Jones for that.
This running with the Joneses, boy,
Just ain't where it's at.
You gonna come back around
To the sad, sad truth, the dirty lowdown.

MAYBE BABY

(MED.)
MAYBE BABY
-NORMAN PETTY/CHARLES HARDIN
INTRO
A
1.,2.
F#-
(GUITARS)
3.
D E A D A E
VERSE
A F#-
May - be, ba - by, I'll have you.
A F#- A
May-be, ba-by, you'll be true. May-be, ba-by, I'll
D E A D A E
have you for me.
TO
(GUITAR)
VERSE
A F#-
It's fun - ny, hon - ey; you don't care.
2nd time, Instrumental
A F#-
You nev - er lis - ten to my prayer.

A
D
E
May - be, ba - by, you will love me some -
A
D
A
- day.
Instrumental ends
Well,
BRIDGE
D
you are the one that makes me glad
A
D
A
and you are the one that makes me sad. A,
D
when some - day you want me, well a
E
1.
I'll be there, wait and see.
2.
D.S. AL
and see.
OUTRO
A
May - be, ba - by, I'll
D
E
A
D
A
have you for me.

(MED. SLOW)

MAYBE I'M AMAZED

— PAUL McCARTNEY

INTRO
A
D/F#
D-/F
E-7
A
(PIANO)

VERSE
Bb
F/A
C
G/C

Ba-by, I'm a-mazed at the way you love me all__ the time,__
2nd & 4th times, Instrumental
May-be I'm a-mazed at the way you're with me all__ the time,__

Bb
F/A
C
N.C.
and may-be I'm a-fraid of the way I love__ you.
and may-be I'm a-fraid of the way I leave__ you.
(PIANO & BASS)

Bb
F/A
C
G
May-be I'm a-mazed at the way you pulled me out__ of time,__ you
May-be I'm a-mazed at the way you help me sing__ my song,__ you

Bb
F/A
Ab
Eb/G
C
To ⊕

hung me on a line.__ May-be I'm a-mazed at the way I real - ly need__ you.__
Instrumental ends
right me when I'm wrong. May-be I'm a-mazed at the way I real - ly need__ you.__

BRIDGE
D
A/D
A-/D
D9/F#
Ba-by, I'm a man, may-be I'm a lone-ly man__ who's in the mid-dle of some - thing_
3rd time, Vocal ad lib.

G
D(add#9)
that he does-n't real - ly un - der-stand.__
(PIANO)

D
A/D
A-/D
D9/F#
May-be I'm a man, and may-be you're the on - ly wom - an who could ev-er help_ me.

G
D/F#
D-/E
3
Ba-by, won't you help me to un - der-stand?_
Vocal ad lib. ends
Ooh,

1., 2.
E-7
A7
3.
E-7
A7
D.S. AL
ah.__
ah.__

OUTRO - GUITAR SOLO
D
A/D
A-/D
D9/F#
G
D
REPEAT AND FADE

(MED.)
MIDNIGHT TRAIN TO GEORGIA
-JIM WEATHERLY
INTRO
Db Ab/C Gb/Bb Gb/Ab
(HORNS)
VERSE
Db F- Gb/Bb Ab Db F-
1.Mm, L.A. proved too much for the man, (Too
* SUNG 2nd x ONLY
Gb/Bb Ab Db F- Gb/Bb Eb9
much for the man, he could-n't make it.) so he's leav-in' the life, mm, he's
Gb/Ab Db F-
come to know, oo. (He said he's go-in',) He said he's go-in' back to find,
Gb/Bb Ab Db F- Gb/Bb Ab Db F-
(go-in' back to find.) oo, what's left of his world, the world he left be-hind
Gb/Bb Eb9 Gb/Ab
not so long a-go.
CHORUS
Db F-
1.He's leav-in'
(2.,3.) he's leav-in'
(Leav-in'.)
Eb-7 Ab7 Db F- Eb-7 Ab7
on that mid-night train to Geor-gia, (Leav-in' on the mid-night train.) mm, yeah,
Db F- Bb-7 Eb9 Gb/Ab
said he's go-in' back (Go-in' back to find.) to a sim-pler place and time. Oh,
(When-ev-er he takes that ride,
Db F- Eb-7 Ab7
yes he is. And I'll be with him (I know you will.) on that mid-night train to Geor-
guess who's gon-na be right by his side.)

Bb-7
Eb9
Gbmaj7
-gia. (Leav-in' on that mid - night train_ to Geor-gia, ___ woo, woo!)
I'd rath-er live in his world_
Gb/Ab
Db
Ab/C
TO ⊕1
TO ⊕2
Gb/Bb
VERSE
F-
than live with-out him in mine.
(Live in his world._ Her world is his, his and hers_ a-lone.)_
2. He kept dream - in'
(Dream - in'.) oo, ___ that_some-day___ he'd be the star,
(A su-per star, but he did-n't get far.)
but he sure_ found out_ the hard___ way
that dreams___ don't_ al -
ways come true, oh no, ah, ah.
(Dreams don't al - ways_ come true, ah, ah, no, ah, ah.
So he pawned all his hopes
Woo, woo, and he e - ven sold________ his_ old car;
woo, ___ woo.
mm, bought a one-way tick-et back_
Woo, woo, woo, _ woo.)
to the life he
D.S. AL ⊕1
once knew._ Oh, yes he did. He said_ he would. 2. Oh, ______
⊕1
D.S. AL ⊕2
his, his and hers_ a-lone.)
3. Mm, ______
⊕2
OUTRO
REPEAT AND FADE (W/ LEAD VOC. AD LIB.)
Oh, ___ hey. ______ For love, _ gon-na board the mid-night train and ride._
his, his and hers___ a - lone.)_ (For love, gon-na board the mid-night train and go.)_

(MED.)
MISS YOU
-ERIC CLAPTON/BOBBY COLOMBY/GREGORY PHILLINGANES
INTRO-GUITAR SOLO
B7#5#9
E- E-/D C G A- E- E-/D C G A-
VERSE
E7sus4
Don't change your mind._ I ain't got the time__ to sit and__
don't say a word._ I al - read - y heard__ that you don't_
A7sus4
won-der.
love me.
E7sus4
I'm do - in' fine;_ if
In your__ state of mind__
you de - cide to leave_ I won't go__
I don't need to hear__ your side of the sto
A7sus4
un - der.
- ry.
PRE-CHORUS
C
You know I've come this far with-out____
Your friends all said we had a fu -
I broke my back to make__ you hap -
G
you.
ture, but
py.
D
It won't be too hard to be__ a - lone.
I don't think I real - ly want_ to know.
Some - time, some - how, some - one's got__ to pay.
A
C
I've got choic - es all a - round__
My friends keep tell - ing me to lose___
If you think you're bet - ter off__ with-out____
G
me, so I
you, and how
me, just re -

E-
B7/F#
won't be spend-ing too much time_ at home._
glad they'll be when you de-cide___ to go._
mem-ber it's a dirt-y world out there._
Still, I'm gon-na
CHORUS
E- E/D C G A- E- E/D C
miss you._ I'm gon-na miss you, ba - by.___
G A- E- E/D C G A-
I can't for-give__ you._ Still, I'm gon-na
E- E/D C TO ⊕ 1. G A- 2. G A-
miss you, ba - by.___ No, Yeah, yeah,
GUITAR SOLO
PLAY 7x, THEN D.S. AL ⊕
E- E/D C G A- E- E/D C G A-
yeah._
⊕ G A- E- E/D C
Yeah,___ I'm gon-na miss the ground_ you walk on.
G A- E- E/D C G A-
Gon-na miss the air__ you breathe.
E- E/D C G A-
I'm giv-in' up for-get-tin' ya, ba - by. I've got
E- E/D C G A-
plans and plans_ for me.___
OUTRO - GUITAR SOLO
REPEAT AND FADE
E- E/D C G A- E- E/D C G A-

(MED. FAST)
MODERN LOVE
—DAVID BOWIE
INTRO
N.C.
PLAY 4x
E-7
(GUITAR)
(KEYS)
Spoken: I know
C6/9
when to go out.
I know when to stay in.
Dsus4
E-7
get things done.
VERSE
C
1. I catch a pa - per - boy, but things don't real - ly change.
2.There's no sign of life it's just the pow - er to
3. Instrumental
4.It's not real - ly work, it's just the pow - er to
G
A-
I'm stand - ing in the wind,
charm. I'm ly - ing in the rain,
charm. Still stand - ing in the wind,
but I
E7
F
nev - er wave bye - bye.
C
G
But I try, I try.
E-
1.
2.
Instrumental ends
Nev - er gon - na fall for...

CHORUS
C
D7
(Mod - ern love...) ...walks be - side_ me._ (Mod - ern love...) ...walks on by._
E-
F
(Mod - ern love...) ...gets me to the church on time._
C
D7
(Church on time...) ...ter - ri - fies_ me._ (Church on time...) ...makes me par - ty.
E-
F
(Church on time...) ...puts my trust in God and man.
C
D7
(God and man.) No con - fes - sions._ (God and man.) No re - li - gion.
E-
F
TO ⊕
D.S. AL ⊕
(TAKE REPEAT)
(God and man.) Don't be - lieve_ in mod - ern love.
OUTRO - CHORUS
C
love. Mod - ern love._ Mod - ern
(Mod - ern love.
D7
E-
love._ Mod - ern love._
Mod - ern love. Mod - ern love.
F
REPEAT AND FADE
Mod - ern love._ Mod - ern
Mod - ern love.)

(MED.)
MONDAY, MONDAY
–JOHN PHILLIPS
INTRO
N.C. (F#) (B/F#) (F#) (B/F#) (F#)
(BKGD. VOC. CONT. SIM.)
VERSE
(Ba, da, ba, da, da, da.)
Mon - day, Mon - day,
so good to me.
can't trust that day.
Mon - day morn - ing, it was all
Mon - day, Mon - day, some-times it
I hoped it would be.
just turns out that way.
Oh, Mon - day morn - ing, Mon-day morn -
Oh, Mon - day morn - ing, you gave me no warn -
- ing could-n't guar - an - tee
ing of what was to be.
that Mon - day eve - ning you would still
Oh, Mon - day, Mon - day, how could you leave
be here with me.
and not take me?
Mon - day, Mon-
Ev -
BRIDGE
- 'ry oth-er day, (Ev-'ry oth-er day.) ev-'ry oth-er day, ev-'ry oth-er day of the week is
fine, yeah. But when-ev-er Mon-day comes, but
(But when-ev-er Mon-day comes,
when-ev-er Mon-day comes, then you can find me cry - in' all of the time, Mon - day, Mon-
you can find me...)

VERSE
(BKGD. VOC. W/ INTRO FIG. SIM.)
- day, so good to me. Mon-day morn - ing, it was all
I hoped it would be. But Mon - day morn - ing, Mon-day morn-
- ing could-n't guar - an - tee that Mon - day eve - ning you would still
be here with me.
BRIDGE
Ev - 'ry oth-er day, (Ev-'ry oth-er day.) ev-'ry
oth-er day, ev-'ry oth-er day of the week is fine, yeah. But
when-ev-er Mon - day comes, but when-ev-er Mon - day comes, then you can find me
(But when-ev-er Mon-day comes, you can find me...)
cry - in' all of the time. Mon - day, Mon -
OUTRO (BKGD. VOC. W/ INTRO FIG. SIM.)
- day, can't trust that day. Mon - day, Mon -
- day, it just turns out that way. Oh, Mon - day, Mon-
REPEAT AND FADE
(W/ LEAD VOC. AD LIB.)

MONY, MONY
(MED.)
—BOBBY BLOOM/TOMMY JAMES/RITCHIE CORDELL/BO GENTRY
INTRO
N.C.
PLAY 3x
P.M.
(BASS & GUITAR)
(BS. & GTR. CONT. SIM.)
VERSE
A
Here she comes now, say, Mo-ny, Mo - ny.
Wake me, shake me, Mo-ny, Mo - ny.
D/A
A
Well, shoot 'em down, turn a-round, come on, Mo - ny.
Shot - gun, get it done, come on, Mo - ny.
Hey, she give me lov-in', I feel all right, now.
Don't stop cook-in', it feels so good, yeah.
You got me toss - in', turn - in' in the mid - dle of the night, and I feel all right, I say yeah!
Hey, well don't stop now, hey, come on, Mo - ny, well come on, Mo - ny, yeah!
D
PRE-CHORUS
E
(Yeah!) Yeah! (Yeah!) Yeah! (Yeah!) Yeah! (Yeah!) Yeah! (Yeah!) Well, you make me
3
CHORUS
feel (Mo-ny, Mo - ny.) so (Mo-ny, Mo - ny.) good. (Mo-ny, Mo - ny.) Yeah!

D
So good. Al-right. Come on.
(Mo-ny, Mo - ny. Mo-ny, Mo - ny. Mo-ny, Mo - ny.
E
Al - right, babe. Say yeah! (Yeah!) Yeah!
Mo-ny, Mo - ny. Mo-ny, Mo - ny.)
(Yeah!) Yeah! (Yeah!) Yeah! (Yeah!) Yeah! (Yeah!) Yeah! Get up!
1. N.C.
2. N.C.
P.M.
(BS & GUITAR)
8VB
(PIANO)
(Oo, I love you
BRIDGE
N.C.
W/ LEAD VOC. AD LIB.
Mo-ny, Mo - Mo - Mo - ny. Oo, I love you Mo-ny, Mo - ny.) Mo - ny, Mo - ny. Yeah!
E
(Yeah!) Ev-'ry-bod-y! (Yeah!) Mm, yeah! (Yeah!) Yeah! (Yeah!) Yeah! (Yeah!) Yeah!
OUTRO
(BKGD. VOC. W/ CHORUS PATTERNS)
A
D
Come on. Come on. Come on. Ev-'ry-bod - y. Al - right.
E
Al - right. Come on. You got it. Yeah! (Yeah!) Yeah!
FADE OUT
(Yeah!) Yeah! (Yeah!) Yeah! (Yeah!) Yeah! (Yeah!) Yeah!

(MED.)
MORE THAN WORDS
—NUNO BETTENCOURT/ GARY CHERONE
INTRO
G G/B Cadd9 A-7 C D Dsus4 G
(GUITAR)
VERSE
G G/B Cadd9 A-7 C D Dsus4 G
(GTR. CONT. SIM.)
Say-ing "I love you" is not the words I want to hear from you.
Now that I've tried to talk to you and make you un-der-stand,
G/B Cadd9 A-7 C D Dsus4 E-
It's not that I want you not to say, but if you on-ly knew
all you have to do is close your eyes and just reach out your hands
A-7 D7 G D/F# Dadd2/F# E-
how eas-y it would be to show me how you feel.
and touch me. Hold me close, don't ev-er let me go.
A-7 CHORUS D7 G7 G7/B C
More than words is all you have to do to make it real.
More than words is all I ev-er need-ed you to show.
C- G E-7
Then you would-n't have to say that you love me, 'cause
A-7 D *(D7b9/A) G Dadd2/F# E-
I'd al-read-y know. What would you do if my heart
*1st X

— was torn— in— two?—
More than words— to show— you feel—
— that your love— for me— is— real.—
What would you say—
— if I took— those words— a - way?—
Then you could - n't make— things new—
INTERLUDE
— just by say - ing "I— love— you."—
La, dee, da,— la, dee, da,—
*BKGD. VOC. 1ST X
— dee, dai,— dai,— da.—
More— than— words.—
La, dee, da,— dai,— da.—
— More— than— words.—
La, dee, dai,— dai,— dai,—
**BKGD. VOC. 2ND & 3RD X
— dee, dai,— dai,— da.—
More— than— words.——
More— than—
(...la,— da, da, da, da,— da.)—
OUTRO
words.— Oo,— oo,— oo,— oo,— oo,— oo,— oo.—
RIT.
FREE TIME GUITAR CADENZA
A TEMPO
RIT.
— More than— words.—

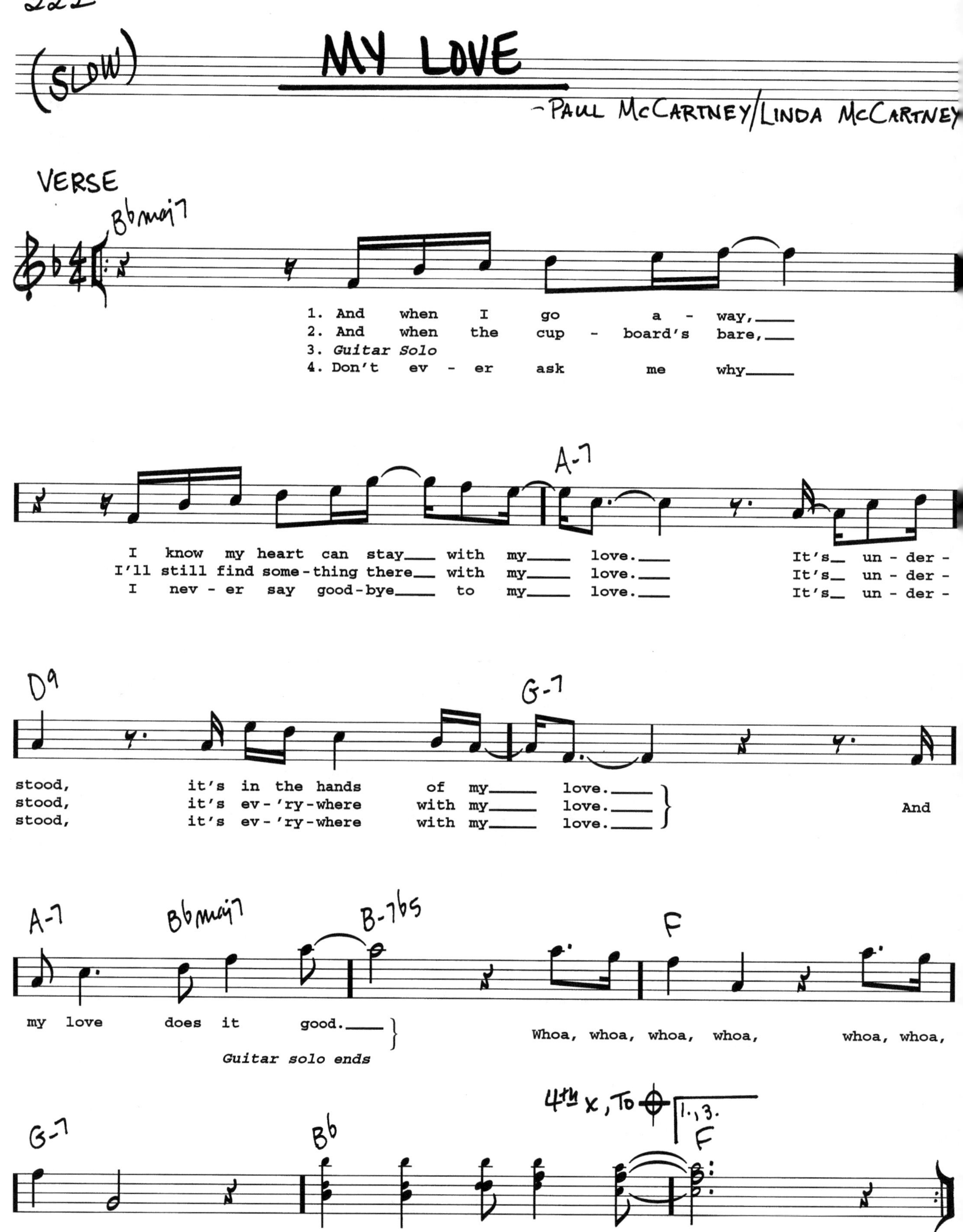

222
(SLOW)
MY LOVE
–PAUL McCARTNEY/LINDA McCARTNEY
VERSE
Bbmaj7
1. And when I go a - way,
2. And when the cup - board's bare,
3. Guitar Solo
4. Don't ev - er ask me why
I know my heart can stay with my love.
I'll still find some-thing there with my love.
I nev - er say good-bye to my love.
A-7
It's un - der -
D9
stood, it's in the hands of my love.
stood, it's ev - 'ry-where with my love.
stood, it's ev - 'ry-where with my love.
G-7
And
A-7
Bbmaj7
my love does it good.
Guitar solo ends
B-7b5
F
Whoa, whoa, whoa, whoa, whoa, whoa,
G-7
whoa, whoa.
Bb
My love does it good.
4th x, To
1., 3.
F

BRIDGE
F
G-7
C7
Whoa, whoa I love, oh, whoa,
F
A+
Bb6
C7
my love, on - ly my love holds the oth - er key
F
A+
G-7
C7
to me. Oh, whoa, my love, oh,
D.C. AL
F
A+
Bb6
C7
F
my love. On - ly my love does it good to me.
OUTRO
F
G-7
C7
Whoa, whoa, I love, oh, whoa,
FREELY
F
A+
Bb
C7
my love. On - ly my love does it good to
A TEMPO
F
A+
Bb6
C6
F
me. Whoa, whoa, whoa, whoa, whoa, whoa, whoa.

(MED. ♫ = ♪♪³)
(YOU MAKE ME FEEL LIKE A) NATURAL WOMAN
—GERRY GOFFIN/CAROLE KING/JERRY WEXLER
INTRO
F/C G-7 F/A
(PIANO)
VERSE
C
Look - in' out on
When my soul was in
G/B Bb
the morn - ing rain, I used to feel so
the lost and found, you came a - long to
F C/E D-7 C
un - in - spired. And when I knew I'd have to
claim it. I did - n't know just what was
G/B Bb
face an - oth - er day, Lord, it
wrong with me, 'til your kiss
F C/E D-7
made me feel so tired.
helped me name it.
PRE-CHORUS
D-9 E-7 D-9
Be - fore the day I met you, life was so un -
Now I'm no long - er doubt - ful of what I'm liv - ing
E-7 D-9
kind. You're the key to
for, and if I make you hap - py

E-7 D-9 G7sus4

my piece of mind,
I don't need to do more,
'cause you make me

CHORUS

C F C F

feel, you make me feel, you make me

C N.C. G7sus4

feel like a nat - u - ral wom - an. (Wom - an.)

BRIDGE

C G-7

Oh, ba - by, what you've done to me. (What you've done to me.)

C G-7

You make me feel so good in - side. (Good in - side.)

Fmaj9 C-7

And I just want to be (Want to be.)

Fmaj9 A-7/E D-7 G7sus4

close to you. You make me feel so a - live! You make me

OUTRO - CHORUS

C F C F

feel, you make me feel, you make me

C N.C. G7sus4 REPEAT AND FADE

feel like a nat - u - ral wom - an. You make me
(Wom - an.)

1999
(MED.)
—PRINCE
F6/C G-/C F6/C G-/C F6/C G-/C F6/C G-/C F6 G-/F
(KEYS)
F6 G-/F F6 G-/F 1. F6 G-/F F6 2. F6 G-/F F6
VERSE
Female: I was
dream - in' when I wrote this, for - give me if it goes a - stray.
dream - in' when I wrote this, so sue me if I go 2 fast.
did - n't come 2 par - ty, don't both - er knock - in' on my door.
Male: But when I woke up this morn - ing, could - 've
Male: But life is just par - ty, and
I got a li - on in my pock - et and,
sworn it was judg - ment day.
par - ties weren't meant 2 last.
ba - by, he's read - y 2 roar.
The
Male: Ev - 'ry -
sky was all pur - ple, there were peo - ple run - nin' ev - 'ry - where;
War is all a - round us, my mind says pre - pare 2 fight.
bod - y's got a bomb, we could all die an - y day.
Both:
try - in' 2 run from the de - struc - tion, U
So if I got - ta die, I'm gon - na
But be - fore I let that hap - pen, I'll
know I did - n't e - ven care.
lis - ten 2 my bod - y 2 - night.
dance my life a - way.
Male: 'Cuz they say two

CHORUS
Bb
D-7
F6 G-/F
ro, par-ty o-ver, oops, out of time. oops, out of time.
TO
F6 G-/F F6
So 2-night I'm gon-na par-ty like it's nine-teen nine-ty-nine.
1. F6 G-/F
F6 G-/F F6
Female: I was
2. F6 G-/F
(KEYS)
INTERLUDE
D.S. AL
Both: If U
Say it one_ more time. Two thou-sand, ze-ro, ze-ro, par-ty
o-ver, oops, out of time.
So 2-night I'm gon-na par-ty like it's
nine-teen nine-ty-nine.
Nine-teen nine-ty-nine._
OUTRO
Don't_ U wan-na go?
Nine-teen nine-ty-nine._
REPEAT AND FADE
(W/ LEAD VOC. AD LIB.)
Don't_ U wan-na go?
Nine-teen nine-ty-nine._

(MED. REGGAE)
NO WOMAN NO CRY
-VINCENT FORD
INTRO
G A-7 G/B C G/B A-7 F C F C G A-7 G/B
(ORGAN)
CHORUS
C G/B A-7 F C F C G A-7 G/B
No wom-an, no cry. No wom-an, no cry.
C G/B A-7 F C F C G A-7 G/B
No wom-an, no cry. No wom-an, no cry. 'Cause, 'cause,
VERSE
C G/B A-7 F
'cause I re-mem-ber a when a we used to sit
said I re-mem-ber a when a we used to sit
C G/B A-7 F
in the gov-ern-ment yard in Trench-town
in the gov-ern-ment yard in Trench-town, yeah.
C G/B A-7 F
o-ba, o-b-serv-ing the hyp-o-crites, yeah,
And then Geor-gie would make a fi-re-light, I say,
C G/B A-7 F C G/B
min-gle with the good peo-ple we meet, yeah. Good friends we have, oh,
a log a wood a burn-in' through the night, yeah. Then we would cook corn-meal
A-7 F C G/B A-7 F
good friends we have lost a-long the way, yeah.
por-ridge, I say, of which I'll share with you. yeah.

C G/B A-7 F
In this bright fu - ture, you can't for - get your past,
My feet is my on - ly car - riage, and so,
C G/B A-7 F TO ⊕ CHORUS C G/B A-7 F
so dry your tears I say, yeah. No wom-an no cry.
I've got to push on through, but while I'm gone:
C F C G A-7 G/B C G/B
No wom - an no cry, hey, yeah. A lit-tle dar-lin',
D.S. AL ⊕
A-7 F C F C G A-7 G/B
don't shed no tears. No wom - an, no cry. Hey, said, said,
⊕ BRIDGE
C G/B A- F
Ev-'ry-thing's gon-na be al-right. Ev-'ry-thing's gon-na be al-right.
C G/B A- F
Ev-'ry-thing's gon-na be al-right. Ev-'ry-thing's gon-na be al-right.
CHORUS
W/ VOC. AD LIB. ON REPEAT
C G/B A-7 F C F C G A-7 G/B
No wom-an, no cry. No wom-an, no cry, I say.
C G/B A-7 F
Oh lit - tle, oh lit - tle dar - lin', don't shed no tears.
C F C G A-7 G/B
No wom - an no cry, hey.
OUTRO - GUITAR SOLO
REPEAT AND FADE
C G/B A-7 F C F C G A-7 G/B

NOTHING FROM NOTHING

(MED.)

—BILLY PRESTON/BRUCE FISHER

F E7 D-7 G7 A-7 G-7 C7
ro is too cold for me.
I'm not try'n' to be your high -
- ing, be - lieve you me.
Don't you re - mem - ber I told
PIANO: W/ INTRO RIFF
F E7 A7 D7 G7 C7
(HORNS)
ness, 'cause that mi - nus is too low to see, yeah.
you I'm a sol - dier in the war on pov - erty? Yeah.
1., 2.
3.
D.S. AL
PIANO: W/ INTRO RIFF
HORNS: W/ VERSE RIFF
C7
That's right, babe. Oh, yeah.
Got - ta have some - thing if you wan - na be
with me. You got - ta bring a lit - tle some - thing, girl, if you wan - na be
REPEAT AND FADE
with me.

(MED.)
OH, PRETTY WOMAN
—ROY ORBISON/ BILL DEES
INTRO
E7
(GUITAR)
PLAY 3X
Pret-ty
VERSE
A
F#-
A
wom - an walk-ing down the street. Pret-ty wom - an, the kind I
wom - an, won't you par-don me? Pret-ty wom - an, I could-n't
wom - an, don't walk on by. Pret-ty wom - an, don't
F#-
D
like to meet. Pret - ty wom - an, I don't be -
help but see. Pret - ty wom - an, that you look
make me cry. Pret - ty wom - an, don't
E
TO
lieve you. You're not the truth. No one could look as good as you.
love-ly as can be. Are you lone - ly just like me?
walk a - way. Hey, o - kay.
E7
Spoken: Mer-cy!
Spoken: Rrr!
1.
Pret-ty
2.
BRIDGE
D-
G7
C
Pret-ty wom - an, stop a - while. Pret-ty wom - an,
A-
D-
G7
C
talk a - while. Pret-ty wom - an, give your smile to me.

D-
G7
C
A-
Pret-ty wom - an, yeah, yeah, yeah.
Pret-ty wom - an, look my way.
D-
G7
C
A
Pret-ty wom - an, say you'll stay with me.
'Cause I
F#-
D-
E
A
need you.
I'll treat you right.
Come to me
F#-
D-
E7
D.S. AL
ba - by.
Be mine to - night.
Pret-ty
If that's the way it must be, o - kay.
I guess I'll
N.C.
go on home; it's late.
There'll be to - mor - row night, but wait!
What do I
E7
see?
Is she walk-ing back to
me?
Yeah,
she's walk - ing back to
A
N.C.
me!
Oh,
pret-ty wom-an.

234
(MED.)
OLD TIME ROCK & ROLL
– GEORGE JACKSON/THOMAS E. JONES III
INTRO
N.C.
(PIANO)
VERSE
F#
Just take those old rec-ords off the shelf, I'll sit and lis-ten to 'em
Tan - go. I'd rath-er hear some blues or
B
by my - self. To - day's mu-sic ain't
funk - y old soul. There's on - ly one sure way to
C#
got the same soul.
get me to go:
F#
I like that old time a rock and roll. Don't try to take me to a
start play-ing old time a rock and roll. Call me a rel-ic, call me
dis - co, you'll nev - er e - ven get me
what you will. Say I'm old-fash-ioned, say I'm
B
out on the floor.
o - ver the hill.
C#
In ten min - utes I'll be late for the door.
To - day's mu - sic ain't got the same soul.
F#
I like that old time a rock and roll.
I like that old time a rock and roll.
Still like that old time a
CHORUS
F#
rock and roll, that kind of mu - sic just
B
soothes the soul.

C#
F#
To ⊕
I rem-i-nisce a-bout the days of old___ with that old___ time a rock and roll.
C#
INSTRUMENTAL SOLO
F#
B
C#
F#
1.
C#
2.
C#
D.S. AL ⊕
Won't go to hear'em play a
Still like that old time a
⊕
C#
BREAKDOWN
N.C.
Still like that old time a rock and roll, that kind of mu-sic just
soothes the soul.__ I rem-i-nisce a-bout the days of old___
C#
with that old______ time a rock and roll. Still like that old time a
CHORUS
F#
B
rock and roll, that kind of mu-sic just soothes the soul.__
C#
I rem-i-nisce a-bout the days of old___ with that old______ time a
F#
C#
OUTRO-INSTRUMENTAL SOLO
F#
rock and roll. Still like that old time a *rock and roll.______
* SUNG 1ST X ONLY
REPEAT AND FADE
B
C#
F#
C#

236
MED. ♫ = ♩♪
ON THE ROAD AGAIN
—ALAN WILSON/FLOYD JON
INTRO/HARMONICA SOLO
E
G A E
Well, I'm so
VERSE
E
tired of cry - in', but I'm out on the road a - gain,
first time I trav - elled out in the rain and snow.
dear moth - er left me when I was quite, young,
G A E
I'm on the road a - gain. Well, I'm so
in the rain and snow. You know the
when I was quite young. And my
tired of cry - in', but I'm out on the road a - gain,
first time I trav - elled out in the rain and snow,
dear moth - er left me when I was quite young,
G A E
I'm on the road a - gain. I ain't got
in the rain and snow, I did - n't have
when I was quite young. She said, "Lord,
no wom - an just to call my spe - cial friend.
no pay - roll, not e - ven no place to go.
have mer - cy on my wick - ed son."

G A E
PLAY 3x
HARMONICA SOLO
E
You know the
And my
1., 2.
3.
VERSE
G A E E E
Take a hint from me, ma - ma, please
go - in' down that
don't you cry no more, don't you cry no more.
long old lone - some road all by my - self.
G A
E
Take a hint from me, ma - ma, please
But I ain't go - in' down that
don't you cry no more, don't you cry no more.
long old lone - some road all by my - self.
G A
E
'Cause it's soon one morn - ing
I can't car - ry you, ba - by, gon - na
down the road I'm gone.
car - ry some - bod - y else.
G A E
But I ain't
OUTRO - HARMONICA SOLO
E
G A E
REPEAT AND FADE

(MED. FAST COUNTRY)
ONE TOKE OVER THE LINE
—MICHAEL BREWER/THOMAS E. SHIPLEY
INTRO - GUITAR SOLO
C C7 F C E- A- D7 F G C
CHORUS
C C7 F C
One toke o-ver the line, sweet Je-sus, one toke o-ver the line.
E- A- D7 F G C
Sit-tin' down-town in a rail-way sta-tion, one toke o-ver the line.
C7 F C
Wait-in' for the train that goes home, sweet Mar-y, hop-in' that the train is on time.
TO 1
TO 2
E- A- D7 F G C
Sit-tin' down-town in a rail-way sta-tion, one toke o-ver the line.
VERSE
C C7 F C
Who do you love? I hope it's me.
I sailed a-way a coun-try mile
D7 F G
I've been chang-in', as you can plain-ly see.
and now I'm re-turn-in', and show-in' off my smile. I

C C7 F
I felt the joy and I learned a-bout the pain that my ma-ma said
met all the girls and I loved my-self a few, when to my sur-prise
C A- D F
if I should choose to make a part of me,
like ev-'ry-thing else that I've been through,
G 1. 2.
would sure-ly strike me dead. And now I'm... And now I'm
it o-pened up my eyes.
GUITAR SOLO
C C7 F C E- A- D7 F G
CHORUS
C C C7
Don't you know I'm just a wait-in' for the train that goes home, sweet Mar-y,
F
hop-in' that the train is on time. Sit-tin' in a
(hop-in' that the train is on time. Sit-tin' down-town in a
A- D7 F G C D.S. AL 2
rail-way sta-tion, one toke o-ver the line. I wan-na be...
2 OUTRO
C E- A- D7 F G
Sit-tin' down-town in a rail-way sta-tion, one toke o-ver the line.
C F D F G C
One toke, one toke o-ver the line.

ONE WAY OR ANOTHER
(MED. FAST)
—DEBORAH HARRY/NIGEL HARRISON
INTRO
(GUITAR IN DROP-D TUNING)
VERSE
One way or an - oth - er, I'm gon - na find ya. I'm gon - na get ya, get ya, get ya, get ya. One way or an - oth - er, I'm gon - na win ya. I'm gon - na get ya, get ya, get ya, get ya. One way or an - oth - er, I'm gon - na see ya. I wan - na meet ya, meet ya, meet ya, meet ya. One day, may - be next week, I'm gon - na meet ya. I'm gon - na meet ya. I'll meet ya.
One way or an - oth - er, I'm gon - na find ya. I'm gon - na get ya, get ya, get ya, get ya. One way or an - oth - er, I'm gon - na win ya. I'll get ya. I'll get ya. One way or an - oth - er, I'm gon - na see ya. How 'bout I meet ya, meet ya, meet ya, meet ya? One day, may - be next week, I'm gon - na meet ya. I'll meet ya. Ah.
One way or an - oth - er, I'm gon - na lose ya. I'm gon - na give you the slip, slip o' the hip or an - oth - er, I'm gon - na lose ya. I'm gon - na trick ya. I'll trick ya. One way or an - oth - er, I'm gon - na lose ya. I'm gon - na trick ya, trick ya, trick ya, trick ya. One way, or an - oth - er, I'm gon - na lose ya. I'm gon - na give you the slip.
To
BRIDGE
I will drive past your house.
And if the lights are all out,

G5 B5 A5 F#5
And if the lights are all down, I'll
I'll fol - low your bus down - town; see
G5 A5 B5 E5 F#5
see who's a - round.
who's hang - ing out.
(DRUM FILL)
GUITAR SOLO
F#5 A5 C#5 F#5
A5 C#5 B5
E5 F#5 G5 G#5 A5
D.S. AL ⊕
A#5 B5 C5 C#5 D5
⊕ OUTRO
HALF-TIME FEEL
D B
(GUITAR)
D B
I'll walk down the mall, stand o - ver by the wall where I can see it all,
Lead you to the su - per - mar - ket, check out some spe - cials and rap; we'd
D
find out who you call. One way or an - oth - er I'm gon - na
get lost in the crowd.
B
1.
END HALF-TIME FEEL
2. - X.
REPEAT AND FADE
get ya. I'll get ya. I'll get ya, get ya, get ya, get ya. get ya, get ya, get ya, get ya.
(Where I can see it all, find out who you call.) find out who you call.)

(MED.)
ONLY WANNA BE WITH YOU
– DARIUS CARLOS RUCKER/ EVERETT DEAN FELBER/ MARK WILLIAM BRYAN/ JAMES GEORGE SONEFEL
INTRO
(GUITAR)
VERSE
You and me, we come from diff-'rent worlds,
You look at me, you got noth-in' left to say.
Put on a lit-tle Dy-lan, sit-tin' on a fence.
Some-times I won-der if we'll ev-er end.
you like to laugh at me when I look at oth-er girls.
I moan and pout at you un-til I get my way.
I say, "That line is great." You ask me what he meant by,
You get so mad at me when I go out with my friends.
Some-times you're cra-zy, and you won-der why
I won't dance; you won't sing.
"Said I shot a man named Gray, took his wife to It-a-ly.
Some-times you're cra-zy, and you won-der why
I'm such a ba-by 'cause the Dol-phins make me cry. But there's
I just wan-na love you, but you want to wear my ring. But there's
She in-her-it a mil-lion bucks, and when she died it came to me. I can't
I'm such a ba-by, yeah the Dol-phins make me cry. But there's
CHORUS
4th x, To
noth-in' I can do, I've been look-in' for a girl like you.
noth-in' I can do, I on-ly wan-na be with you.
help it if I'm luck-y." I on-ly wan-na be with you.
noth-in' I can do, I on-ly wan-na be with you.
You can

BAdd2
C#add4
(GTR.)
F#
B6add2
call me a fool,
I only wan-na be with you.
F#
B6add2
3.
F#
B6add2
(GTR.)
F#
B6add2
Badd4
Ain't Bob-by so cool?
C#add4
GUITAR SOLO
F#
B6add2
F#
B6add2
PLAY 6X
F#
B6add2
I on-ly wan-na be with you.
Yeah, I'm
CHORUS
G#7add4
Badd2
F#
B6add2
(GTR.)
tang-led up in blue,
I on-ly wan-na be with you.
F#
B6add2
Badd2
(GTR.)
C#add4
You can call me a fool.
I
D.S. AL
F#
B6add2
F#
B6add2
F# B6add2
F# B6add2
(GTR. W/ INTRO PATTERN)
on-ly wan-na be with you.
F#
B6add2
Badd2
C#add4
(GTR.)
You can call me a fool,
F#
B6add2
F#
B6add2
I on-ly wan-na be with you.
Yeah, I'm
Badd2
C#add4
tang-led up in blue,
I on - ly wan-na be with you.
OUTRO
F#
B6add2
F#
B6add2
F#
B6add2
PLAY 3X
(GTR.)
I on-ly wan-na be with you.

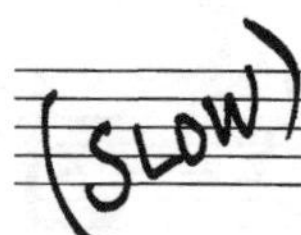

OUR HOUSE

(SLOW)

—GRAHAM NASH

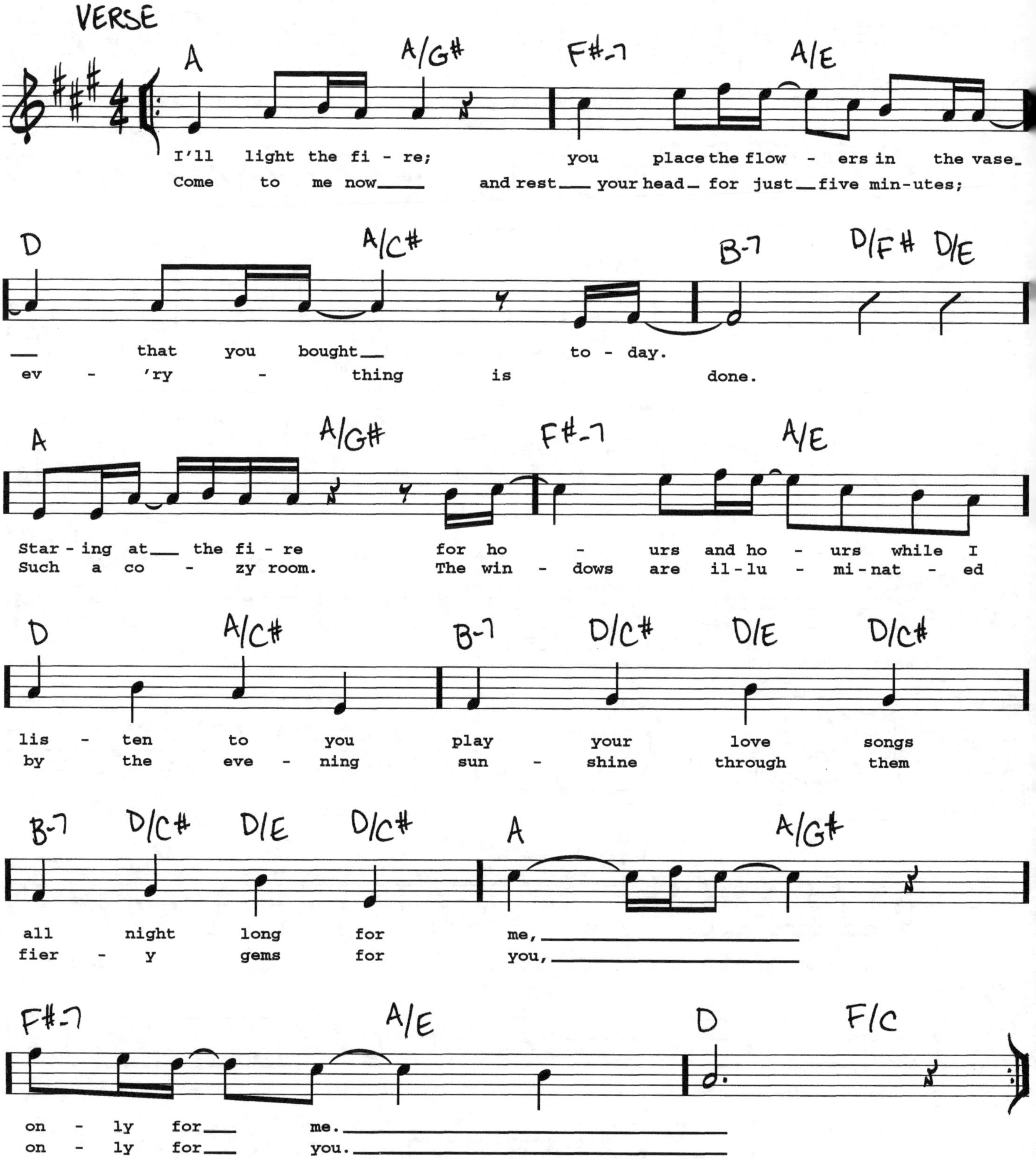

VERSE
A A/G# F#-7 A/E
I'll light the fi - re; you place the flow - ers in the vase
Come to me now and rest your head for just five min-utes;
D A/C# B-7 D/F# D/E
that you bought to - day.
ev - 'ry - thing is done.
A A/G# F#-7 A/E
Star - ing at the fi - re for ho - urs and ho - urs while I
Such a co - zy room. The win - dows are il - lu - mi - nat - ed
D A/C# B-7 D/C# D/E D/C#
lis - ten to you play your love songs
by the eve - ning sun - shine through them
B-7 D/C# D/E D/C# A A/G#
all night long for me,
fier - y gems for you,
F#-7 A/E D F/C
on - ly for me.
on - ly for you.

CHORUS
A A/G# F#-7 A/E
Our house is a ver-y, ver-y, ver-y fine house, with
D A/C# D A/C#
two cats in the yard._ Life used to be_ so hard;_ now ev-
D A/C# D
-'ry-thing_ is eas - y 'cause of you
2nd X, SLOWER
B-7 D TO INTERLUDE A A/G#
and our... La, la, la, la, la, la, la,___
F#-7 A/E 1. D A/C#
__ la, la, la, la,__ la, la, la, la, la, la, la, la, la,_ la, la,_ la,
B-7 D/F# D/E 2. D F/C D.S. AL
la, la, la,_ la, la, la, la, la. la, la, la, la, la,_ la, la, la.
OUTRO
A A/G# F#-7 A/E
I'll light the fi-re, while you place the flow - ers in the vase_
D F/C A
_ that you bought_ to - day.___

PAPA WAS A ROLLIN' STONE

(MED.)

–NORMAN WHITFIELD/BARRETT STRONG

Additional Lyrics

2. Hey Mama, is it true what they say, that Papa never worked a day in his life?
   And Mama, there's some bad talk go'n' around say'n' Papa had three outside children
   And another wife, and that ain't right.
   Heard some talk about Papa doin' some store-front preachin', talkin' about savin' souls,
   And all the time leachin'.
   Dealin' in dirt and stealin' the name of the Lord.
   Spoken: Mama just hung her head and said, "Pop;

3. Hey Mama, I heard Papa call himself a jack of all trades.
   Tell me, is that what sent Papa to an early grave?
   Folks say Papa would beg, borrow, steal to pay his bills.
   Hey Mama, folks say Papa never was much on thinkin',
   Spent most of his time chasin' women and drinkin'.
   Mama, I'm dependin' on you to tell me the truth.
   Spoken: Mama looked up with a tear in her and and said, "Son...

(FAST)
PART TIME LOVER
—STEVIE WONDER
INTRO
(SYNTH) Bb- Ab Gbmaj7 F-7
Voc. 2nd x ONLY
Da, da, da, da, da, da, da, da, da, da, da, da, da, da, da, da, da,
Eb-7 F-7 Bb-7 1. Eb-7 F-7 2. Eb-7 F-7
da, da, da, da, da, da, da, da, da, da, da, da.
Call up, ring
VERSE
Bb- Ab Gbmaj7
once, hang up the phone to let me know you made it home,
friends and we should meet, just pass me by don't e - ven speak,
thing that I must tell; last night some - one rang our door - bell
F-7 Eb-7 F-7 Ab Bb-
don't want noth - ing to be wrong with part - time lov - er.
know the word's "dis - creet" with part - time lov - ers.
and it was not you, my part - time lov - er.
Ab Gbmaj7
If she's with me, I'll blink the lights to let you know to - night's the night
But if there's some e - mer - gen - cy, have a male friend to ask for me
And then a man called our ex - change but did - n't want to leave his name,
F-7 Eb-7 F-7 Ab Bb- To ⊕
for me and you, my part - time lov - er.
so then she won't peek, it's real - ly you my part - time lov - er.
I guess that two can play the game of part - time lov - ers.
Ab-7 Db7 𝄋 CHORUS Gb Db
We are un - der - cov - er pas - sion on the run,

Eb-
F- G-7b5 Ab Bb- Ab-7 Db7
chas-ing love, up a-gainst the sun. We are
Gb Db
stran-gers by day, lov-ers by night, know-ing it's so
Eb-6 Fadd4 1., 3. N.C. 2. N.C.
wrong, but feel-ing so right. If I'm with Oh.
I've got some-
INTERLUDE
Bb- Ab Gbmaj7 F-7
Da, da, da, da, da, da, da, da, da, da, da, da, da, da, da, da, da,
(Oo, oo, oo, oo,
Eb-7 F-7 Ab/Bb Bb- 1. Eb-7 F-7 2. Ab-7 Db7 D.S. AL CODA
da, da, da, da, da, da, da, da, da, da, da, da.
oo. Part-time lov-er.) We are
Eb-7 F-7 Ab Bb-
You and me, part-time lov-ers.
Eb-7 F-7 Ab Bb- Ab Bb- N.C.
But she and he, part-time lov-ers.
OUTRO
Bb- Ab Gbmaj7 F-7
Da, da, da, da, da, da, da, da, da, da, da, da, da, da, da, da, da,
(Oo, oo, oo, oo,
REPEAT AND FADE
Eb-7 F-7 Ab/Bb Bb- Eb-7 F-7
da, da, da, da, da, da, da, da, da, da, da, da.
oo. Part-time lov-er.)

(MED. FUNK)

PICK UP THE PIECES

—JAMES HAMISH STUART/ALAN GORRIE/ROGER BALL/
ROBBIE McINTOSH/OWEN McINTYRE/MALCOLM DUNCAN

C7#9
Shouted: Pick up the pie - ces, uh huh,
pick up the piec - es, al - right. Pick up the piec - es, uh huh, pick up the piec - es.
E SAX SOLO
Ab/Bb
PLAY 4X
(GTR.)
(SAXES)
(GTR. CONT. RHY. SIM.)
F-7
2nd X, D.S. AL ⊕
⊕2 F
Ab/Bb
CONT. RHY. SIM.
PLAY 3X
C7#9
G GTR. W/ B RIFF
F-7
1., 2.
Pick up the piec - es. Pick up the piec - es. Pick up the
3.
Ow!
(SAXES)

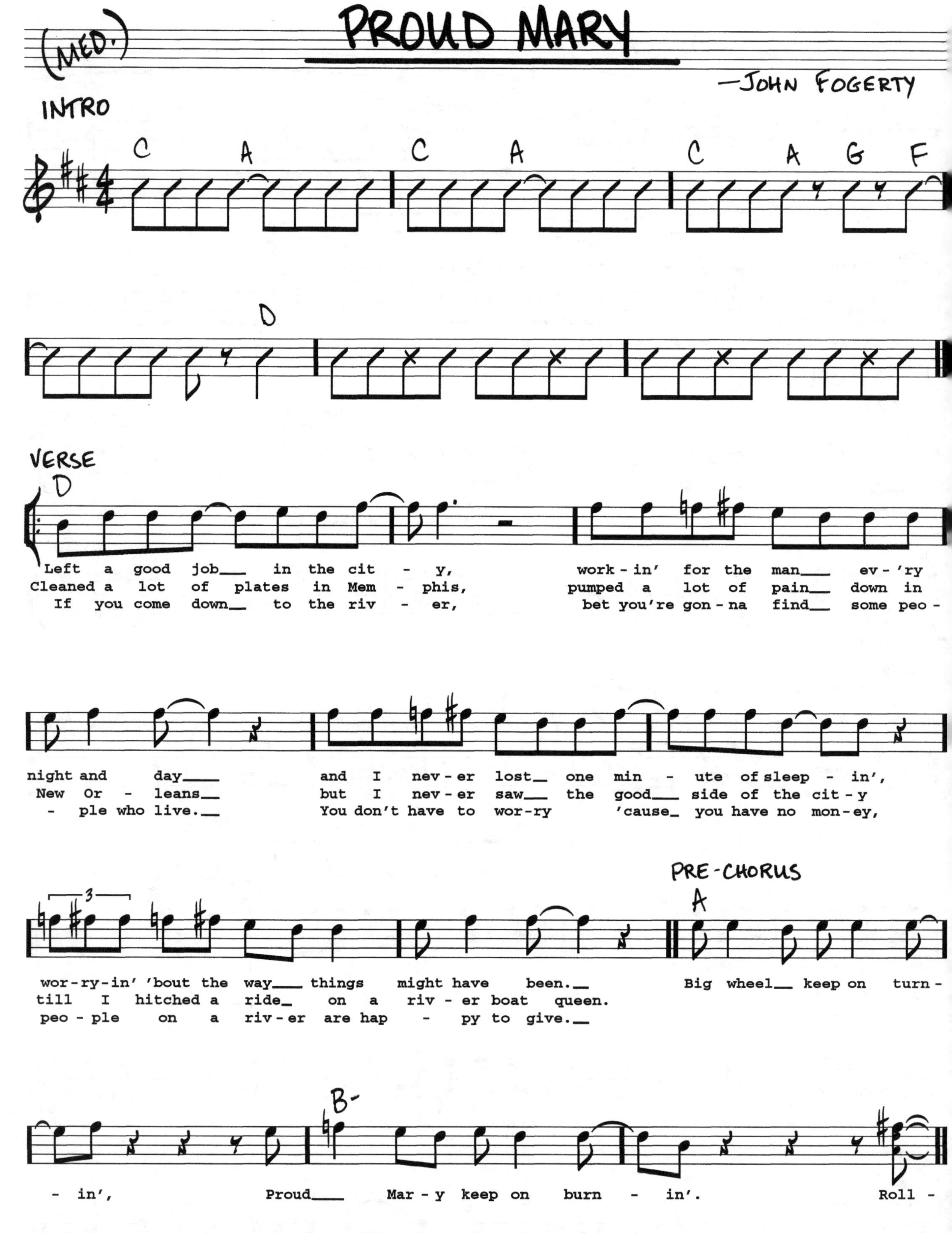
(MED.)
PROUD MARY
—JOHN FOGERTY
INTRO
C A C A C A G F
D
VERSE
D
Left a good job__ in the cit - y, work - in' for the man__ ev - 'ry
Cleaned a lot of plates in Mem - phis, pumped a lot of pain__ down in
If you come down__ to the riv - er, bet you're gon - na find__ some peo -
night and day____ and I nev - er lost__ one min - ute of sleep - in',
New Or - leans__ but I nev - er saw__ the good__ side of the cit - y
- ple who live.__ You don't have to wor - ry 'cause_ you have no mon - ey,
3
wor - ry - in' 'bout the way__ things might have been.__
till I hitched a ride_ on a riv - er boat queen.
peo - ple on a riv - er are hap - py to give.__
PRE-CHORUS
A
Big wheel__ keep on turn -
B-
- in', Proud__ Mar - y keep on burn - in'. Roll -

CHORUS

D

To ⊕

- in', roll - in', roll - in' on a riv - er.

INTERLUDE

C A C A C A G F

D

GUITAR SOLO

D

A B-

Roll -

CHORUS

D

D.C. AL ⊕

- in', roll - in', roll - in' on a riv - er.

⊕

OUTRO

D

Roll - in', roll - in', roll -

REPEAT AND FADE

- in' on a riv - er. Roll -

RAMBLIN' MAN
(FAST)
INTRO
-DICKEY BETTS
8VA
(GUITARS)
CHORUS
*2nd x, SUBSTITUTE C
Lord, I was born a ram - blin' man.
Instrumental
Try'n to make a liv-ing, and do-in' the best I can. An'
when it's time for leav - in' I hope you'll un - der - stand
that I was born a ram - blin' man. Well, my
Instrumental ends I'm
VERSE
fath-er was a gam - bler down in Geor - gia, and he
on my way to New Or - leans this morn - in' a
wound up on the wrong end of a gun. And
leav-in' out of Nash - ville, Ten-nes - see. They're

C G E- C
I was born in the back seat of a Grey-hound bus,
al-ways hav - in' a good time down on the bay-ou, Lord. Them
G D G
roll-in' down High - way For - ty - one.
del - ta wom-en think the world of me.
CHORUS
G F C G
Lord, I was born a ram - blin' man.
C D
Try'n to make a liv-ing, and do-in' the best I can. An'
C G E- C
when it's time for leav - in' I hope you'll un - der-stand
G D G 1. D 8VA N.C.
that I was born a ram - blin' man.
(GTRS.)
INTERLUDE
G D G
2.
CHORUS
G F C G
Lord, I was born a ram - blin' man.
(GTRS.)
OUTRO - GTR. SOLO
G F C G
REPEAT AND FADE
(GTRS.)

(MED.)

RAPTURE

– DEBORAH HARRY/CHRIS STEIN

INTRO (GUITAR) E-7

(BASS)

𝄋 VERSE

E-7

Toe__ to__ toe,__ dancing very close,__ body breathing,__ almost comatose.__
Back__ to__ back,__ sacroiliac__ spineless movement__ and a wild attack.__

Wall__ to__ wall,__ people hypnotized,__
Face__ to__ face,__ sightless solitude,__

F A C E- F A C G E-7

and they're stepping lightly,__ hang each night in rapture.__
and it's finger popping,__ twenty-four hour shopping in__ rapture.__

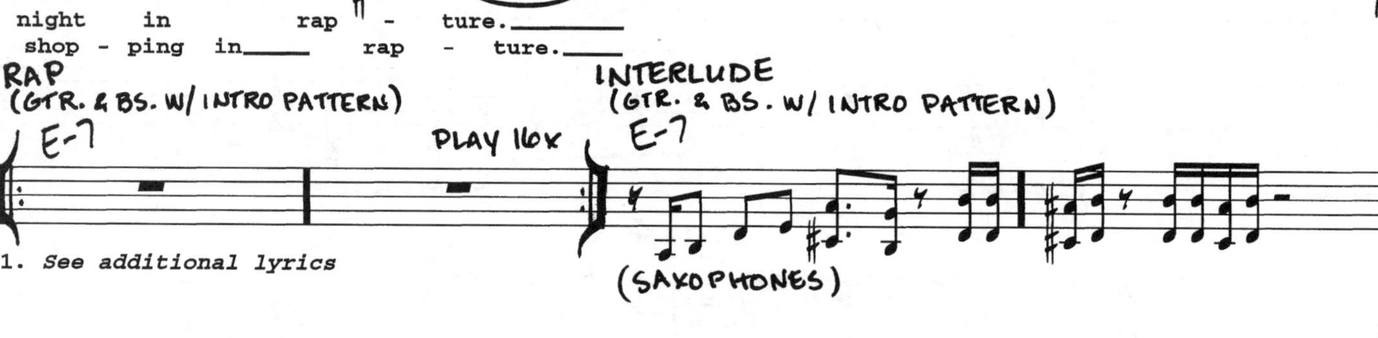

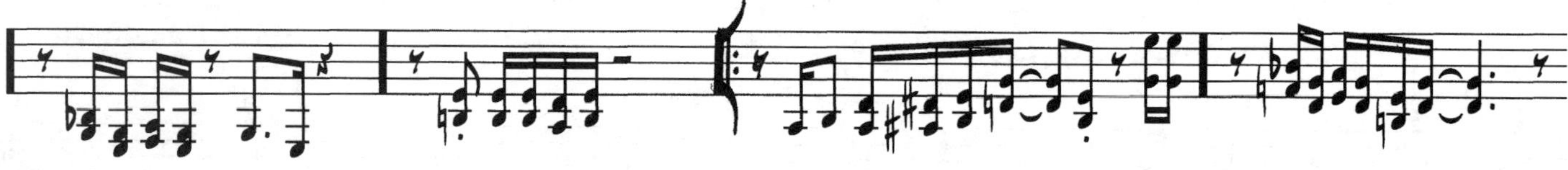

Rap Lyrics

Rap 1 *Fab five Freddy told me everybody's fly,*
DJ spinnin' I said, "My my."
Flash is fast, flash is cool,
Francois, c'est pas flache non due.
And you don't stop, sure shot.
Go out to the parking lot and
Get in your car and drive real far.
And you drive all night and then you see a light,
And it comes right down and it lands on the ground,
And out comes the man from Mars.
And you try to run but he's got a gun,
And he shoots you dead and he eats your head.
And then you're in the man from Mars.
You go out at night eating cars.
You eat Cadillacs, Lincolns too,
Mercuries and Subaru and you don't stop.
You keep on eatin' cars.
Then when there's no more cars you go out at night
And eat up bars where the people meet,
Face to face, dance cheek to cheek,
One to one, man to man.
Dance toe to toe, don't move too slow
'Cause the man from Mars is through with cars,
He's eating bars.
Yeah, wall to wall, door to door,
Hall to hall, he's gonna eat 'em all.
Rapture, be pure, take a tour
Through the sewer.
Don't strain your brain, paint a train.
You'll be singin' in the rain.
I said, "Don't stop, do punk rock."

Rap 2 *Well, now you see what you wanna be,*
Just have your party on TV
'Cause the man from Mars won't eat up bars
Where the TV's on.
And now he's gone back up to space
Where he won't have a hassle with the human race.
And you hip hop, and you don't stop,
Just blast off. A sure shot,
'Cause the man from Mars stopped eatin' cars
And eatin' bars, and now he only eats guitars.
Get up.

REBEL 'ROUSER

D
F#
B
F#
C#7
F#
E
G
(GUITAR)
C
G
D7
G
F
G
(SAX)
C
G
(GUITAR)
D7
G
REPEAT AND FADE

(MED. REGGAE)
RED, RED WINE
—NEIL DIAMOND
VERSE
Red, red, wine, goes to my head,
makes me for - get that I still need her so.
Red, red wine, it's up to you.
All I can do, I've done, mem - 'ries won't
go. Mem - 'ries won't go. I'd have
BRIDGE
sworn that with time thoughts of you would leave - my head.
I was wrong, now I find just one

𝄋 VERSE
Gb
Ab
Db
Gb
thing makes me___ for - get.___ Red, red wine,___
Ab/Eb
Gb/Ab
Db
Gb
Ab/Eb
Gb/Ab
Db
Gb
stay close_ to me.___ Don't let_ me be a - lone;
Ab/Eb
Gb/Ab
Ab
Gb
Ab
Db
Gb
it's tear - ing__ a - part___ my blue_ heart.___
Absus4/Eb
Ab
Db
Gb
1.
Absus4/Eb
Ab
2.
Absus4/Eb
Ab
D.S. AND FADE
I'd have Red, red

262
MED. ♫ = ♩♪ (triplet)
REELING IN THE YEARS
–WALTER BECKER/DONALD FAGEN
INTRO - GUITAR SOLO
N.C.
Gadd9
Aadd9
PLAY 4x
* Key signature denotes A Mixolydian.
(GUITAR)
VERSE
D
A/C#
B-7
A
D
Your ev-er last-in' sum-mer you can see it fad-in' fast. So you
You've been tell-in' me you're a gen-ius since you were sev-en - teen. In
I've spent a lot of mon-ey and I've spent a lot of time. The
A/C#
B-7
A
A7/E
grab a piece of some-thin' that you think is gon-na last. Well you would -
all the time I've known you I still don't know what you mean. The
trip we made to Hol-ly-wood is etched up - on my mind. Af-ter all
Ebo
D-
A/C#
D
n't e-ven know a dia - mond if you held it in your hand. The
week-end at the col-lege did-n't turn out like you planned. The
the things we've done and seen, you find an-oth-er man. The
A/C#
B-7
A
things you think are pre-cious I can't un - der-stand.
things that pass for know-ledge I can't un - der-stand.
things you think are use-less I can't un - der-stand.
Are you reel-in' in the
CHORUS
Gadd9
Aadd9
years, stow-in' a-way the time?
Gadd9
Are you gath-er-in' up the tears? Have you had e-nough of

Aadd9
Gadd9
mine?
Are you reel - in' in the years,
Aadd9
Gadd9
stow-in' a-way the time?
Are you gath-er-in' up the tears?
F#-7
TO
1.
2.
Have you had e-nough of mine?
(GUITAR)
INTERLUDE
Gadd9
Aadd9
1.
2.
Gadd9
Aadd9
(GUITARS)
GUITAR SOLO
Gadd9
Aadd9
PLAY 4X, THEN D.S. AL
INTERLUDE
Gadd9
GUITARS
Aadd9
1.
2.
OUTRO - GUITAR SOLO
Gadd9
Aadd9
REPEAT AND FADE

(MED.)
RESPECT
—OTIS REDDING
INTRO
(SAXES)
(GUITAR)
VERSE
C7 F7 G7 F7
What you want, ba - by, I got.
(Oo, oo.
G7 F7 G7
What you need, do you know I got it? All I'm ask-in'
Oo, oo. Oo,
F7 C7 F7
is for a lit-tle re-spect when you come home, hey, ba-by, when you get home,
oo. Just a lit-tle bit, just a lit-tle bit.
C7 F7 VERSE G7
mis - ter. I ain't go'n' do you wrong
Just a lit-tle bit, just a lit - tle bit.)
F7 G7 F7
while you're gone. Ain't go'n' do you wrong 'cause I don't wan - na.
(Oo.
G7 F7 C7
All I'm ask-in' is for a lit-tle re-spect when you come home, ba -
Oo, oo. Just a lit - tle bit,
F7 C7 F7
by, when you come home, yeah.
VERSE just a lit - tle bit. Just a lit - tle bit, just a lit - tle bit.)
G7 F7 G7
I'm a-bout to give you all of my mon-ey and all I'm ask-in'

F7
G7
F7
C7
in re-turn, hon-ey, is to give me my prop-ers when you get home, yeah,
(Just a, just a, just a, just a,
F7
C7
F7
ba-by, when you get home, yeah.
just a, just a, just a, just a. Just a lit-tle bit, just a lit-tle bit.)
SAX SOLO
F#.
1. B
2. G7
VERSE
G7
F7
G7
F7
Oo, your kiss-es, sweet-er than hon-ey. And guess what? So is my mon-ey.
(Oo. Oo, oo.
G7
F7
3
C7
All I want you to do for me is give it to me when you get home, yeah,
Oo, oo. Re - re - re - re -
F7
C7
F7
ba-by, whip it to me when you get home.
re - re - re - re - re-spect. Just a lit-tle bit, just a lit-tle bit.)
OUTRO
C7
F7
C7
F7
R-E-S-P-E - C-T, find out what it means to me. R-E-S-P-E - C-T, take care of T - C-B.
C7
F7
A lit-tle re - spect.
(Sock it to me, sock it to me, sock it to me, sock it to me, sock it to me, sock it to me, sock it to me, sock it to me.
C7
F7
REPEAT AND FADE
W/ LEAD VOC. AD LIB.
Whoa, yeah, a lit-tle re - spect.
Just a lit - tle bit, just a lit - tle bit.)

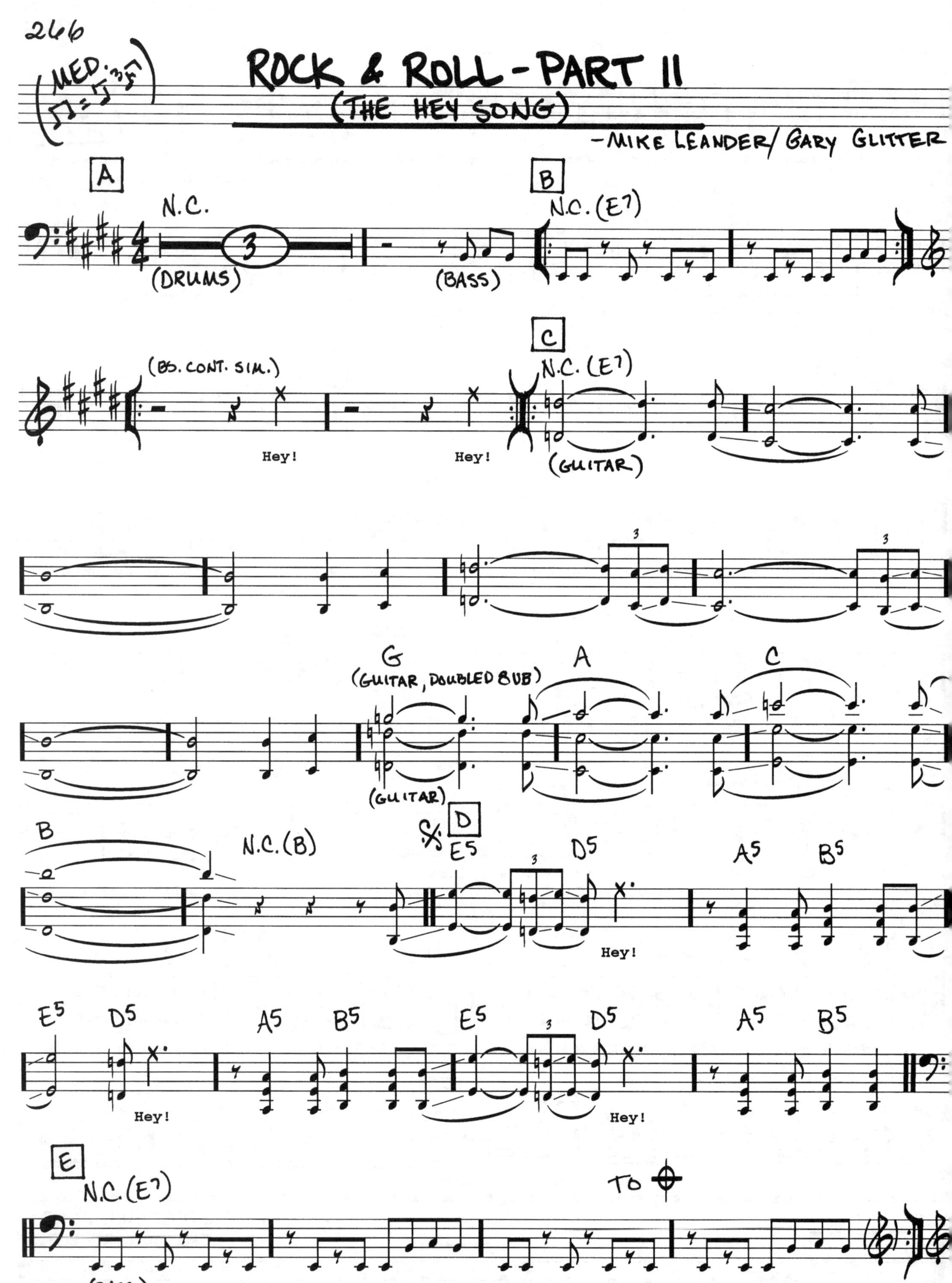
266
MED.
ROCK & ROLL - PART II
(THE HEY SONG)
-MIKE LEANDER/ GARY GLITTER
A
N.C.
(DRUMS)
(BASS)
B
N.C. (E7)
(BS. CONT. SIM.)
Hey!
Hey!
C
N.C. (E7)
(GUITAR)
G
(GUITAR, DOUBLED 8VB)
A
C
(GUITAR)
B
N.C. (B)
D
E5
D5
Hey!
A5
B5
E
N.C. (E7)
(BASS)
TO

F
N.C. (E7)
(BS. CONT. SIM.)
Hey, hey!
(Hey, hey!)
Hey, hey, hey!
(Hey, hey, hey!)
Hey, hey, hey, hey, yeah! (Hey, hey, hey, hey, yeah!) Hey, hey, hey, hey, yeah! (Hey, hey, hey, hey, yeah!) Hey, hey.
(Hey, hey.
Hey, hey.
Hey, hey.)
D.S. AL
(GTR.)
(BS. CONT. SIM.)
G
N.C. (E7)
Hey, hey, hey, hey, yeah! (Hey, hey, hey, hey, yeah!) Hey, hey, hey, hey, yeah! (Hey, hey, hey, hey, yeah!) Hey, hey, yeah! (Hey, hey, yeah!) Hey, hey, yeah! (Hey, hey, yeah!) Hey, hey.
(Hey, hey.)
REPEAT AND FADE
Hey.
(Hey.)

(MED.)

ROCK ME

—JOHN KAY

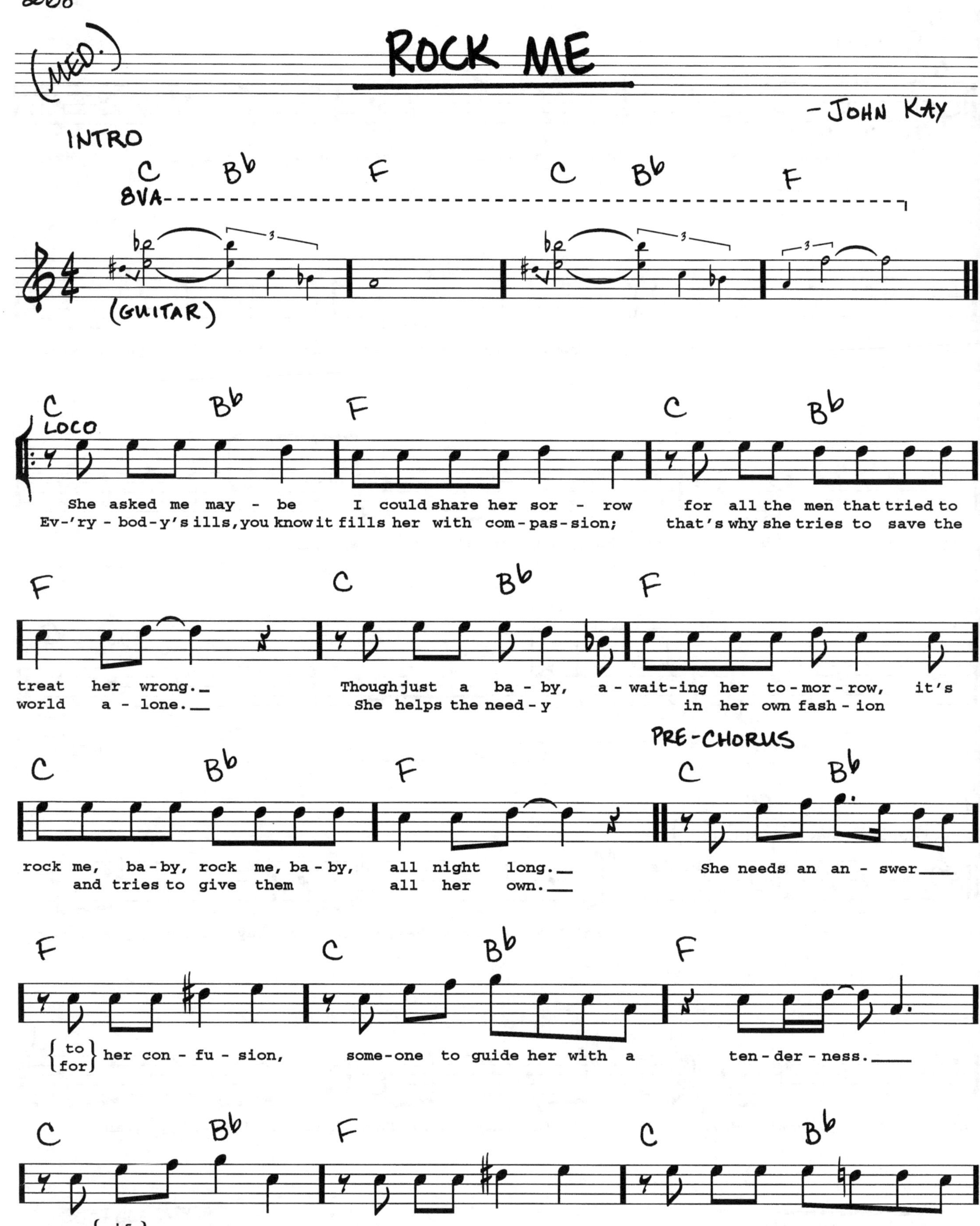
INTRO
C
Bb
F
C
Bb
F
8VA
3
3
3
(GUITAR)
C
LOCO
Bb
F
C
Bb
She asked me may - be I could share her sor - row for all the men that tried to
Ev-'ry - bod-y's ills, you know it fills her with com-pas-sion; that's why she tries to save the
F
C
Bb
F
treat her wrong.
world a - lone.
Though just a ba - by, a - wait-ing her to-mor-row, it's
She helps the need - y in her own fash - ion
C
Bb
F
PRE-CHORUS
C
Bb
rock me, ba-by, rock me, ba-by, all night long.
and tries to give them all her own.
She needs an an - swer
F
C
Bb
F
{to for} her con - fu - sion, some-one to guide her with a ten-der-ness.
C
Bb
F
C
Bb
But {if when} she's ask - in' for a so - lu - tion, all that she gets, you know, is

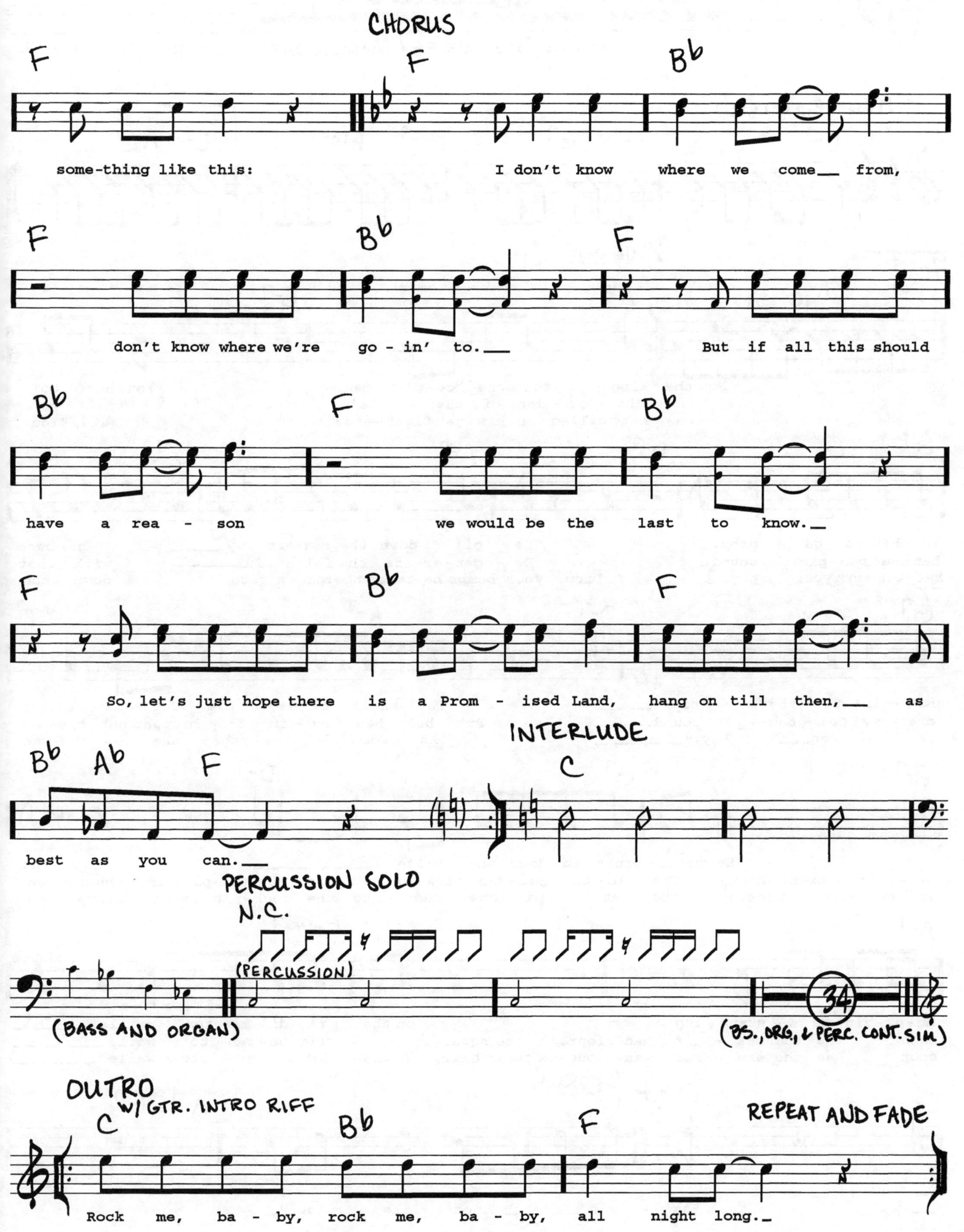
CHORUS
F
F
Bb
some-thing like this:
I don't know where we come__ from,
F
Bb
F
don't know where we're go - in' to.__
But if all this should
Bb
F
Bb
have a rea - son
we would be the last to know.__
F
Bb
F
So, let's just hope there is a Prom - ised Land, hang on till then,__ as
INTERLUDE
Bb
Ab
F
C
best as you can.__
PERCUSSION SOLO
N.C.
(PERCUSSION)
(BASS AND ORGAN)
34
(BS., ORG., & PERC. CONT. SIM.)
OUTRO
W/ GTR. INTRO RIFF
C
Bb
F
REPEAT AND FADE
Rock me, ba - by, rock me, ba - by, all night long.__

(MED.)
ROCK THE CASBAH
–JOE STRUMMER/MICK JONES/TOPPER HEADON
INTRO - PIANO SOLO
VERSE
Now the king told the boo-gie men, "You have to let that ra - ga drop.
Sha - or - der of the et, we ban that boo-gie sound.
king called out his jet fight-ers. He said, "You bet-ter earn your pay.
The oil down the des-ert way has been shak - in' to the top."
De - gen-er-ate the faith - ful with that cra - zy Cas - bah sound.
Drop your bombs be-tween the min - a-rets down the Cas - bah way."
The sheik, he drove his Cad - il - lac. He went a - cruis - in' down the ville.
But the Bed - ou - in, they brought out the e - lec-tric cam-el drum, The lo-cal gui - tar pick-er got his gui-tar-pick-ing thumb.
As soon as the sha - rif was chauf-feured out-ta there, the jet pi - lots tuned to the cock-pit ra-di-o blare.
The mu-ez-zin was a - stand - ing on the ra - di - a - tor grille.
As soon as the sha - rif had cleared the square, they be-gan to wail.
As soon as the sha - rif was out-ta their hair, the jet pi-lots wailed.
TO CHORUS
Sha - rif don't like it.

E-7 Fmaj7 E-7 A/C A- D-7 A-7 G7
Rock-in' the Cas - bah. Rock the Cas - bah. Sha - rif don't like it.
E-7 Fmaj7 1. E-7 A/C A- 2. E-7 A/C A- BRIDGE A-7
Rock-in' the Cas - bah. Rock the Cas - bah. By Rock the Cas - bah. Now, o-ver at the tem-ple,
N.C. A-7 N.C. A-7
oh, they real-ly pack 'em in. The in-crowd say it's cool
N.C. A-7 N.C. Fmaj7
to dig this chant-ing thing. But as the wind changed di-rec-tion
N.C. Fmaj7 N.C. G7 A-7
and the tem-ple band took five, the crowd caught a whiff
N.C. A-7 N.C. CHORUS D-7
of that cra-zy Cas - bah jive. Sha - rif don't like it.
A-7 G7 E-7 Fmaj7 E-7 A/C A- D-7
Rock-in' the Cas - bah. Rock the Cas - bah. Sha - rif don't like it.
A-7 G7 E-7 Fmaj7 E-7 A/C A- D.S. AL CODA
Rock-in' the Cas - bah. Rock the Cas - bah. The
OUTRO-CHORUS REPEAT AND FADE
D-7 A-7 G7 E-7 Fmaj7 E-7 A/C A-
rif don't like it. Rock-in' the Cas - bah. Rock the Cas - bah. Sha -

MED.
ROSANNA
-DAVID PAICH
INTRO
(GUITAR)
G Gsus4 G Gsus2 G Gsus4 G Gsus2
P.M.
VERSE
G Gsus4 G Gsus2 G Gsus4 Gsus2
All I wan-na do when I wake up in the morn-ing is see your eyes, Ro-
I can see your face still shin-in' through the win-dow on the oth-er side, Ro-
G Gsus4 G Gsus2 Fsus2
san-na, Ro-san-na. Nev-er thought that a girl like you could ev-er
san-na, Ro-san-na. I did-n't know that a girl like you could make me
E-7 G Gsus4 G Gsus2 G Gsus4 G C5
care for me, Ro-san-na.
feel so sad, Ro-san-na.
F5
All I wan-na do in the mid-dle of the eve-nin' is hold you tight, Ro-
All I wan-na tell you is now you'll nev-er ev-er have to com-pro-mise, Ro-
Ebsus2
san-na, Ro-san-na. I did-n't know you were look-in' for more than I
san-na, Ro-san-na. I nev-er thought that los-in' you could ev-
D-7
PRE-CHORUS
DOUBLE-TIME FEEL
G-
could ev-er be. Not quite a year since she
er hurt so bad.
F/A Bb Eb/Bb Bb F G-
went a-way, Ro-san-na, yeah. Now she's gone and I

END DOUBLE-TIME FEEL
F/A Bb Eb5 Bb5 F5 F7 Bb/F
have to say: Meet you
CHORUS
Bb/C C-7 Bb/C C-7 Ebadd2 Bb F F7 G-7 Bb/C C-7 Bb/C C-7 Eb5
all the way, meet you all the way, Ro - san -
Bb5 F5 F7 G-7 Bb/C C-7 Bb/C C-7 Ebadd2 Bb F F7 G-7
- na, yeah. Meet you all the way, meet you
Bb/C C-7 Bb/C C-7 Eb5 Bb5 F5 TO
all the way, Ro - san - na, yeah.
KEYBOARD SOLO
G Fadd2 E-7 G C5
GUITAR SOLO
F Eb D- D.S. AL
F7 G-7 Bb/C C-7 Bb/C C-7 Ebadd2 Bb F F7 G-7
Meet you all the way, meet you
Bb/C C-7 Bb/C C-7 Eb5 Bb F F7 G-7
all the way, Ro - san - na, yeah. Meet you
Bb/C C-7 Bb/C C-7 Ebadd2 Bb F F7 G-7 Bb/C C-7 Bb/C C-7 Eb5
all the way, meet you all the way, Ro - san -
Bb F
- na, yeah.
OUTRO-INSTRUMENTAL SOLO
G7
REPEAT AS DESIRED

RUBY BABY

—Jerry Leiber/Mike Stoller

INTERLUDE
E
Hey, hey. Hey, hey. Hey, hey.
A7
Hey, hey. Hey, hey. Hey, hey.
E
B7
Hey, hey. Hey, hey. Hey, hey.
A7
TO ⊕
E
D.S. AL ⊕
(NO REPEAT)
Hey, hey. Hey, hey. Well, I tell you. Now
⊕
E
OUTRO
E
Hey, hey. Ah, lis-ten, lis-ten, lis-ten now. Ru-by, Ru-by, ba - by,
FADE OUT
Ru - by, will you be mine?

(MED.)
RUNAWAY
—DEL SHANNON/MAX CROOK
INTRO
A-
(GUITAR)
(PIANO)
(GUITAR CONT. SIM.)
VERSE
A-
G
As I walk a - long, I won - der a
F
E7
what went wrong with our love, a love that was so strong.
A-
G
And as I still walk on, I think of the
F
E7
things we've done to - geth - er, a while our hearts were young.
CHORUS
A
F#-
I'm a-walk-in' in the rain. Tears are fall - in' and I
A
F#-
feel a pain, a - wish - in' you were here by me to end this

(GTR. & PIANO)
A
CONT. SIM.
F#-
mis - er - y. And I won - der, I wo - wo - wo - wo - won - der
A
F#-
(GTR. & PIANO)
why, why, why, why, why, why she ran a - way
D
E7
and I won - der where she will stay,
TO
A
D
A
my lit - tle run - a - way, a run - run - run - run - run - a - way.
MUSITRON SOLO
E7
A-
G
(MUSITRON)
F
E7
A-
G
F
E7
D.S. AL
A
D
A
REPEAT AND FADE
run - a - way, a run - run - run - run - run - a - way, a

278
SAN FRANCISCO
(BE SURE TO WEAR SOME FLOWERS IN YOUR HAIR)
(MED.)
—JOHN PHILLIPS
INTRO
G
(GTR.)
VERSE
E- C
If you're go - ing to
G D E- C
San Fran - cis - co, be sure to wear some
G D E- G
flow - ers in your hair. If you're go - in' to
C G B-
San Fran - cis - co, you're gon - na meet some
E- D
gen - tle peo - ple there.
VERSE
2nd X (A- C G E-)
E- C G D
For those who come to San Fran - cis - co,
For those who come to San Fran - cis - co,
E- C G D
sum-mer - time will be a love - in there.
Be sure to wear some flow - ers in your hair.

E- G C G
In the streets of San Fran - cis - co,
If you come to San Fran - cis - co,
B- E- TO D
gen-tle peo - ple with flow - ers in their hair.
sum-mer - time will be a love-in
BRIDGE
F
All a-cross the na - tion, such a strong vi-bra - tion:
G F
people in mo - tion. There's a whole gen-er-a-
-tion with a new ex-pla-na - tion,
G D D.S. AL
peo-ple in mo - tion, peo-ple in mo - tion.
OUTRO
G E- F#- A
there. If you come to
D A C#- F#-
San Fran - cis - co, sum-mer - time will ba a love-in
A F#- A D A
there.

(SLOW)
SARA SMILE
—DARYL HALL/JOHN OATES
INTRO
VERSE
Ba-by hair with a wom-an's eyes, I can feel you watch-ing
in the night. All a-lone with me and we're wait-ing for the
sun-light.
PRE-CHORUS
When I feel cold you warm me, and when I feel I can't go on, you come and hold me.
And when you feel cold I'll warm you, and when you feel you can't go on, I'll come and hold you.
It's you and me for-ev-er Sar-a
TO ⊕ CHORUS
Smile.
(Smile.
A, won't you smile a while for me, Sar-a.
Smile.)

VERSE
D-7
A-/C
If you feel like leav - ing,
you know you can go,
B♭maj7
G/A
A
but why don't you__ stay un - til to - mor - row?
D-7
A-/C
If you want to be free,
you know,
B♭maj7
G/A
A
D.S. AL ⊕
all you got__ to do__ is say__ so.
⊕ CHORUS
D-7
A-7
G-7
B♭/C
C#9
Smile.
A, won't you
(Smile.
D-7
A-7
1.
G-7
B♭/C
smile a while__ for me,
Sar - a.
Sar - a
Smile.
2.
G-7
B♭/C
G-7
B♭
C
D-
C/E
F
B♭
C#o7
(STRINGS)
OUTRO - CHORUS
W/ LEAD VOC. AD LIB.
REPEAT AND FADE
D-7
A-7
G-7
B♭/C
C#9
D-7
A-7
G-7
B♭/C
(Smile.
Smile.
Oo.)

282
(MED. SLOW)
SEARCHIN'
-JERRY LIEBER/MIKE STOLLER
INTRO
Db7
(Gon-na find her, gon-na find her,
gon-na find her, gon-na find her.)
Well, I've been
VERSE
W/BKGD. VOC. SIM.
Db7
search-in', I've been search - in', oh, yeah,
search-in' ev - 'ry which a way, yeah, yeah. Oh, yes,
Gb7
search-in', search-in',
Db7
search-in' ev - 'ry which a way,
yeah, yeah. But I'm like that
Ab7
Norh - west Moun - tie,
N.C.
you know I'll
bring her in
Db7
some - day.
(Gon - na find her, gon - na find her.)
Well, now

VERSE

Db7

if I have to swim a riv-er, a you know I will.__ A and a
Sher-lock a Holmes, Sam Spade__ a got noth-ing, child, on me.__

if I have to climb a moun-tain, a you know I will.__ A and a
Sar-geant Fri-day, Char-lie Chan__ and Bos-ton Black-ie, a no

if she's a hid-ing up on a blue-ber-ry hill,__
mat-ter where she's a hid-ing, she's a gon-na hear me a com-in'. I'm gon-na

am I gon-na find her, child, you know____ I will.__ 'Cause I've__ been
walk right down that street a like Bull-dog Drum-mond, 'Cause I've been

Gb7

search-in'. Oh,____ yeah,____ search-in'. My good-ness,____
search-in'. Oh,____ Lord,__ now, search-in'. Mm,____ child,__

Db7

search-in' ev-'ry which____ a way,__ yeah, yeah.

Ab7

But I'm like that North-west Moun-tie,__

N.C.

you know I'll

Db7

bring her in some-day.
(Gon-na find her, gon-na find her.)

1. 2.

OUTRO

Db7

REPEAT AND FADE

Well, (Gon-na find her.) (Gon-na

284
SEE YOU LATER, ALLIGATOR
(MED. FAST)
-ROBERT GUIDRY
INTRO
N.C.
Spoken: See you later, alligator.
Well, I saw my ba - by
VERSE
Eb
(SAX)
walk-ing with an-oth-er man to - day;
told me, near - ly made me lose my head;
dad-dy, I know you mean it just for play."
Eb7
Ab7
well, I saw my ba-by walk-ing with an-oth-er man to -
when I thought of what she told me, near - ly made me lose my
She said, "I'm sor-ry, pret-ty dad-dy, I know you mean it just for
Eb
Bb7
day. Now when I asked her what's the mat-ter,
head. Yeah, the next time that I saw her,
play." Don't you know you real-ly hurt me,
Eb
N.C.
To
a this is what I heard her say:
re-mind-ed her of what she said:
and this is all I have to say:
"See you lat-er, al-li -
CHORUS
Eb
ga-tor. Well, af-ter 'while, croc-o - dile.

Eb7
Ab7
See you lat-er al-li-ga-tor. Well af-ter 'while,_ croc-o-
Eb
Bb7
dile._ Now don't you know you're in my way now?
Eb
1. N.C.
A can't you see you cramp my style?" Now when I thought of what she
2. N.C.
INSTRUMENTAL SOLO
Eb
Eb7
Ab7
Go!
Eb
Bb7
Eb
N.C.
D.S. AL
She said, "I'm sor-ry, pret-ty
OUTRO - CHORUS
Eb
Eb7
ga-tor. Well, af-ter 'while, croc-o-dile. See you lat-er, al-li-
Ab7
F-7
Bb7
ga-tor. Fare-well._ So long._ Good-bye."_
Eb
Eb7/Db
Ab/C
B7
Bb7
N.C.
Eb

SHE DRIVES ME CRAZY

-DAVID STEELE/ROLAND GIFT

INTRO

N.C. (GUITAR) D G B- A

(SYNTH DOUBLED 15 VB)

(GTR.)
(SYNTH CONT. SIM.)

VERSE

D G B- A D G B- A

I can't stop___ the way I feel._
I can't get___ an - y rest._

D G B- A D G B- A

Things you do___ don't seem real.__
Peo - ple say___ I'm ob - sessed._

D G B- A D G

Tell me what you've got in mind,__ 'cause we're run - ning
Ev - 'ry-thing you say is lies.__ But to me that's

B- A D G B- A

out of time.__ Won't you ev - er set me free?____
no sur - prise._ What I had__ for you was true.____

D G B- A

This wait - ing 'round's kill - ing me.______ } She
Things go wrong they al - ways do.______ }

CHORUS
D G B- A D G B- A
drives me cra - zy like no one else._ She
D G B- A D G B- A
drives me cra-zy, and I can't help_ my - self._______
INTERLUDE
(SYNTH W/ INTRO RIFF)
D G B- A D G B- A
(GTR.)
VERSE
D G B- A D G B- A
(GTR. CONT. SIM.)
I won't make_ it on_ my own._
D G B- A D G B- A
No one likes_ to be a - lone._ She
OUTRO - CHORUS
D G B- A D G B- A
drives me cra-zy like no one else._ She
REPEAT AND FADE
D G B- A D G B- A
drives me cra-zy, and I can't help_ my - self._______ She

(MED.)
SIGNED, SEALED, DELIVERED I'M YOURS
-STEVIE WONDER/SYREETA WRIGHT/LEE GARRETT/LULA MAE HARDAWAY
INTRO
F /Eb /D /C /Bb /A F
(SITAR)
VERSE
F
Like a fool, I went and stayed
Then that time I went and said
Seen a lot of things in this
Oo, wee babe, you set my soul
D-7
F
too long.
good - bye.
old world.
on fire.
Now I'm won - d'rin' if your love's
Now I'm back and not a - shamed
When I touched them they did
That's why I know you're my one and on -
D-7
F
Bb
still strong.
to cry.
noth - in', girl.
ly de - sire.
Oo, ba - by, here I am,
Bb/C
1.,3.
F /Eb /D /C /Bb /A F
signed, sealed, de-liv-ered, I'm yours.
2.,4.
F
CHORUS
F
Eb/G
Here I am, ba - by,
(Here I am, ba - by,
Bb
Bb/C
F
Eb/G
you got my fu - ture in your hands.
signed, sealed, de-liv-ered, I'm yours,
yeah.

Bb Bb/C F Eb/G
Here I am, ba - by,
Here I am, ba - by,
Bb Bb/C F Eb/G
you got my fu - ture in your hands.
signed, sealed, de-liv-ered, I'm yours, yeah.)
To ⊕
Bb Bb/C F /Eb /D /C
I've done a lot of fool - ish things, a that I real-ly did - n't mean.
/Bb /A F /Eb /D /C /Bb /A F
D.S. AL ⊕
Hey, hey, yeah, yeah, did-n't I, oh, ba-by.
⊕ /Bb /A F /Eb /D /C
I could be a bro - ken man, but here I am
/Bb /A F
OUTRO
F Eb/G
with your fu - ture, got your fu - ture, babe.
(Here I am, ba - by,
REPEAT AND FADE
W/ LEAD VOC. AD LIB
Bb Bb/C F Eb/G Bb Bb/C
Here I am, ba - by. Here I am, ba-
signed, sealed, de-liv-ered, I'm yours, yeah.)
(Here I am,

MED. SLOW

SINCE I DON'T HAVE YOU

–JAMES BEAUMONT/JANET VOGEL/JOSEPH VERSCHAREN/
WALTER LESTER/LENNIE MARTIN/JOSEPH ROCK/JOHN TAYLOR

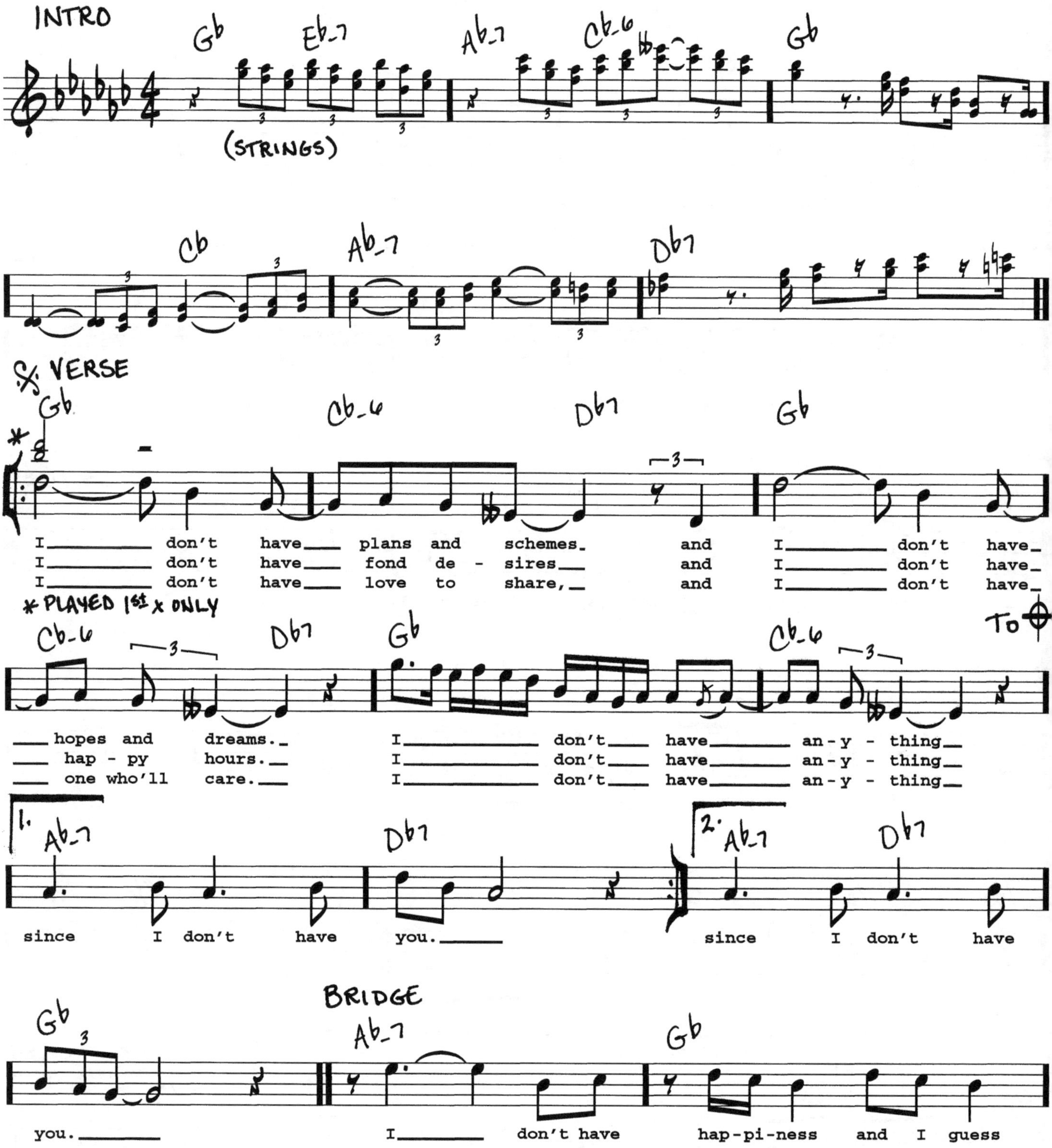

INTRO

Gb Eb-7 Ab-7 Cb-6 Gb

(STRINGS)

Cb Ab-7 Db7

VERSE

Gb Cb-6 Db7 Gb

I ___ don't have ___ plans and schemes. ___ and I ___ don't have ___
I ___ don't have ___ fond de - sires ___ and I ___ don't have ___
I ___ don't have ___ love to share, ___ and I ___ don't have ___

* PLAYED 1st x ONLY

Cb-6 Db7 Gb Cb-6 To ⊕

___ hopes and dreams. ___ I ___ don't ___ have ___ an-y - thing ___
___ hap - py hours. ___ I ___ don't ___ have ___ an-y - thing ___
___ one who'll care. ___ I ___ don't ___ have ___ an-y - thing ___

1. Ab-7 Db7 2. Ab-7 Db7

since I don't have you. ___ since I don't have

Ab-7 Gb
I never will ever again.
Ab-7 Gb
When you walked out on me, in walked the mis-er-y,
Ab-7 Db7
D.S. AL ⊕
and he's been here since then. A,
Ab-7 Db7
OUTRO
Gb Eb-7
since I don't have you, you,
Ab-7 Db7 Gb Eb-7 Ab-7 Db7 Gb Eb-7
you, you, you, you, you, you, you, you,
Ab-7 Db7 Gb Gb6/9
8VA
you, you, you.

(MED.)
SMELLS LIKE TEEN SPIRIT
-KURT COBAIN/KRIST NOVOSELIC/DAVE GROHL
INTRO
F5 Bb5 Ab5 Db5 F5 Bb5 Ab5 Db5
PLAY 3X
RIFF A (GUITAR)
END RIFF A
*CHORDS IMPLIED BY BASS (UNTIL CHORUS).
VERSE
GTR: W/ RIFF A (2 TIMES)
Load up on guns, bring your friends. It's fun to lose and to pretend. She's o - ver - bored, self - as - sured. Oh, no, I know a dirt - y word.
I'm worse at what I do best, and for this gift I feel blessed. Our lit - tle group has al - ways been and al - ways will un - til the end.
And I for - get just why I taste. Oo, yeah, I guess it makes you smile. I found it hard; it's hard to find. Oh, well, what-ev - er, nev - er mind.
PRE-CHORUS
Hel-lo, hel-lo, hel-lo. How low? Hel-lo, hel-lo, hel-lo. How low?
RIFF B
END RIFF B
(GUITAR)

GTR: W/ RIFF B
F5 Bb5 Ab5 Db5 F5 Bb5 Ab5 Db5
Hel-lo, hel-lo, hel-lo. How low? Hel-lo, hel-lo, hel-lo. With the lights
CHORUS
F5 Bb5 Ab5 Db5 F5 Bb5 Ab5 Db5
out it's less dan - g'rous. Here we are now; en-ter-tain us. I feel stu-
F5 Bb5 Ab5 Db5 F5 Bb5 Ab5 Db5
- pid and con-ta - gious. Here we are now; en-ter-tain us. A mu-lat-
F5 Bb5 Ab5 Db5 F5 Bb5 TO ⊕ Ab5 Db5
- to, an al-bi - no, a mos-qui - to, my li-bi - do. Yeah!
INTERLUDE
F5 E5 F5 Gb5 N.C. F5 E5 F5 Bb5 Ab5 F5 E5 F5 Gb5 N.C. F5 E5 F5 Bb5 Ab5
Yay. Yah.
GUITAR SOLO
F5 Bb5 Ab5 Db5
PLAY 8X
INTERLUDE
F5 Bb5 Ab5 Db5 F5 Bb5 Ab5 Db5
D.S. AL ⊕
(GTR.)
⊕ Ab5 Db5 F5 Bb5 Ab5 Db5 F5
PLAY 4X
- do. A de-ni - al, a de-ni - al. A de-ni - al.

294
SMOKIN' IN THE BOYS ROOM
(MED.)
-MICHAEL KODA/MICHAEL LUTZ
INTRO
C#5 D5 C#5 D5 C#5
(GUITAR)
D5 C#5 1.,2. D5 C#5 3. D5 C#5
See additional lyrics
VERSE
D5 C#5 D5 A5
Sit - tin' in the class - room, think - in' it's a drag.
Check - in' out the halls, mak - in' sure the coast is clear.
put me to work in the school book store
Bb5 A5 Bb5 C#5
Lis-ten-in' to the teach - er rap just ain't my bag.
Look-in' in the stalls, no there ain't no - bod - y here. A,
check - out count - er, and I got bored.
D5 C#5 D5 A5
Noon bells ring, you know that's my cue. I'm
my bud - dy Fang, and me and Paul, to
Teach - er was look - in' for me all a - round.
Bb5 A5 Bb5
gon - na meet the boys on floor num - ber two.
get caught would sure - ly be the death of us all.
Two hours la - ter you know where I was found.
CHORUS
G5 G6 G5 G6 G5 G6 G5 G6 D5 D6 D5 D6
Smok-in' in the boys room. Smok-in' in the boys room.
D5 D6 D5 D6 A5 A6 A5 A6 A5 G5 G6 G5 G6 G5
Now, teach-er, don't you fill me up with your rules, a

Additional Lyrics

Intro Spoken: *How you doin' out there?*
You ever seem to have one of those days
Where it just seems like everybody's gettin' on your case,
From your teacher all the way down to your best girlfriend?
Well, you know, I used to have 'em just about all the time.
But I found a way to get out of 'em. Let me tell you about it!

296
MED.
(SHE'S) SOME KIND OF WONDERFUL
—JOHN ELLISON
INTRO
D
(BASS)
(BS. CONT. SIM.)
I don't need
VERSE
D
a whole lots of mon - ey. I don't need a big, fine
her in my arms, you know she sets my soul on fire.
car. I got ev - 'ry-thing that a man could want. I got more
Oo, when my ba - by kiss - es me, my
than I could ask for.
heart be-comes filled with de - sire.
3
G
I, I don't have to
When she wraps her lov-in' arms a-round
run a - round. I don't have to stay out all night.
me, it 'bout drives me out of my mind.
D
'Cause I got me a sweet, a sweet lov-in' wom - an, and she knows
Yeah, when my ba - by kiss - es me, chills
just how to treat me right.
run up and down my spine.
PRE-CHORUS
A
Well, my ba - by, she's al - right.
G
Well, my ba - by, she's clean out of sight. Don't you know that she's,
know that she is
CHORUS
D
G
she's some kind of won-der-ful.
D
She's some kind of

G D G
wonder-ful. Yeah, she is, she's, she's some kind of won-der-ful. Yeah, yeah, yeah,
1. D 2. D
yeah. When I hold yeah Now is there an-y-bod-
VERSE
D
-y got a sweet lit-tle wom-an like mine? There's got to be some-
-bod-y got a, got a sweet lit-tle wom-an like mine. Yeah. Now, can I get a
BRIDGE
D B-
wit-ness? Can I get a wit-ness? Well, can I get a
D B-
wit-ness? One more time, now. Can I get a wit-ness?
...wit-ness? Can I get a wit-ness?
D
Oh, can I get a wit-ness? Yeah,
Can I get a wit-ness? Can I get a
OUTRO
B- D
yeah. I'm talk-in', talk-in' 'bout my ba-by,
wit-ness?) (She's some kind of
G D REPEAT AND FADE
won-der-ful.) talk-in' 'bout my ba-by. (She's some kind of won-der-ful.) Talk-in' 'bout my

(SLOW)

SOMEONE SAVED MY LIFE TONIGHT

– ELTON JOHN / BERNIE TAUPIN

INTRO
Ab/Eb
Db
(PIANO)
VERSE
Ab/Eb
Db/Eb
Ab/Eb
When I think of those East End lights,
I nev - er real - ized the pass - ing hours
Db
Ab/C
Gb/Bb
Db/Ab
mug - gy nights, the cur - tains drawn in the lit - tle room down - stairs,
of eve - ning show - ers, a slip - noose hang - ing in my dark - est dreams. I'm
Gb6
Ab
Gb6
Ab
pri - ma don - na, lord, you real - ly should have been there,
sit - ting like a prin - cess perched in her e - lec -
stran - gled by your haunt - ed so - cial scene,
just a pawn out - played by a dom - i - nat -
Db
3
Db
- tric chair.
And it's one more beer, and I don't hear you
ing queen.
It's four o' - clock in the morn - ing. Damn it!
Bb7
Db
an - y - more.
We've all gone cra - zy late - ly, my
Lis - ten to me good.
I'm sleep - ing with my - self to - night.
Bb/D
Ab/Eb
Eb
friends out there roll - ing 'round the base - ment floor.
(Oo, oo.)
Saved in time, thank God my mu - sic's still a - live.
(Ah, ah.)
CHORUS
Db
Ab/C
Bb
Ab/C
Db
Ab/C
And some - one saved my life to - night, sug - ar bear. (Sug - ar bear.)
You al - most had your hooks in me,

Bb- Ab/C Dbmaj7 Ab/C Db Bb/D
did - n't you dear? You near - ly had me roped ___ and tied, ___ al - tar bound, hyp - no - tized. ___ Sweet free -
Ab/Eb Bb7/F Db
- dom whis - pered in ___ my ear, "You're a but - ter - fly, and but - ter - flies ___ are free ___ to fly,
Bb/D Ab/Eb C7 Db Ab/C Bb- Bb-/Ab
fly a - way, high a - way, ___ bye, ___ bye." (Oo.) ___
INTERLUDE
W/PIANO INTRO RIFF
TO ⊕
Gb Gb/Db Ab/Eb Db Ab/Eb Db
BRIDGE
Bb- Ab/C F-11
And I would have walked ___ head on ___ in - to the deep end of a riv - er, cling - ing to your stocks and bonds, ___ pay - ing your
Db/Ab Bb- Ab/C
H. P. de - mands for - ev - er. They're com - ing in the morn - ing with a truck ___ to take ___ me home. ___
F-11 Db/Ab F-11
Some - one saved my life ___ to - night, some - one saved my life ___ to - night. ___ Some - one saved my life ___ to - night,
D.S. AL ⊕
Db/Ab F-11 Db/Ab Bb7 Ab/C
some - one saved my life ___ to - night. ___ Some - one saved my life ___ to - night, so save your strength ___ and run the field ___ you play a - lone. ___
⊕ OUTRO
W/PIANO INTRO RIFF
REPEAT AND FADE
Ab/Eb Db
Some - one saved, some - one saved, some - one saved my life ___ to - night. ___

(SLOW)
SORRY SEEMS TO BE THE HARDEST WORD
—ELTON JOHN/ BERNIE TAUPIN
INTRO
VERSE
What have I got to do to make you love me?
What do I do to make you want me?
What have I got to do to make you care?
What have I got to do to be heard?
What do I do when light-ning strikes me
What do I say when it's all o - ver?
and I wake to find that you're not there?
Sor-ry seems to be the hard - est word.
CHORUS
It's sad, (So sad.) so sad.
It's a sad, sad sit - u - a - tion,
and it's get-ting more and more ab - surd.
It's sad, (So sad.) so sad.
Why can't we talk it o - ver?
Al-ways seems to me that
TO

INTERLUDE
C- A-7b5 D7 G- G-7 C-7
sor-ry seems to be the hard - est word.
(ACCORDIAN & VIBES)
F Eb/Bb Bb A-7b5 D7 G- G-7
C-7 F F7 Bb F/A
D.S. AL ⊕
⊕
OUTRO - VERSE
C- D7 G- G-7 C-7
sor-ry seems to be the hard - est word. What do I do to make you love me?
F Eb/Bb Bb A-7b5 D7
What have I got to do to be heard?
G- G-7 C-7 A-7b5 D7
What do I do when light-ning strikes me? What have I got to do?
G- C-7 A-7b5 D7
What have I got to do when sor-ry seems to be the hard - est
G-/F E-7b5 Ebmaj7 G-/D C-6 D7sus4 D7 G-7
word?
(PIANO)
RIT.

SOUL MAN
(MED.)
INTRO
—ISAAC HAYES/DAVID PORTER
G F Bb C D
(GUITAR)
(HORNS)
G A-G A-G A-G A-G
GTR. CONT. SIM.
Com- in'
VERSE
G A-G A-G A-G
to you on a dust - y road, good lov-in', I got a
what I got the hard way and I'll make it bet - ter each and
brought up on a side street. I learned how to love be -
A-G A-G A-G
truck - load. And when you get it you got some, so
ev - 'ry day. So, hon - ey, don't you fret, 'cause
fore I could eat. I was ed - u - cat - ed at Wood - stock. When
A-G A-G
CHORUS
G
don't wor - ry 'cause I'm com - in'.
you ain't seen noth - in' yet.
I start lov - in', oh, I can't stop.
I'm a soul man,
F G
8VA
(HORNS)
(GUITAR)
I'm a soul man
I'm a

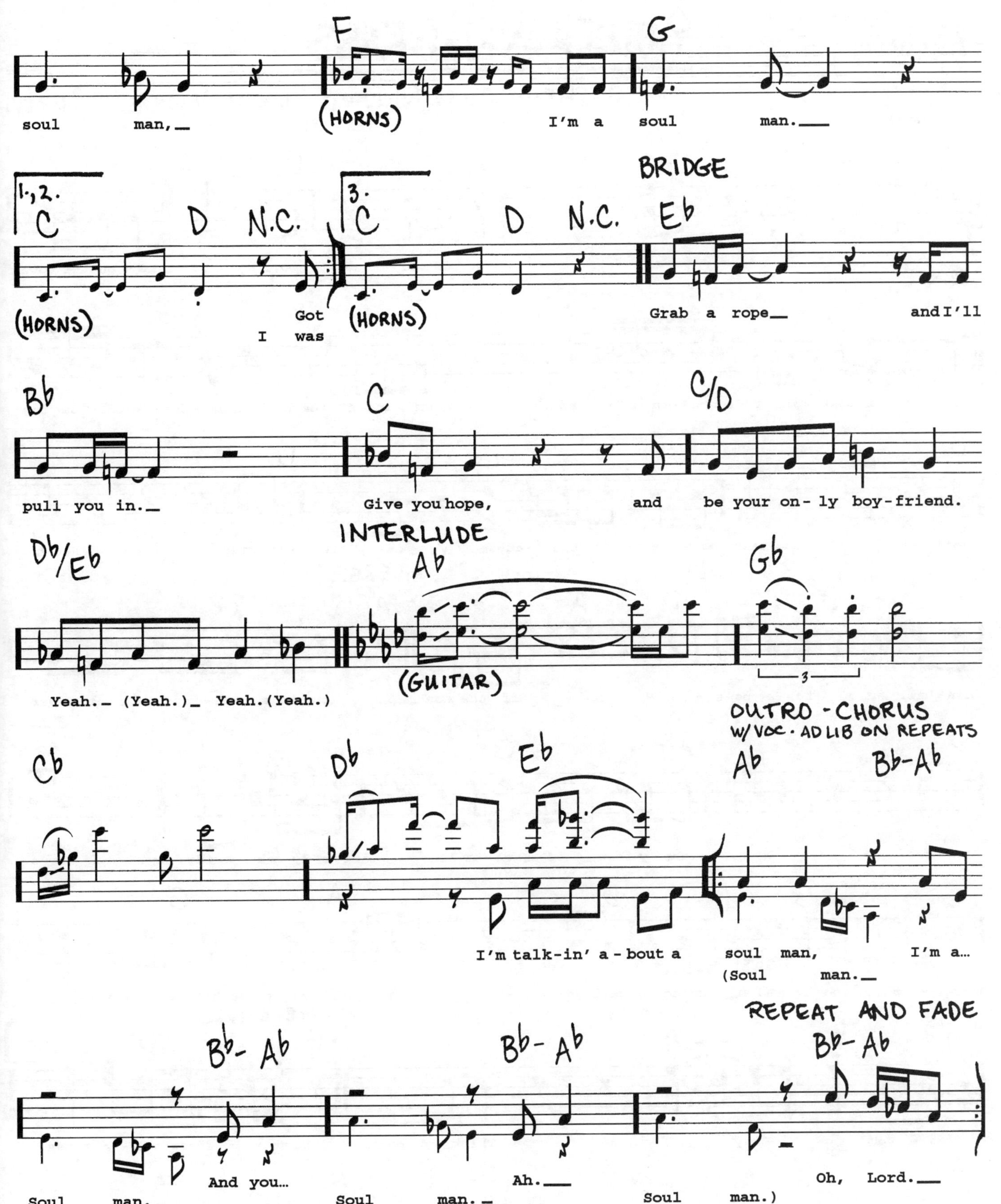
F
G
soul
man,
(HORNS)
I'm a
soul
man.
BRIDGE
1., 2.
C
D
N.C.
3.
C
D
N.C.
Eb
(HORNS)
Got
I
was
(HORNS)
Grab
a
rope
and I'll
Bb
C
C/D
pull
you
in.
Give you hope,
and
be your
on-
ly
boy-friend.
INTERLUDE
Db/Eb
Ab
Gb
Yeah.
(Yeah.)
Yeah.
(Yeah.)
(GUITAR)
OUTRO - CHORUS
W/VOC. AD LIB ON REPEATS
Cb
Db
Eb
Ab
Bb-Ab
I'm talk-in' a - bout a
soul
man,
I'm a...
(Soul
man.
REPEAT AND FADE
Bb- Ab
Bb- Ab
Bb- Ab
And you...
Ah.
Oh,
Lord.
Soul
man.
Soul
man.
Soul
man.)

(MED.)
SOUTHERN CROSS
–STEPHEN STILLS/RICHARD CURTIS/MICHAEL CURTIS
INTRO
(Oo, oo. Oo, oo, oo.) Got out of town
VERSE
on a boat goin' to south-ern is - lands, sail-ing a reach be-fore a fol-low-ing
sea. She was mak-ing for the trades on the out-side and the
down-hill run to Pa-pe-e - te.
VERSE
Off the wind on this head-ing lie the Mar -
que-sas. We got eight-y feet of a wat-er line nice-ly mak - ing way. In a
nois-y bar in Av-a-lon I tried to call you, but on a mid-night watch I re-al-ized why
twice you ran a-way. Think a-bout...
PRE-CHORUS
Think a-bout how man-y times
I have fa - all-en. Spir-its are us-ing me, larg-er voic - es ca - all-in'.

G D G A
What heav-en brought you and me can-not be for-go - ot-ten. I have been a
CHORUS
W/ LEAD VOC. AD LIB.
D G A D G A
round the world. Look-in' for that wom-an, girl,
D G A N.C.
who knows love can en - dure. And you know it will
A G D A G To D A
Mm.
And you know it will.
When you see
VERSE
A G D A G
the South-ern Cross for the first time, you un-der-stand now why you come this
sail-ing for to-mor-row, my dreams are a dy - ing. And my love is an an - chor tied to you,
D A G D
way. 'Cause the truth you might be run-ning from is so small, but it's as
tied with a sil-ver chain. I have my ship and all her flags are a fly-ing. She is
2nd X, D.S. AL
A G D B- A
big as the prom-ise, the prom-ise of a com-in' day. So I'm
all that I have left and mu - sic is her name. Think a-bout...
OUTRO-GUITAR
W/ LEAD GTR. AD LIB.
REPEAT AND FADE
D A A G D A G D A
(GUITARS)

(MED.)
SPINNING WHEEL
-DAVID CLAYTON THOMAS
INTRO
D7#9
(HORNS)
VERSE
E7 A7 D7 G7
What goes___ up must come___ down,
You got no mon - ey, and you, you got no home,___
E7 A7 D7 G7
spin - ning wheel got to go 'round._
spin-ning wheel all a - lone.___
E7 A7 D7 G7
Talk - in' 'bout your trou - bles, it's a cry - in' sin,______
Talk - in' 'bout your trou - bles and you, you nev-er learn,_
D7 N.C. D7#9
ride a paint - ed po - ny, let the spin - ning wheel__ spin.__
ride a paint - ed po - ny, let the spin - ning wheel__ turn.__
BRIDGE
Cadd9 Bbadd9 Abadd9
Did you find___ the di - rect-ing sign on the straight and__ nar - row
Gadd9 Cadd9
high - way?______ Would you mind______ a re -

Bbadd9
Abadd9
G
Ab/G
flect-ing sign? Just let it shine with-in your mind, and show you the
Bb6
C
Dsus2
col-ors that are real.
F7sus4
F-11
N.C.
(DRUM FILL)
VERSE
E7
A7
D7
G7
Some-one is wait-ing just for you, spin-ning wheel
spin-ning true. Drop all your trou-bles by the riv-er-side,
TO
D7 N.C.
D7#9
GUITAR SOLO
2nd x, D.S. AL
catch a paint-ed po-ny on the spin-ning wheel ride.
REPEAT AND FADE
OUTRO
D7 N.C.
E7#9
A13
Eb7
Gmaj9
ride a paint-ed po-ny let the spin-ning wheel fly.
(HORNS)

308
MED.
STAGGER LEE
-LLOYD PRICE/HAROLD LOGAN
INTRO
FREELY
Eb
C-
The night was clear and the moon was yel - low and the
(Oo.)
F-7
A TEMPO
Bb7
VERSE
Eb7
leaves came tum - bling down. I was stand - ing on the cor -
told Bil -
went to the
Ab7
- ner when I heard my bull - dog bark. He was bark -
ly, "I can't let you go with that. You have won
bar - room and he stood a - cross the bar - room door. Said, "Now no -
Eb7
Bb7
Eb7
- in' at the two men who were gam - blin' in the dark.
all my mon - ey and my brand new Stet - son hat."
- bod - y move," and he pulled his for - ty - four.
Bb7
Eb7
It was Stag - ger Lee and Bil -
Stag - ger Lee went home
"Stag - ger Lee," cried
Ab7
ly, two men who gam - ble late. Stag - ger Lee
and he got his for - ty - four. Said, "I'm go -
Bil - ly, "Oh, please don't take my life. I got three

Eb7 Bb7 Eb7 To ⊕
drew a sev-en, Bil-ly swore that he drew eight.
in' to the bar-room just to pay that debt I owe. Spoken: Go
lit-tle chil-dren and a ver - y sick-ly wife.
SAX SOLO
Bb7 Eb7 Ab7
Stag-ger Lee
on, Stag - ger Lee. (Oo, wah. Oo, wah.
Eb7 Bb7 Eb7 Bb7 D.S. AL ⊕
Stag-ger Lee
Oo, wah. Wah.)
Bb7 VERSE Eb7
Stag-ger Lee shot Bil-ly, oh he shot
Ab7 Eb7
that poor boy so bad, till the bul - let came through Bil-ly and it broke
Bb7 Eb7 Bb7 OUTRO - SAX SOLO W/ LEAD VOC. AD LIB. Eb7
the bar - tend-er's glass. Spoken: Now, look out, Stag, go! (Go, Stag-ger Lee.
Ab7 Eb7
Go, Stag-ger Lee. Go, Stag-ger Lee. Go, Stag-ger Lee. Go, Stag-ger Lee.
Bb7 Eb7 Bb7 REPEAT AND FADE
Go, Stag-ger Lee. Go, Stag-ger Lee. Go, Stag-ger Lee.)

STAND BY ME

–JERRY LEIBER/MIKE STOLLER/BEN E. KING

TO
E
A
stand by me.
stand by me.
So, darling, darling,
And darling, darling,
Instrumental ends
Darling, darling,
CHORUS
A
F#-
stand by me, oh, stand by
D
E
me. Oh, stand, stand by me,
A
1.
2.
D.S. AL
stand by me. If the sky
OUTRO-CHORUS
A
F#-
stand by me, oh, stand by
D
E
me, oh stand, now, stand by me, stand
A
REPEAT AND FADE
(W/ LEAD VOC. AD LIB.)
by me. Whenever you're in trouble, won't you

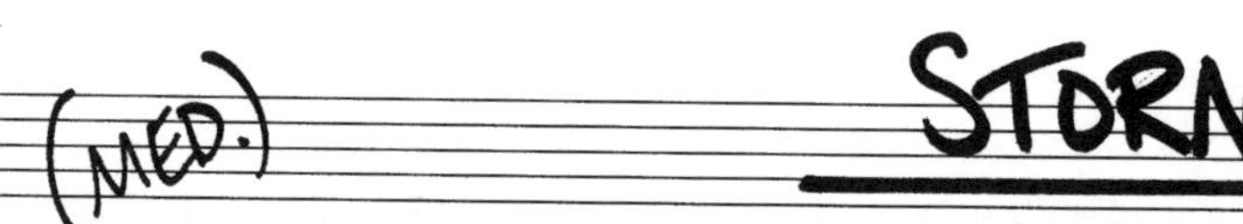
STORMY
(MED.)

-J.R. COBB/ BUDDY BUIE

INTRO

A-7
Gmaj7
A-7
Gmaj7
Oo.
Oo.

VERSE

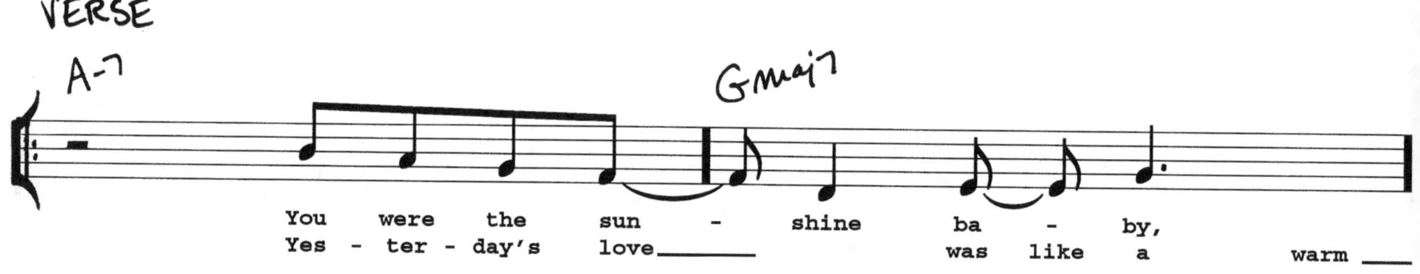
A-7
Gmaj7
You were the sun - shine ba - by,
Yes - ter - day's love was like a warm

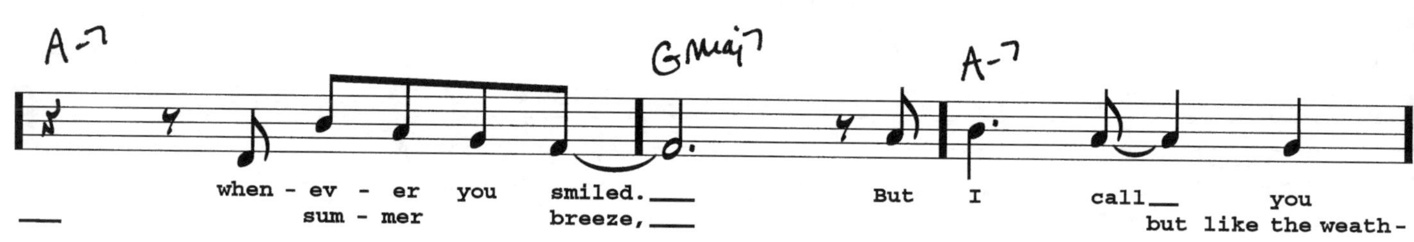
A-7
Gmaj7
A-7
when - ev - er you smiled. But I call you
sum - mer breeze, but like the weath -

Gmaj7
Cmaj7
Storm - y to - day.
- er you changed.

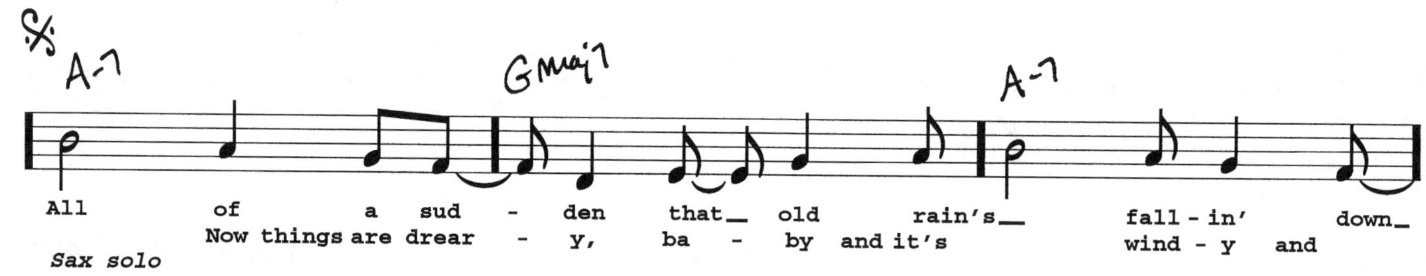
A-7
Gmaj7
A-7
All of a sud - den that old rain's fall - in' down
Now things are drear - y, ba - by and it's wind - y and
Sax solo

Gmaj7
A-7
Gmaj7
Cmaj7
and my world is cloud - y and gray.
cold. And I stand a - lone in the rain
B-
B
You've gone a - way.
call - in' your name.
Sax solo ends
Oh,
CHORUS
E-9
A13
E-9
Storm - y, oh, Storm - y,
A13
C
B-7
bring back that sun - ny day.
E-9
TO
1.
A13
2.
A13
D.S. AL
A13
C
B-7
Bring back that sun - ny day.
OUTRO
E-9
A13
E-9
A13
REPEAT AND FADE
Oh, Storm - y. Oh,

(MED. ROCKABILLY)
STRAY CAT STRUT
—BRIAN SETZER
INTRO
N.C.
(BASS)
(GUITAR)
(C-) (Bb7) (Ab7) (G7) C- Bb7 1.-3. Ab7 G7 4. Ab7 G7
PLAY 2nd X
Oo. Black
VERSE
C- Bb7 Ab7 G7 C- Bb7 Ab7 G7
and or-ange stray cat sit-tin' on a fence. Ain't
C- Bb7 Ab7 G7 C- Bb7 Ab7 G7
got e-nough dough to pay the rent. I'm
C- Bb7 Ab7 G7 C- N.C.
flat broke but I don't care, I strut right by with my tail in the air.
CHORUS
F- Eb Db C7 F- Eb Db7 C7
Stray cat strut, I'm a... I'm a fe-line Ca-sa-no-va. Get a
(La-dies' cat. Hey! Man, that's sad.)
F- Eb Db7 C7 F- N.C.
shoe thrown at me from a mean old man. Get my din-ner from a gar - bage can.
INTERLUDE
C- Bb7 Ab7 G7 C- Bb7 Ab7 G7
(Me - ow.) Yeah. Yeah, don't cross my path!

GUITAR SOLO
C- Bb7 Ab7 G7 PLAY 3x C- N.C.
BRIDGE
F-7 C-
I don't both-er chas-in' mice a-round. Whoa, no! I
F-7 D7
slink down the al-ley, look-in' for a fight, howl-in' to the moon-light on a
G7b9 VERSE C- Bb7 Ab7 G7
hot sum-mer night. Sing-in' the blues while the la-dy cats cry, "Wild
C- Bb7 Ab7 G7 C- Bb7
stray cat, you're a real gone guy." I wish I could be as
Ab7 G7 C- N.C. TO
care-free and wild, but I got cat class and I got cat style.
INTERLUDE
C- Bb7 Ab7 G7 C- Ab7 G7#5 PLAY 4x
GUITAR SOLO
C- Bb7 Ab7 G7 PLAY 3x C- N.C. D.S. AL
OUTRO
N.C. C-13
(BASS) (GUITAR)
N.C.

(MED.)
SULTANS OF SWING
—MARK KNOPFLER
INTRO - GUITAR SOLO
D-
PLAY 7x
VERSE
(GUITAR)
(GTR. CONT.)
1. You get a shiv - er in the dark, it's rain-ing in the park, but mean - time,
Gui - tar George, he knows all the chords,
south of the riv-er you stop, and you hold ev - 'ry-thing.
mind, he's strict-ly rhy-thm, he does-n't want to make it cry or sing.
A band is blow-ing Dix-ie dou-ble four time, you feel al - right when you hear the mu - sic ring.
Yes, and an old gui-tar is all he can af - ford when he gets up un-der the lights to play his thing.
(GTR.)
VERSE
2. Well, now you step in - side, but you don't see too man - y fac - es, com-ing in out of the rain they hear the jazz go down.
4. And Har-ry does-n't mind if he does-n't make the scene he's got a day - time job, he's do-ing al - right.
5.,6. See additional lyrics
C
Bb
A
A7
F

Additional Lyrics

5. Then a crowd of young boys, they're foolin' around in the corner,
Drunk and dressed in their best brown baggies and their platform soles.
They don't give a damn about any trumpet-playin' band.
It ain't what they call rock and roll.
And the Sultans, yeah, the Sultans are playing Creole.

6. And then the man, he steps right up to the microphone
And says at last just as the time bell rings,
"Goodnight, now it's time to go home."
Then he makes it fast with one more thing,
"We are the Sultans, we are the Sultans of Swing."

(MED. FUNK)

SUPERSTITION

– STEVIE WONDER

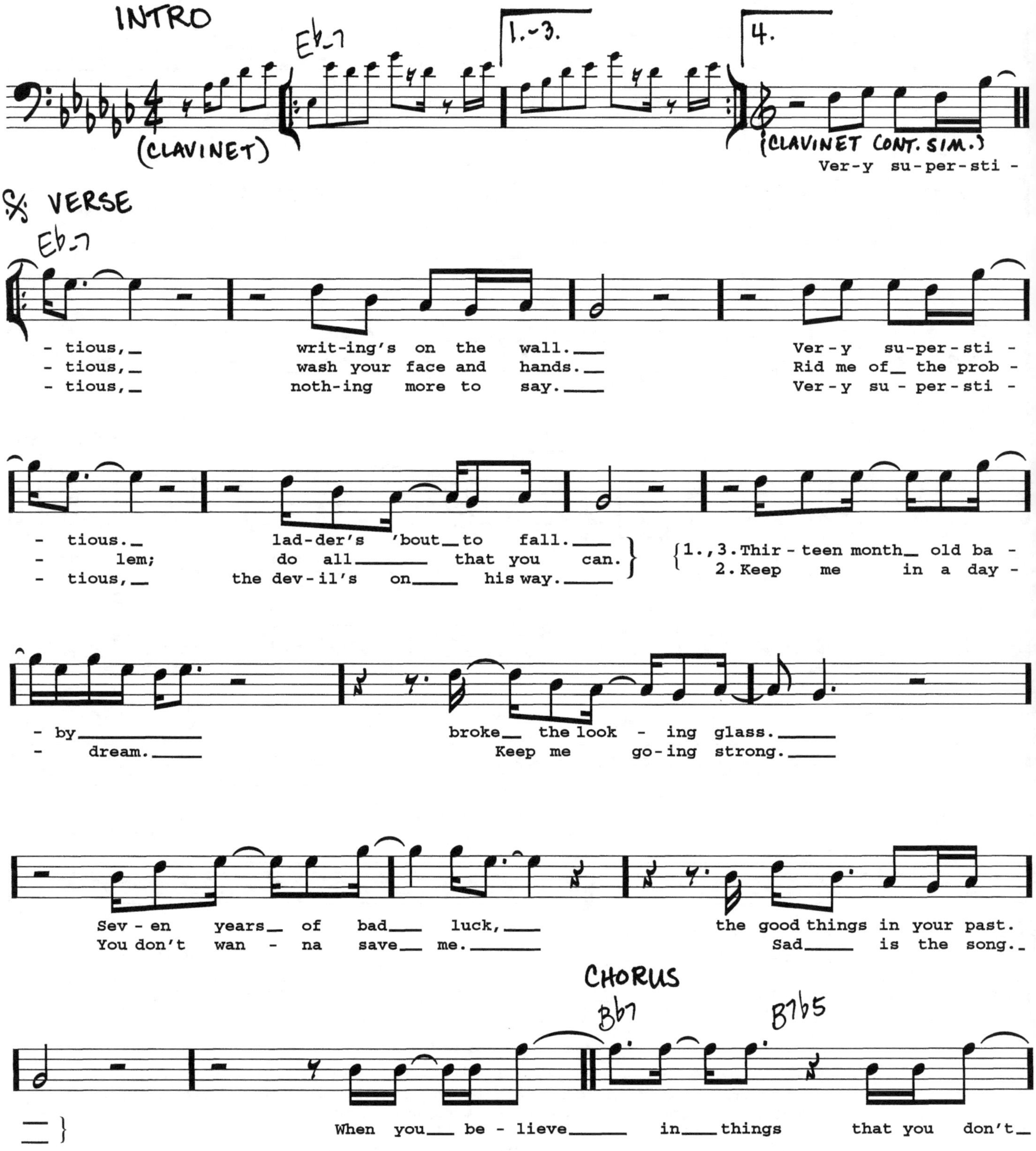

INTRO
Eb-7
1.-3.
4.
(CLAVINET)
(CLAVINET CONT. SIM.)
Ver-y su-per-sti -
VERSE
Eb-7
- tious, writ-ing's on the wall. Very su-per-sti -
- tious, wash your face and hands. Rid me of the prob -
- tious, noth-ing more to say. Ver-y su - per-sti -
- tious. lad-der's 'bout to fall.
- lem; do all that you can.
- tious, the dev-il's on his way.
1., 3. Thir - teen month old ba -
2. Keep me in a day -
- by broke the look - ing glass.
- dream. Keep me go-ing strong.
Sev - en years of bad luck, the good things in your past.
You don't wan - na save me. Sad is the song.
CHORUS
Bb7
B7b5
When you be - lieve in things that you don't

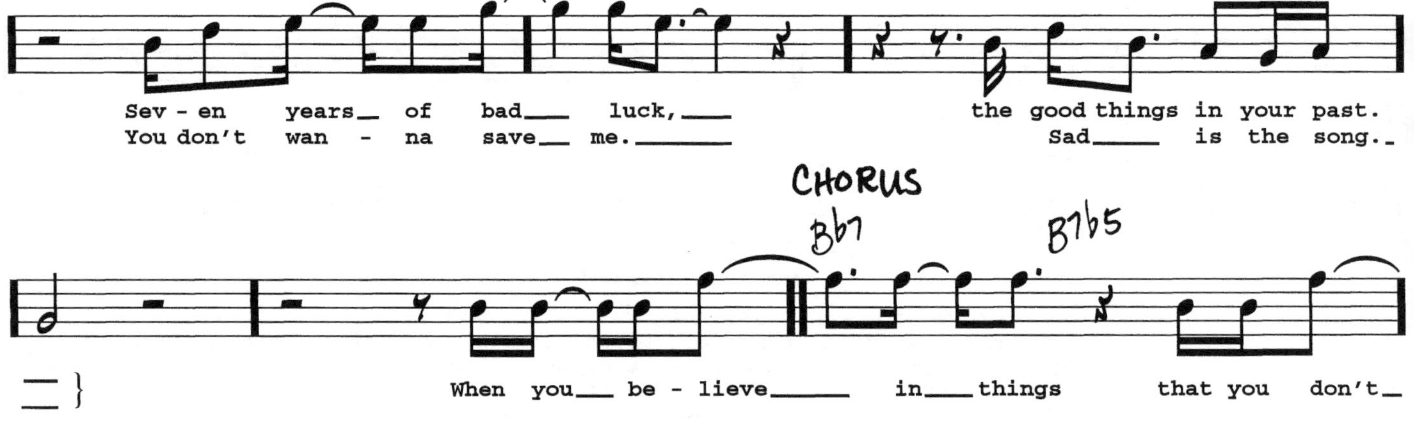

Bb7
A7b5
Ab7
under - stand, then you suf - fer.
Bb7#5
W/ CLAVINET RIFF
Eb-7
(HORNS)
Su - per - sti - tion ain't the way.
TO ⊕
1.
2.
Oo, ver - y su - per - sti -
Bb7
B7b5
Bb7
A7b5
Ab7
Bb7#5
(HORNS)
INTERLUDE
W/ CLAVINET RIFF
Eb-7
D.S. AL ⊕
Ver - y su - per - sti -
⊕ OUTRO
Eb-7
REPEAT AND FADE

(MED. FAST)
SURFIN' U.S.A.
-CHUCK BERRY
INTRO
Eb
N.C.
(GUITAR)
If ev-'ry-bod-y had an
VERSE
Bb7
N.C.
Eb
o - cean a - cross the U. S. A.,
route we're gon - na take real soon.
N.C.
Bb7
N.C.
Eb
then ev-'ry-bod-y'd be surf - in' like Cal - i - for - ni - a.
We're wax-in' down our surf - boards, we can't wait for June.
N.C.
Ab
N.C.
You'd see them wear-in' their bag - gies, huar - a - chi san-dals too.
We'll all be gone for the sum - mer, we're on sa - fa - ri to stay.
Eb
N.C.
Bb7
Ab
N.C.
A bush-y, bush-y blonde hair - do, surf-in' U. S. A.
Tell the teach-er we're surf - in', surf-in' U. S. A.
Eb
VERSE
Bb7
You'll catch 'em surf - in' at Del Mar,
At Hag-gar-ty's and Swam - i's
Eb
Ven - tu - ra Coun - ty Line,
Pa - cif - ic Pal - i - sades,
San - ta Cruz and
San O - no-fre and

Bb7
Tres - sels, Aus - tra - lia's Nar - ra - been,
Sun - set, Re - don - do Beach, L. A.,
Eb
Ab
all o - ver Man - hat - tan
all o - ver La Jol - la,
Eb
and down Do - he - ny way,
at Wai - a - me - a Bay,
ev - 'ry - bod - y's gone
Bb7
Ab
N.C.
surf - in', surf - in' U. S. A.
1.
Eb
N.C.
We'll all be plan-nin' out a
2.
Eb
ORGAN SOLO
Bb7
Eb
GUITAR SOLO
Ab
Eb
Ev - 'ry - bod - y's gone
OUTRO
REPEAT AND FADE
Bb7
Ab
N.C.
Eb
N.C.
surf - in', surf-in' U. S. A. Ev - 'ry - bod - y's gone

(MED.)
SWEET HOME ALABAMA
—RONNIE VAN ZANT/ED KING/GARY ROSSINGTON
INTRO
(GUITAR)
VERSE
Big wheels keep on turn - in',
car-ry me home to see my kin.
Sing-in' songs a - bout the south - land.
I miss ole 'Bam - ee once a - gain and I think it's a sin, yes.
INTERLUDE
(GTR.)
VERSE
Well, I heard Mis - ter Young sing a - bout her.
In Bir-ming - ham they love the gov - 'nor, boo, boo, hoo.
Now, Mus - cle Shoals has got the Swamp - ers an' they been known to pick a song or two. (Yes, they do!)
Well, I heard old Neil put 'er down.
Now we all did what we could do.
Well, I hope Neil Young will re - mem - ber,
Now Wa - ter - gate does not both - er me,
Lord, they get me off so much,

D
Cadd2
G
a south-ern man___ don't need him a - round an - y - how.
does your con - science both - er you?___ Tell the truth.
they pick me up___ when I'm feel - in' blue___ 'n' now how 'bout you?
CHORUS
D5 D6 D5 C5 C6 C5 G5 G6 G5 C5
Sweet__ home Al - a - bam - a,
D5 D6 D5 C5 C6 C5 G5 C5 D5 D6 D5 C5 C6 C5 G5 G6 G5 C5
where the skies are so blue.___ Sweet__ home Al - a - bam - a,
D5 D6 D5 C5 C6 C5 TO ⊕1 G5 G6 F C/E TO ⊕2
GUITAR SOLO
D Cadd2 G
2nd X, D.S. AL ⊕1
Lord, I'm com-in' home to you.
PLAY 8X, THEN D.S.S. AL ⊕2
(TAKE REPEAT)
⊕1
G5 G6 G5 G6 G5
GUITAR SOLO
D5 D6 D5 C5 C6 C5 G5 G6 G5 G6 G5
you. Here I come, Al - a - bam - a!
⊕2
D5 D6 D5 C5 C6 C5 G5 G6 G5 C5 D5 D6 D5 C5 C6 C5
Sweet__ home Al - a - bam - a, oh, sweet home,__ where the skies are so blue_
G5 C5 D5 D6 D5 C5 C6 C5 G5 G6 G5 C5
__ and the gov-'nor's true. Sweet__ home Al - a - bam - a, Lord - y.
D5 D6 D5 C5 C6 C5 G5 G6 G5 G6 G5
Lord, I'm com - in' home to you. Yeah.___
OUTRO-PIANO SOLO
REPEAT AND FADE
D5 D6 D5 C5 C6 C5 G5 G6 G5 G6 G5

(MED.)

TAKE ME TO THE RIVER

–AL GREEN/ MABON HODGES

INTRO

E

(DRUMS) 2 (BASS)

D A

(GUITAR)
(BS. CONT. SIM.)

VERSE

E D A E
I don't know why I love you like I do, all the chang-es
I don't know why I love you like I do, all the trou-ble

D A E D A
you put me through. Take my mon-ey, my cig-ar-ettes,
you put me through. Six-teen can-dles there on my wall,

E D A PRE-CHORUS C
I have-n't seen the worst of it yet. I wan-na know, oh, can you
and here am I, the big-gest fool of them all.

G A D E-7
tell me, am I in love to stay? Take me to the

CHORUS
E
(GTR.) (GTR. CONT. SIM.)
riv-er, drop me in the wa-ter.

{Push / Dip} me in the riv-er, {dip / drop} me in the

TO ⊕
BRIDGE
C#–
wa - ter, washing me down, washing me. Hold me,
A
C#–
A
G/D
squeeze me, love me, tease me till I can't,
till I can't, I can't take no more. Dip me in the
CHORUS
E
(GTR. CONT. SIM.)
(GTR.)
wa - ter, drop me in the riv - er. Push me in the
wa - ter, drop me in the riv - er, wash-ing me down, wash-ing me down.
INTERLUDE
E5
1.
2.
D.S. AL ⊕
D
A
rake
rake
rake
rake
(ORGAN & GTR.)
⊕
wash - ing me down.
OUTRO
W/ LEAD VOC. AD LIB.
E
(BASS)
1.–5.
6.
D
A
E
RIT.

TAKIN' CARE OF BUSINESS
(MED.)
-RANDY BACHMAN
INTRO-GUITAR SOLO
C7 Bb7 F7 1.-3. C7 4. C7
(GUITAR)
(GTR. CONT. SIM.)
1. They
VERSE
C7 Bb7 F7
(3.) get up ev-'ry morn-in' from the a - larm clock's warn-in', take the eight fif - teen in - to the
eas - y as fish-in', you could be a mu - si-cian if you could make sounds loud or
C7 Bb7
cit - y. There's a whis-tle up a - bove and peo - ple push - in', peo - ple shov - in' and the
mel - low. Get a sec - ond-hand gui - tar, chanc - es are you'll go far if you
F7 C7
girls who try to look pret - ty. And if your train's on time you can
get in with the right bunch of fel - lows. Peo - ple see you hav-in' fun just a
Bb7 F7 C7
get to work by nine and start your slav-in' job to get your pay. If you
ly - in' in the sun. Tell them that you like it this way. It's the
Bb7 F7
ev - er get an-noyed, look at me, I'm self - em - ployed. I love to work at noth-in' all day.
work that we a - void and we're all self - em - ployed. We love to work at noth-in' all day.
C7 CHORUS C7 Bb7
And I've
And we've
been tak-in' care of busi - ness, ev - 'ry day. Tak -
F7 C7
- in' care of busi - ness, ev - 'ry way.
1., 3. I've
2. We've
been tak - in' care of busi - ness,

Bb7
F7
3rd x, TO ⊕ 2
C7
it's all mine.
Tak - in' care of busi - ness and work - in'
o - ver - time, work out.
o - ver - time.
GUITAR SOLO
C7
Bb7
F7
4th x, TO ⊕ 1
1.
C7
2.
C7
D.S. AL ⊕ 1
(TAKE REPEAT)
2. There's work
⊕ 1
C7
INTERLUDE
(W/ LEAD VOC. AD LIB.)
N.C.
3
C5
(GTR.)
F5
Eb7
1.-3.
Bb5
C5
4.
Eb5
Bb5
GUITAR SOLO
C7
Bb7
F7
1.
C7
2.
C7
D.S. AL ⊕ 2
3. They
⊕ 2
C7
OUTRO
N.C.
(GTR.)
work - in' o - ver - time.
Tak - in' care of busi - ness.
Tak - in' care of busi - ness.
C5
N.C.
Bb5
N.C.
F5
Tak - in' care of busi - ness,
ev - 'ry day.
it's all mine.
Tak -
N.C.
C5
1.
N.C.
C5
2.
N.C.
- in' care of busi - ness,
ev - 'ry way.
Tak - work - in' o - ver - time, woo!
C7
Bb7
F7
C7
REPEAT AND FADE
Tak - in' care of busi - ness.
- in' care of busi - ness.
Tak - in' care of busi - ness.
We've been tak - in' care of busi - ness.
We've been tak-
Woo! Tak-

328
(MED. COUNTRY ROCK)
TEACH YOUR CHILDREN
—GRAHAM NASH
INTRO/PEDAL STEEL SOLO
D G D A
VERSE
You who are on the road__ must have a code.
that_ you can live by, and
so be- come_ your - self, be-cause_ the past
is just a good - bye.
CHORUS
Teach your chil - dren well; their fa - ther's
Teach your par - ents well; their chil - dren's
hell did slow - ly go__ by.
hell will slow - ly go__ by.
And
feed them on__ your dreams, the one__ they
picked, the one__ you'll know__ by.

D
G
Don't you ev - er ask them why; if they told you, you would
D
B-
cry, so just look at them and sigh
G
A
D
TO
and know they love you.
PEDAL STEEL SOLO
G
D
A
And
VERSE
D
G
you of ten-der years can't know the
(Can you hear? Do you care?
D
A
fears that your el-ders grew by. And so, please
Can you see you must be free to
D
G
help them with your youth. They seek the
teach your chil - dren what you be - lieve in?
D.S. AL
D
A
truth be-fore they can die.
Make a world that we can live in.)
OUTRO/PEDAL STEEL SOLO
G
D
A
D
A D

(MED. FAST LATIN)
TEQUILA
—CHUCK RIO
A
E D E D E D E D
(GUITAR)
E D E D E D E
1.,2.
D
3.
D
(BASS)
(GUITAR CONT.)
(SAX)
B
E D E D E D E
1.-3.
D
4.
D
* SAX SOLO ON D.S.
END SAX SOLO
C
E°7
E6
1.,2.
3.
F#7
E N.C.
Spoken: Tequila!
D
E D E D E D E
4th X, TO ⊕
1.
D
2.
D.S. AL ⊕
D (TAKE REPEATS)
D
E
E D E D
1.-3.
E D E
(GUITAR)
D
4.
E D E
N.C.
Spoken: Tequila!

(MED.)
WE CAN WORK IT OUT
-JOHN LENNON/PAUL McCARTNEY
VERSE
D Dsus4 D Dsus4 C D
Try to see it my way, do I have to keep_ on talk-ing till I can't_ go on?
Think of what you're say - ing, you can get it wrong_ and still you think_ that it's_ al - right.
Dsus4 D Dsus4 C D
While you see it your way, run the risk of know-ing that our love may soon be gone._
Think of what I'm say-ing, we can work it out_ and get it straight, or say good-night._
G D G A
We can work it out,_ we can work it out._
BRIDGE
B-
Life is ver - y short,_
B-/A G F#sus4 F#
_ and there's no time_ for fuss - ing and
B- B-/A B-/G B-/F# B- B-/A
fight-ing, my friend. I have al-ways thought_ that it's a crime,_
G F#sus4 F# B- B-/A B-/G B-/F#
_ so I will ask you once a - gain.
VERSE
D Dsus4 D Dsus4 C D
Try to see it my way, on-ly time will tell if I_ am right or I am wrong.
Dsus4 D Dsus4 C D
While you see it your way, there's a chance that we might fall a - part_ be-fore too long.
G D G A
We can work it out,_ we can work it out._
OUTRO
D
8VB
(HARMONIUM)

THAT'LL BE THE DAY

(MED. ♫ = ♩♪ triplet)

—JERRY ALLISON/NORMAN PETTY/BUDDY HOLLY

INTRO

N.C. (GUITAR) | A E7 |

𝄋 CHORUS

D
Well, that-'ll be the day when you say good - bye. Yes,___
A
that - 'll be the day when you make me cry. Ah, you
D
say you're gon - na leave, you know it's a lie,__ 'cause
A
that-'ll be the day_____
N.C. E7 A
when I die._ { Well, you / Well, a

VERSE

D
give me all your lov - in' and your
A
tur - tle - dov - in', a,

when Cu - pid shot his dart,
he shot it at your heart.

D
A
all your hugs an' kiss - es an' your mon - ey, too.___ Well,__ a
So if we ev-er part then I'll leave you.

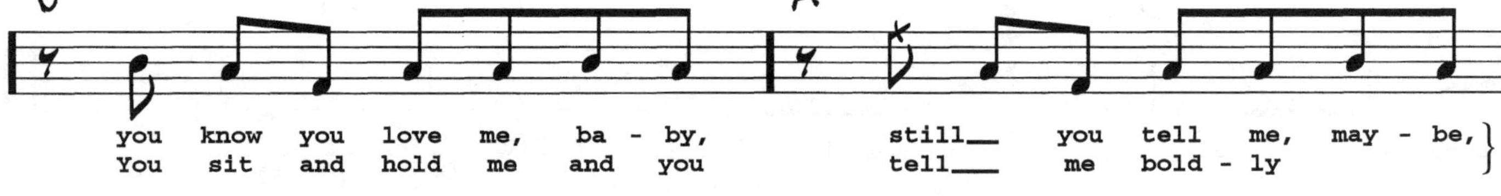
D
A
you know you love me, ba - by, still___ you tell me, may - be, }
You sit and hold me and you tell___ me bold - ly

CHORUS
B E7 D
that some day, well, I'll be blue. Well, that-'ll be the day when
A
you say good - bye. Yes, that-'ll be the day when
D
you make me cry. Ah, you say you're gon-na leave, you know it's a lie 'cause
A TO N.C. E7 A
that - 'll be the day when I die.
GUITAR SOLO
A7 D7
D.S. AL
A7 E7 D7 A7 E7
Well,
N.C. E7 A
OUTRO
D
when I die. Well, that-'ll be the day, hoo, hoo. Well,
A 1. 2. N.C. A
that-'ll be the day, hoo, hoo. Well,
(GTR.)

334
(SLOW)
THREE TIMES A LADY
-LIONEL RICHIE
INTRO
(PIANO)
VERSE
Thanks for the times that you've giv - en me.
The mem-'ries are all in my mind.
And now that we've come to the end of our rain - bow,
there's some - thing I must say out loud:
CHORUS
You're once, twice, three times a la - dy,
and I love you.
Yes, you're once, twice, three times a la - dy,
and I love you,

Eb/C
Eb/Bb
Ab
Eb/Ab
Db/Ab
Db/Eb
I love you. When
VERSE
Ab
Eb/Ab
Db/Ab
Db/Eb
Ab
we are to - geth - er, the mo - ments I cher-ish with ev - 'ry beat
Eb/Ab
Db/Ab
Db/Eb
Ab
Eb/Ab
Db/Ab
of my heart; to touch you, to hold you, to feel you, to
Db/Eb
Ab
Eb/Ab
Db/Ab
Db/Eb
need you, there's noth - ing to keep us a - part.
GUITAR SOLO
Ab
Eb/Ab
Db/Ab
Db/Eb
Ab
Eb/Ab
Db/Ab
Db/Eb
INTERLUDE
Ab
Eb/Ab
Db/Ab
Db/Eb
Ab
(Oo, oo, oo,
(Oo, oo,
Eb/Ab
Db/Ab
OUTRO-CHORUS
Ab
oo.)
oo.)
You're once,
Eb/G
Gb
Db/F
Bb-7
Ab
twice, three times a la - dy, and I love
Eb
Eb/Db
Eb/C
Eb/Bb
RIT.
Ab
3
you, I love you.

TONIGHT'S THE NIGHT
(GONNA BE ALRIGHT)
-ROD STEWART
MED.
INTRO-INSTRUMENTAL SOLO
FREELY
Cmaj7 D-7 F-6 C G/A E
VERSE
A TEMPO
B Emaj7 B Emaj7
Stay a-way from my win-dow; stay a-way from my back door, too.
B Emaj7 B Emaj7
Dis-con-nect the tel-e-phone line; re-lax, ba-by, and draw that blind.
Amaj7 F#7 E/G# F#/A#
VERSE
B Emaj7
Kick off your shoes and sit right down
Come on, an - gel, my heart's on fire;
Don't say a word, my vir - gin child;
B Emaj7 B
and loos-en up that pret-ty French gown. Let me pour you a
don't de - ny your man's de-sire. You'd be a fool to
just let your in-hi - bi-tions run wild. The se - cret is a -
Emaj7 B Emaj7
good long drink; ooh, ba - by, don't you hes - i - tate.
stop this tide; spread your wings and let me come in - side.
bout to un-fold up - stairs be-fore the night's too old.
'Cause

Additional Lyrics

Outro Spoken: *J'ai un peu peur.*
Qu'est-ce que va dire maman?
Mon amour viens plus près, embrasse-moi.
Oh, Je t'adore beaucoup.
Cette nuit, mon ami,
Oui, cette nuit, mon ami,
Je t'aime Je t'aime Je t'aime ...

(Translation)
I'm scared.
What will my mom say?
My love come closer, kiss me.
Oh, I adore you a lot.
Tonight, my friend,
Yes, tonight, my friend,
I love you I love you I love you...

TOWN WITHOUT PITY

(MED.)

—DIMITRI TIOMKIN/NED WASHINGTON

INTRO

B- E- G7

(GUITAR & HORNS)

F#7sus4 F#7#5

VERSE

B-

When you're young and so in love as we, and be-
stop to gaze up-on a star, people

E-

wil-dered by the world we see. Why do
talk a-bout how bad we are. Ours is

C6 B7 E-7 G-6

peo-ple hurt us so? On-ly those in love would know what a
not an eas-y age; we're like ti-gers in a cage. What a

1. A6 Ab6 A-7 G7 F#7sus4 F#7#5

town with-out pit-y can do. If we

2. A6 Ab6 A7 A13 D C/E D7/F#

town with-out pi-ty can do. Though young

BRIDGE

G G6

have prob-lems, man-y

Gmaj7 G6 G G7 Esus4 E

prob-lems, we need an un-der-stand-ing heart. Why don't they

A A6 Amaj7 F#-7 B- N.C. E7 N.C.

help us, try to help us, be-fore this clay and gran-ite plan-et falls a-

A7 F#7#5
VERSE
B-
part? Take these ea - ger lips and hold me fast. I'm a -
E- C6 B7
fraid this kind of joy can't last. How can we keep love a - live? How can
E-7 G-6 A6 Ab6 G6
an - y - thing sur - vive when these lit - tle minds tear you in
F#sus4 F# G A D (SAXES) G7#5
two? What a town with - out pit - y can do.
INTERLUDE
C- C-6 C-(maj7) C- F- F-6 F-(maj7) F-
How can
OUTRO
Db6 C7 F-7 Ab-6 Bb6 A6 Ab6
we keep love a - live? How can an - y - thing sur - vive when these lit - tle minds tear you in
Gsus4 G Ab G7
two? What a town with - out pit - y can do. No, it
C- B° C-/Bb A-7b5 Ab7 G7 N.C.
is - n't ver - y pret - ty what a town with - out pit - y can
FREELY
A TEMPO
C- F- C-(maj7)
do.

340
(MED.)
TURN ME LOOSE
—PAUL DEAN/DUKE RENO
INTRO
GAdd2
(BASS)
Fadd9
GAdd2
2nd X, W/ GTR. AD LIB.
G-7
(GUITAR)
(BS. CONT. SIM.)
Fadd9
G-7
1.
2.
% VERSE
G-7
I was born to run, I was born to dream. The
came a - round, tried to tie me down. I
here to please, I'm e - ven on my knees mak - ing
Guitar solo
cra - zi - est boy you've ev - er seen. I've got-ta do it my way,
was such a clown. You had to have it your way,
love to who - ev - er I please. I've got-ta do it my way,
Fadd9
G-7
or no way at all. And I was
or no way at all. But I've had
I've go - ta do it my way. And when you

here to please, I'm e - ven on my knees making love to who - ev - er I please.
all I can take, I can't take it no more. I'm gon-na pack my bags and fly
came a - round, you tried to tie me down, I was such a clown.
Fadd9
G-7
I've got to do it my way, or no way at all.
it my way, or no way at all.
You had to have it your way, well, I'm say - in' no way.
1.
2., 3., 4.
4th x, To ⊕ 2
CHORUS
G-7
And then you
Solo ends
So why don't you turn me loose? Turn me loose.
Fadd9
1., 3.
Turn me loose. I've got-ta do it my way, or no way at all.
G-7
2., 4.
G-7 To ⊕ 1
Why don't you I wan-na fly.
INTERLUDE
E5
N.C.
PLAY 3x
E+
D.S. AL ⊕ 1
(GTR.)
P.M.
I'm
⊕ 1
D.S. AL ⊕ 2
⊕ 2 OUTRO-CHORUS
G-7
Oh, yeah. turn me loose? Turn me loose.
Fadd9
Turn me loose. I've got - ta do it my way
G-7
REPEAT AND FADE
(W/ LEAD VOC. AD LIB.)
or no way at all. Why don't you

342
TWIST AND SHOUT
(MED.)
-BERT RUSSELL/PHIL MEDLEY
INTRO
D G A D G A
(GUITAR)
CHORUS
D G A
Well, shake it up ba - by, now. (Shake it up ba - by.) Twist and
D G A
shout. (Twist and shout.) Come on, come on, come on, come on,
D G A
ba - by, now. Come on and work it on out.
(Come on ba - by.)
D G A
(Work it on out.) 1. Well, work it on out.
2.,3. You know you're a twist - y lit - tle girl.
VERSE
D G A
(Work it on out.) You know you look so
(Twist, lit - tle girl.) You know you twist so
D G A
good. (Look so good.) You know you got me
fine. (Twist so fine.) Come on and twist a lit - tle

D G A
go - in' now, (Got me go - in'.) just like I knew you would.
clos - er now, (Twist a lit-tle clos - er.) and let me know that you're
D G To ⊕ 1. A 2. A
(Like I knew you would.) Well, shake it up ba -
mine. (Let me know you're mine.)
INTERLUDE
D G A 1.,2.,3. G 4.
(GUITARS)
BRIDGE
A
(Ah, ah,
D.S. AL ⊕
ah, ah.) Whoa, yeah, yeah. Ba -
⊕
A
CHORUS
D G
Well, shake it, shake it, shake it, ba - by, now.
(Shake it up, ba -
A D G
Well, shake it, shake it, shake it, ba - by, now.
- by.) (Shake it up, ba -
A D G A
Well, shake it, shake it, shake it, ba-by, now.
- by.) (Shake it up, ba - by.)
OUTRO
A N.C. D9
(Ah, ah, ah, ah.)
(GTR.)

(MED.)

WAH WATUSI

—KAL MANN/DAVE APPELL

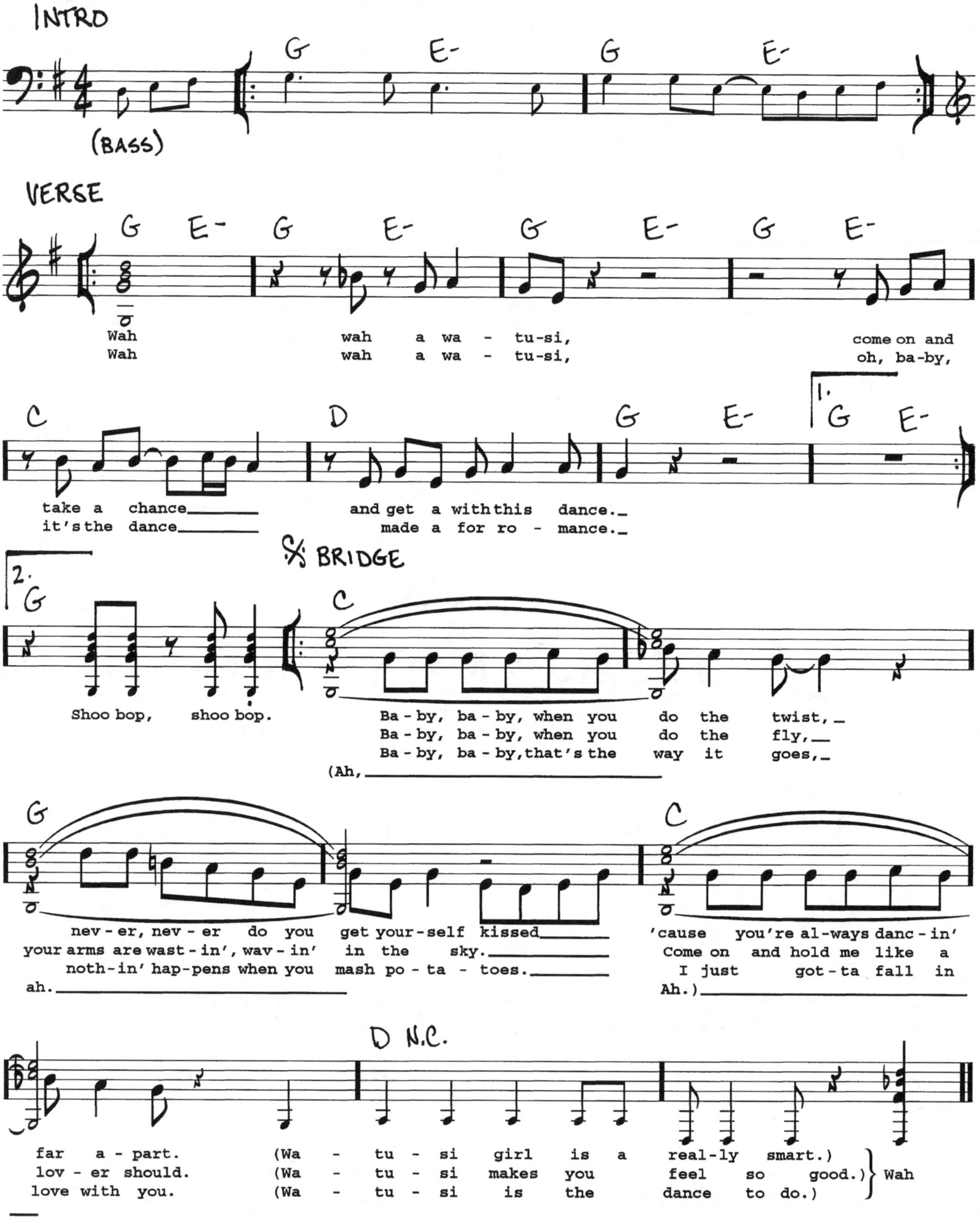

INTRO

G E- G E-

(BASS)

VERSE

G E- G E- G E- G E-

Wah wah a wa - tu-si, come on and
Wah wah a wa - tu-si, oh, ba-by,

C D G E- 1. G E-

take a chance____ and get a with this dance._
it's the dance____ made a for ro - mance._

2. G

Shoo bop, shoo bop.

𝄋 BRIDGE

C

Ba - by, ba - by, when you do the twist,_
Ba - by, ba - by, when you do the fly,_
Ba - by, ba - by, that's the way it goes,_
(Ah,____

G C

nev - er, nev - er do you get your-self kissed____ 'cause you're al-ways danc - in'
your arms are wast - in', wav - in' in the sky.____ Come on and hold me like a
noth-in' hap-pens when you mash po - ta - toes.____ I just got-ta fall in
ah.____ Ah.)____

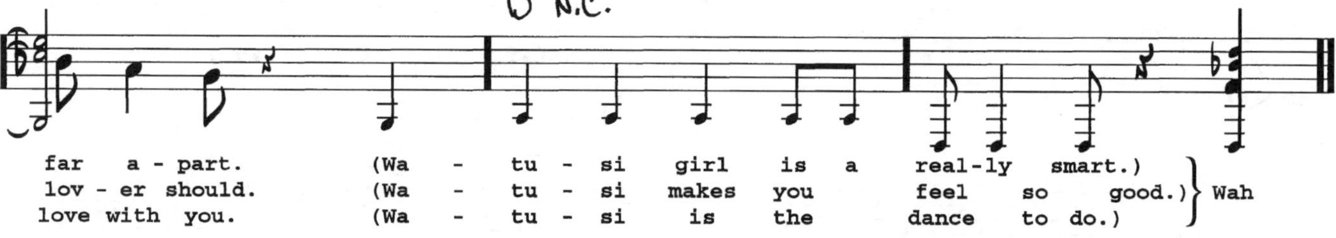

VERSE
G E- G E- G E- G E-
wah wah a wa - tu-si,
1.,3. come on and
2. oh, ba-by,
C D TO 1. G E- G
take a chance and get a with this dance.
it's the dance made a for ro - mance.
Shoo bop, shoo bop.
2. G C G N.C.
SAX SOLO
G E- G E-
Yay!
C D G E- G
D.S. AL
Shoo bop, shoo bop.
G E- G E-
OUTRO - VERSE
G E- G E-
Wah wah a wa -
G E- G E- C
tu - si, oh, ba - by, it's the dance
D G E- G
FADE OUT
made a for ro - mance.

FAST
WAKE UP LITTLE SUSIE
-BOUDLEAUX BRYANT/FELICE BRYANT
INTRO
CHORUS
Wake up, lit-tle Su - sie, wake up.
Wake up, lit-tle Su - sie, wake up.
VERSE
We've both been sound a - sleep, wake up lit-tle Su-sie and weep. The mov - ie's o - ver, it's four o' - clock and we're in trou-ble deep.
The mov - ie was-n't so hot, it did - n't have much of a plot. We fell a - sleep, our goose is cooked, our rep - u - ta-tion is shot.
Wake up, lit-tle Su - sie. Wake up, lit-tle Su - sie. Well

BRIDGE
A E7 A E7
what are we gon - na tell your ma - ma? What are we gon - na tell your pa?
A E7 A
What are we gon - na tell our friends when they say,
N.C. D To
"Ooh la la"? Wake up, lit - tle Su - sie.
A7 D A7
Wake up, lit - tle Su - sie. Well, I
VERSE
D D7
told your ma - ma that you'd be in by ten. Well,
G
Su - sie, ba - by, looks like we goofed a - gain. Wake up, lit - tle
A7 G A7 N.C.
Su - sie. Wake up, lit - tle Su - sie. We got - ta go
INTERLUDE
D F G F D F G F D.S. AL
home.
A7 D
Wake up, lit - tle Su - sie.
INTERLUDE
D F G PLAY 4x
OUTRO
D F G F REPEAT AND FADE

WALK LIKE A MAN

–BOB CREWE/ BOB GAUDIO

INTRO

Bb Eb Bb Eb Bb Eb Bb Eb

(GUITAR)

Oo.

Bb Eb Bb Eb Bb Eb Bb Eb

(Walk, walk, walk, walk.) Oo.

Bb Eb/Bb Bb F7

Walk like a man.

𝄋 VERSE

Bb C-7 Bb C-7 Bb C-7

Oh, how you tried_ to cut me down to size,_ tell-in' dirt-y lies_ to my

Bye,_ ba - by, I don't a mean_ may - be. Gon - na get a - long_ some -

Bb C-7 Bb C-7 Bb C-7

friends. But my own fa - ther said, "Give her up, don't both - er. The

how._ Soon, you'll be cry - ing, on ac - count of all your ly - ing. Oh

Bb C-7 Bb N.C. CHORUS Eb Ab

world is - n't com - ing to an end." (He said it.) "Walk like a man,

yeah, just look who's laugh - ing now. (I'm gon - na...) ...walk like a man,

Eb Ab Eb G- F- Bb
3
talk like a man, walk like a man, my son.
fast as I can walk like a man from you.
Eb Ab Eb Ab Eb G-
No wom-an's worth crawl-in' on the earth, so walk like a man, my
I'll tell the world, "For-get a - bout it, girl," and walk like a man from
Ab F7 TO INTERLUDE Bb Eb Bb Eb
son."
you.
Oo.
Bb Eb Bb Eb Bb Eb
(Walk, walk, walk, walk.
Oo.
Bb Eb Bb F7 D.S. AL
Oo, oo.)
OUTRO
Bb Eb Bb Eb Bb Eb Bb Eb
Oo.
(Walk, walk, walk, walk.
Bb Eb Bb Eb Bb Eb Bb Eb
REPEAT AND FADE
(BKGD. VOC. CONT. SIM.)
Oo.
Walk, walk, walk, walk, walk, walk, walk, walk.)

350
MED ♫ = ♪³♪
THE WAY YOU DO THE THINGS YOU DO
—WILLIAM "SMOKEY" ROBINSON/ROBERT ROGERS
INTRO
(GUITAR)
You got a smile so
VERSE
bright, you know you could-'ve been a can - dle.
are, you know you could-'ve been a flow - er.
I'm hold-ing you so tight, you know you could-'ve been a
If good looks caused a min-ute, you know that you could be an
han - dle. The way you swept me off my feet,
hour. The way you stole my heart,
you know you could-'ve been a broom. The way you smell so
you know you could-'ve been a cool crook. And, ba-by, you're so
sweet, you know you could-'ve been some per - fume.
smart, you know you could-'ve been a school book.
CHORUS
Well, you could-'ve been an-y-thing that you want-ed to and I can

Bb
Ab N.C.
Eb Ab Eb Ab
tell.
The way you do the things you do.
Ah, ba -
1.
Eb Ab Eb Ab Eb N.C.
- by.
As pret - ty as you
2.
Eb Ab Eb Ab Eb N.C.
- by.
Yes!
SAXOPHONE SOLO
E A E A E A E A B E B E A D A D E A E A E N.C.
You make my life so
VERSE
E A E A E A E A E A E A
rich,
you know you could - 've been some mon - ey.
E A E A E A E A E A E A
And, ba - by, you're so sweet,
you know you could - 've been some
E A E A E B
hon - ey.
Well, you could - 've
CHORUS
B
been an - y - thing that you
A
want - ed to and I can
B
tell.
A N.C.
The way you do the things you
OUTRO
W/ LEAD VOC. AD LIB.
E A E A E
REPEAT AND FADE
do.
(The way you do the things you do.)

352
(MED.)
WE WILL ROCK YOU
—BRIAN MAY
N.C.
*(HAND CLAPS)
*(FOOT STOMPS)
VERSE
* CONTINUE THROUGHOUT ENTIRE SONG
N.C.
Bud-dy, you're a boy, make a big noise play-ing in the street, gon-na be a big man some-day. You got
Bud-dy, you're a young man, hard man, shout-ing in the street, gon-na take on the world some-day. You got
Bud-dy you're an old man, poor man, plead-ing with your eyes, gon-na make you some peace some-day. You got
mud on your face, you big dis-grace, kick-ing your can all__ o-ver the place__ sing-ing,
bloodon your face, you big dis-grace, wav-ing your ban-ner all__ o-ver the place._
mud on your face, big dis-grace, some-bod-y bet-ter put you back in-to your place.
CHORUS
N.C.
"We will, we will rock you. We will, we will
1.,2.
rock you."
3.
rock you. Ev-'ry-bod-y; we will, we will
rock you. Uh._ We will, we will
C5
rock you.
A5
Al-right.
OUTRO - GUITAR SOLO
A5
(GUITAR)
D
A
D A D A D A
D A D
REPEAT SIM. AND FA

WHEN WILL I BE LOVED

(MED.)

WE'RE NOT GONNA TAKE IT

-DANIEL DEE SNIDER

CHORUS

N.C.

We're not gon - na take __ it. No, we ain't gon - na take __ it.

E5 D#5 C#5 B5

We're not gon - na take __ it an - y - more. __

E5 D#5 C#5 B5

𝄋 VERSE

E5 B5

We've got the right to choose_ and
Oh, you're so con - de - scend - ing,
Guitar solo

E5 A5 E5 B5

there ain't no way we'll lose_ it. __ This is our life; __ this is __ our song. _
your gall is nev - er - end - ing. __ We don't want noth - in', not a thing _ from you. _

E5 B5 E5 B5

We'll fight the pow'rs that be, __ just
Your life is trite and ja - ded,

E5 A5 E5 B5

don't pick our des - ti - ny, _ 'cause _ you don't know us, ___ you don't be - long. _
bor - ing and con - fis - cat - ed. ___ If that's your best, __ your best won't _

1.

E5 B5

CHORUS

E5 B5

We're not gon - na take __ it.

E5
A5
E5
B5
No, we ain't gon-na take__ it.
We're not gon - na take__ it an - y - more._
E5
D#5
C#5
B5
2.
E5
D#5
C#5
B5
do.
BRIDGE
D5
C#5
B5
D5
C#5
B5
E5
Whoa,
whoa.
We're right, (Yeah!)_ we're
F5
F#5
N.C. B5
To
free, (Yeah!)_ we'll fight, (Yeah!)_ you'll see.
Whoa.
CHORUS
E5
B5
E5
A5
We're not gon - na take__ it.
No, we ain't gon - na take_
E5
B5
__ it.
We're not gon - na take__ it an - y - more._
D.S. AL
(TAKE 2nd ENDING)
1.
E5
B5
2.
E5
D#5
C#5
B5
OUTRO - CHORUS
1st X, BAND TACET (1st 7 MEAS.)
E5
B5
E5
A5
We're not gon - na take__ it.
No, we ain't gon-na take__ it.
E5
B5
E5
B5
REPEAT AND FADE
(W/ LEAD VOC. AD LIB.)
We're not gon - na take__ it an - y - more.__

(MED.)
WHAT A FOOL BELIEVES
-MICHAEL McDONALD/KENNY LOGGINS
INTRO
VERSE
PRE-CHORUS
He came from some - where back in her long a - go.
The sen-ti-men-tal fool don't see, try-in' hard to re-cre-ate what had yet to be cre-at - ed once in her life.
She mus-ters a smile for his nos - tal-gic tale, never com-in' near what he want-ed to say, on-ly to re - al - ize it nev - er real - ly was.
some-where back in her long a - go where he can still be - lieve there's a place in her life. Some - day, some - how, she will re - turn.
She had a place in his life.

Bb-7
Ab9b5
Gb/Ab
He never made her think twice.
Eb-7
Gb/Ab
Dbmaj7
B7
Bb7
Eb-7
Gb/Ab
Bb-7
As she ris - es to her a - pol - o - gy, an - y - bod - y else would sure - ly know
G-7b5
he's watching her go.
But what a fool be - lieves
CHORUS
2nd & 3rd X, W/ LEAD VOC. AD LIB.
F#-7
A/B
he sees,
no wise man has the pow - er
E
to rea - son a - way.
C#-7
N.C.
(KEYS)
8VB
(BASS)
What seems
F#-7
A/B
to be
is al - ways bet - ter than noth - ing,
E
C#-7
1. and noth - ing at all.
2., 3. and noth - ing at all.
1.
N.C.
8VB
keeps send - ing him
2.
N.C.
8VB
D.S. AND FADE
(TAKE 2nd ENDING)
What a fool be - lieves.

358
(MED. R&B)
WHAT'S GOING ON
—RENALDO BENSON/ALFRED CLEVELAND/MARVIN GAYE
Emaj7
(SAX)
VERSE
Emaj7
1.Moth - er, moth - er, there's_ too_ man - y
2. Fa - ther, fa - ther, we___ don't_ need to
3.Moth - er, moth - er, ev - 'ry - bod - y
C#-7
of you cry - ing.
es - ca - late.
thinks we're wrong.
You see,
Ah, but
Emaj7
Broth - er, broth - er, broth - er, there's far too man - y
war is not_ the an - swer, for on - ly love can
who are they_ to judge_ us sim - ply 'cause our
C#-7
of you_ dy - ing.
con - quer_ hate.
hair is_ long.
You_ know_ we've
F#-7
got to find_ a way_
(1.,2.) to bring some
(3.) to bring some un - der -
1. B7sus4
lov - in' here to - day,
B13
yeah.
2.,3. B7sus4
lov - in' here to - day,
stand - ing here to - day,
B13
oh.
oh.

CHORUS
F#-7
A/B
Pick - et lines_ and pick - et signs_ don't
F#-7
A/B
pun - ish me with___ bru - tal - i - ty.
F#-7
A/B
B13
Talk to me so you can see, oh, what's
Emaj7
C#-7
go - ing on,____ what's go - ing on,____ yeah, what's
To ⊕
Emaj7
C#-7
go - ing on,____ oh, what's go - ing on.____
INTERLUDE
W/ LEAD VOC. AD LIB.
A-7
(STRINGS)
D.S. AL ⊕
A/B
B13
⊕ OUTRO
W/ LEAD VOC. AD LIB.
A-7
(STRINGS)
REPEAT AND FADE
A/B
B13

WHITE RABBIT

(MED.)
WHITE RABBIT
—GRACE SLICK
INTRO
F#
G
(BASS)
(GUITAR)
(BASS CONT. SIM.)
VERSE
One ___ pill makes you larg-er and _______ one pill __ makes you small. And the
you go chas-ing rab-bits and you know you're ____ go-ing to fall, tell'em a
ones that moth-er gives you ___ don't do ______ an-y-thing __ at all. ____ Go ask
hoo-kah smok-in' cat-er-pil-lar_ has ______ giv-en you ____ the call. ____ Call
A
C
D
1.
2.
A-lice when she's ten feet tall. And if
A-lice when she was just small.

BRIDGE
E
A
When the men on the chess - board get up and tell you where to go, and you've
E
A
just had some kind of mush - room, and your mind is mov-ing low, go ask
F#
A - lice, I think she'll know. When
VERSE
F#
G
log - ic and pro - por - tion have fall - en slop - py
F#
dead, and the white knight is talk - ing back - wards, and the
G
A
red queen's off with her head, re - mem - ber
C
D
A
E
A
what the dor - mouse said, "Feed your head,
E
A
feed your head."

WHITE ROOM
(MED.)
-JACK BRUCE/PETE BROWN
INTRO
G- F D- C
(GUITARS)
G- F D- C
VERSE
A-7 N.C. D5 Csus2 G/B Bb5 C5 D5 Csus2
CONT. SIM.
In a white room with black cur-tains near the sta-tion.
no strings could se-cure you at the sta-tion.
At the par-ty, she was kind-ness in the hard crowd.
G/B Bb5 C5 D5 Csus2 G/B Bb5 C5 D5 Csus2
Black-roof coun-try, no gold pave-ments, tired_ star-lings.
Plat-form tick-et, rest-less die-sels, good-bye win-dows.
Con-so-la-tion for the old wound now for-got-ten.
G/B Bb5 C5 D5 Csus2 G/B Bb5 C5 D5 Csus2
Sil-ver hors-es run down moon-beams in your dark eyes.
I walked in-to such a sad time at the sta-tion.
Yel-low ti-gers crouched in jung-les in her dark eyes.
G/B Bb5 C5 D5 Csus2 G/B Bb5 C5 D5 Csus2
Dawn light smiles_ on you leav-ing my con-tent-ment.
As I walked out, felt my own need just be-gin-ning.
She's just dress-ing, good-bye win-dows, tired_ star-lings.

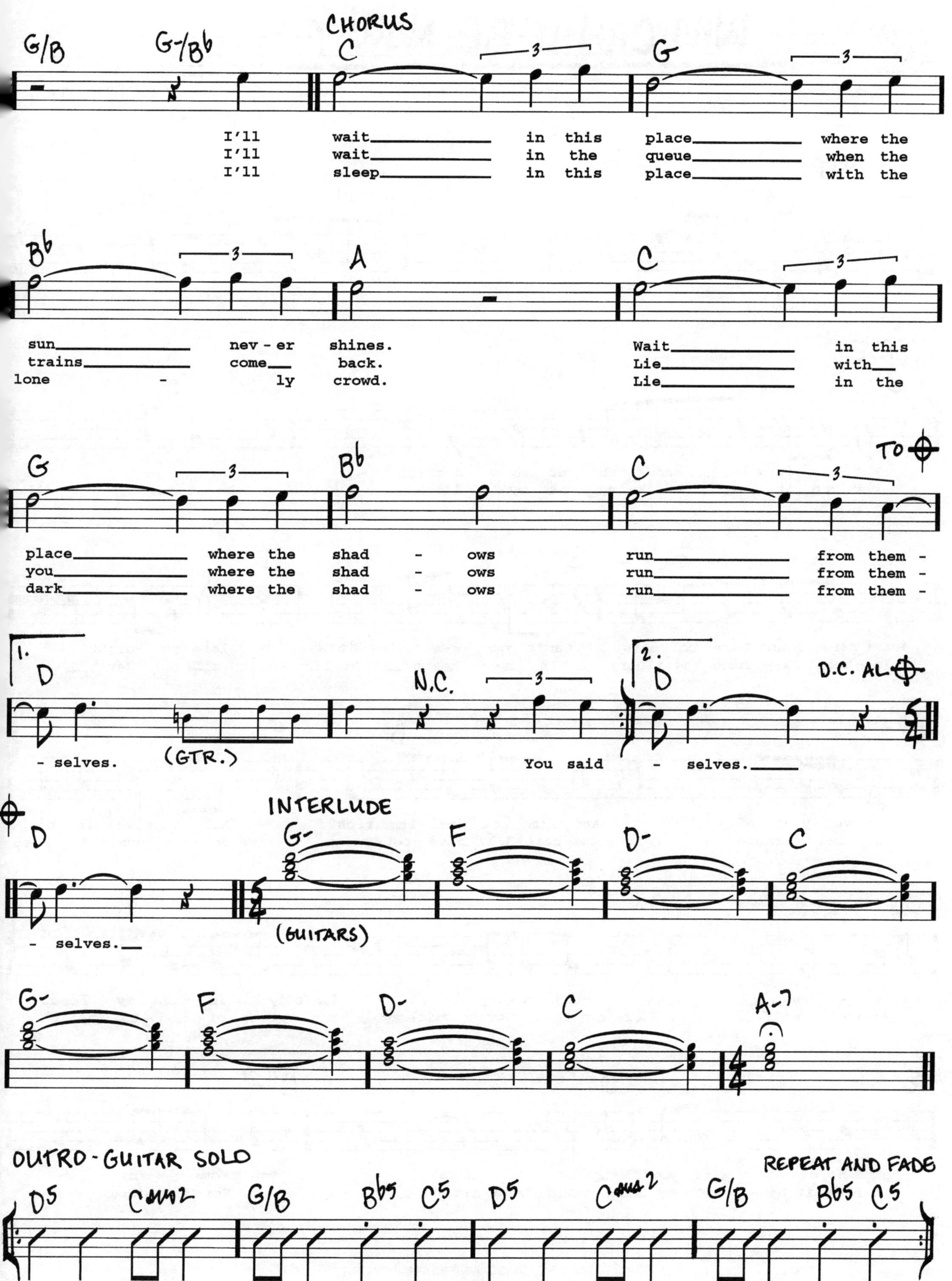
CHORUS
G/B
G-/Bb
C
G
I'll wait in this place where the
I'll wait in the queue when the
I'll sleep in this place with the
Bb
A
C
sun nev - er shines.
trains come back.
lone - ly crowd.
Wait in this
Lie with
Lie in the
G
Bb
C
TO
place where the shad - ows run from them -
you where the shad - ows run from them -
dark where the shad - ows run from them -
1.
D
N.C.
2.
D
D.C. AL
- selves.
(GTR.)
You said
- selves.
D
INTERLUDE
G-
F
D-
C
- selves.
(GUITARS)
G-
F
D-
C
A-7
OUTRO - GUITAR SOLO
REPEAT AND FADE
D5
Cadd2
G/B
Bb5
C5
D5
Cadd2
G/B
Bb5
C5

(MED.)

WHO CAN IT BE NOW?

—COLIN HAY

CHORUS
BKGD. VOC. SUNG 2nd & 3rd x
B
C#-7
I'll on - ly run and hide.
those feel - ings a - gain!
Who can it be now?
(SAX)
Bsus4
C#-7
Who can it be now?
Who can it be now?
Bsus4
TO BRIDGE
F#-7
Who can it be now?
Is it the man come to
Bsus4
F#-7
Bsus4
F#-7
take me a - way?
Why do they fol - low me?
It's not the fu - ture that
Bsus4
F#-7
Bsus4
I can see,
It's just my fan - ta - sy.
SAX SOLO
E
D/E
PLAY 4x, THEN D.S. AL
OUTRO
B
Aadd9
Oh.
Who can it be now?
B
1. Aadd9
2. Aadd9
Oh.
Who can it, who can it... Yeah, yeah, yeah.

(MED. IN 2)
WHY CAN'T WE BE FRIENDS
-SYLVESTER ALLEN/HAROLD R. BROWN/MORRIS DICKERSON/LONNIE JORDAN/
CHARLES W. MILLER/LEE OSKAR/HOWARD SCOTT/JERRY GOLDSTEIN
INTRO
(KEYS)
(Oo, oo, oo, oo. Oo, oo, oo, oo.
Oo, oo, oo, oo. Oo, oo, oo, oo.)
Ha, la, la la, la, la,
ha, la, la, la, la, la. Why can't
CHORUS
we be friends? Why can't we be friends? Why can't
we be friends? Why can't we be friends?
3. I

Additional Lyrics

5. I'd kinda like to be the President
So I can show you how your money's spent.

6. Sometimes I don't speak right,
But yet I know what I'm talking about.

7. I know you're working for the CIA.
They wouldn't have you in the Mafia.

(MED.)
WILL IT GO ROUND IN CIRCLES
-BILLY PRESTON/ BRUCE FISHER
INTRO
N.C. (Ab7)
(PIANO)
VERSE
Ab7
1.,5. I've got a song, I ain't got no
2. I've got a sto - ry, ain't got no
3. I've got a dance, I ain't got no
4. Instrumental
Bb7 Eb7 Ab7
mel - o - dy.
mor - al.
steps, no.
How'm I gon - na sing it to my friends?
Let the bad guy win ev - 'ry once in a while.
I'm gon - na let the mu - sic move me a -
Bb7 Eb7 Ab7
round.
I've got a song, I ain't got no
I've got a sto - ry, ain't got no
I've got a dance, I ain't got no
Bb7 Eb Ab7
mel - o - dy.
mor - al.
steps.
How'm I gon - na sing it to my friends?
Let the bad guy win ev - 'ry once in a while.
I'm gon - na let the mu - sic move me a -
CHORUS
Ab7 Db7 Ab7 Db7
round.
Instrumental ends
Will it go 'round in cir - cles?
Will it fly high like a
Ab7 Db7 Ab7 Db7 Ab7 Db7
bird up in the sky?
Will it go 'round in cir - cles?

Ab7
Db7
N.C. (Ab-7)
PLAY 5x
Will it fly high like a bird up in the sky?
Will it go round in circles?
Go down in cir - cles.
Oo!
OUTRO - INSTRUMENTAL SOLO
REPEAT AND FADE

WITH A LITTLE HELP FROM MY FRIENDS

MED.

—JOHN LENNON/PAUL McCARTNEY

VERSE

E B F#-7
What would you think__ if I sang__ out of tune, would you stand_
What do I do__ when my love__ is a - way? (Does it wor -
(Would you be - lieve_ in a love__ at first sight?) Yes, I'm cer -

B7 E
__ up and walk__ out on me?__
- ry you to be__ a - lone?)__
- tain that it hap - pens all the time.__

B F#-7 B7
Lend me your ears_ and I'll sing__ you a song, and I'll try__ not to sing__ out of key._
How do I feel_ by the end__ of the day? (Are you sad__ be-cause you're on your own?)
(What do you see__ when you turn__ out the light?) I can't tell__ you, but I know_ it's mine._

CHORUS

E D A
__ Oh,__ / No,__ / Oh,__ I get by with a lit-tle help from my friends.

E D A
__ Mm,__ I get high__ with a lit-tle help from my friends.

E A
__ Mm,__ gon - na try__ with a lit-tle help from my friends.

1. E B
(GUITAR)

2., 3.
E
BRIDGE
C#-7
F#7
(Do you need ___ an - y - bod - y?)
I
I
E D A C#-7
need some - bod - y to love. ___
just need some - one to love.
(Could it be ___ an - y - bod -
F#7 E D To ⊕ A D.C. AL ⊕
- y?) I want some - bod - y to love. ___
CHORUS
A D A
___ Oh, ___ I get by ___ with a lit - tle help from my friends. ___
E D A
___ Mm, ___ gon - na try ___ with a lit - tle help from my friends. ___
E A
___ Oh, ___ I get high ___ with a lit - tle help from my friends. ___
E D
___ Yes, ___ I get by ___ with a lit - tle help from my friends, ___
A C/G A-6 E
___ with a lit - tle help from my friends. ___
(Ah.) ___

(SLOW)
WITHOUT YOU
—PETER HAM/TOM EVANS
INTRO
Esus2
E
(PIANO)
(PIANO CONT. SIM)
No, I
VERSE
can't for-get this eve - ning or your face as you were leav - ing, but I
guess that's just the way the sto - ry goes. You al - ways
smile, but in your eyes your sor-row shows. Yes it
shows.
No I
VERSE
can't for-get tom-mor - row when I think of all my sor - row, when I
can't for-get this eve - ning or your face as you were leav - ing, but I
had you there but then I let you go. And now it's on -
guess that's just the way the sto - ry goes. You al - ways

C#- C#-/B F#/A# F#
- ly fair that I should let you know what you should know.
smile, but in your eyes your sor-row shows. Yes, it
EAUS2 E TO B7SUS2 B7 B7SUS2 B7
I can't
shows.
CHORUS
EAUS2 E C#-
live if liv-ing is with-out you. I can't
F#-(add9) F#- B7SUS2 B7
live, I can't give an - y more. I can't
EAUS2 E C#-
live if liv-ing is with-out you. I can't
F#-(add9) F#- B7SUS2 B7 D.S. AL
give, I can't give an - y - more. Well, I
OUTRO-CHORUS W/VOC. AD LIB.
B7SUS2 B7 B7SUS2 B7 EAUS2 E
I can't live if
C#- F#-(add9) F#-
liv-ing is with-out you. I can't live, I can't
B7SUS2 B7 REPEAT AND FADE
give an - y more. I can't

WONDERFUL TONIGHT
(MED. SLOW)
-ERIC CLAPTON
INTRO
G D/F# C D (E-) (D7/F#) (A-7)
(GUITAR)
G D/F# C D (E-) (D7/F#) (A-7)
VERSE
G D/F# C
It's late in the eve - ning. She's won-d'ring what clothes
We go to a par - ty and ev - 'ry - one turns
It's time to go home now and I've got an ach-ing
D G D/F#
to wear. She puts on her make - up
to see. This beau-ti-ful la - dy
head. So I give her the car keys
C D C
and brush-es her long blond hair. And then she asks
is walk-in' a - round with me. And then she asks
and she helps me to bed. And then I tell
D G D/F# E-
me, "Do I look al - right?" And I say,
me, "Do you feel al - right?" And I say,
her, as I turn out the light, I say, "My
C D TO ⊕ 1. G
"Yes, you look won-der - ful to - night."
"Yes, I feel won-der - ful to - night."
darlin', you were won-der - ful to - night."

D/F#
C
D (E-)(D7/F#)(A-7)
2.
G
I feel
BRIDGE
C
D
G
D/F#
E-
won-der-ful__ be-cause I see_ the love__ light in__ your eyes. And the
C
D
C
D
won-der of it all___ is that you just don't re-al-ize___ how much_ I love_
INTERLUDE
G
D/F#
C
D (E-)(D7/F#)(A-7)
you.
D.S. AL
G
D/F#
C
D (E-)(D7/F#)(A-7)
G
D/F#
E-
D
C
D
Oh, my dar-lin', you were won-der-ful___ to-night._
OUTRO
G
D/F#
C
D (E-)(D7/F#)(A-7)
HOLD BEND
G
D/F#
C
D (E-)(D7/F#)(A-7) G
RIT.

Y.M.C.A.
(MED. DISCO)
—JACQUES MORALI/HENRI BELOLO/VICTOR WILLIS
INTRO
B/C#
(HORNS)
VERSE
F#
D#-
Young man, there's no need to feel down. I said, young man, pick your-
Young man, are you list-'ning to me? I said, young man, what do
Young man, I was once in your shoes, I said, I was down and
B
self off the ground. I said young man, 'cause you're in a new town, there's no
you wan-na be? I said, young man, you can make real your dreams, but you've
out with the blues. I felt no man cared if I were a-live. I felt
C#/E# B/D# C# B F#/A# C#/G# F#
need to be un-hap-py. Young man, there's a
got to know this one thing. No man does it
the whole world was so jive. That's when some-one
D#-
place you can go, I said, young man, when you're
all by him-self, I said, young man, put your
came up to me and said, "Young man, take a
B
short on your dough. You can stay there and I'm
pride on the shelf and just go there to the
walk up the street. It's a place there called the
C#/E# B/D# C#
sure you will find man-y ways to have
Y. M. C. A. I'm sure they can help
Y. M. C. A. They can start you back

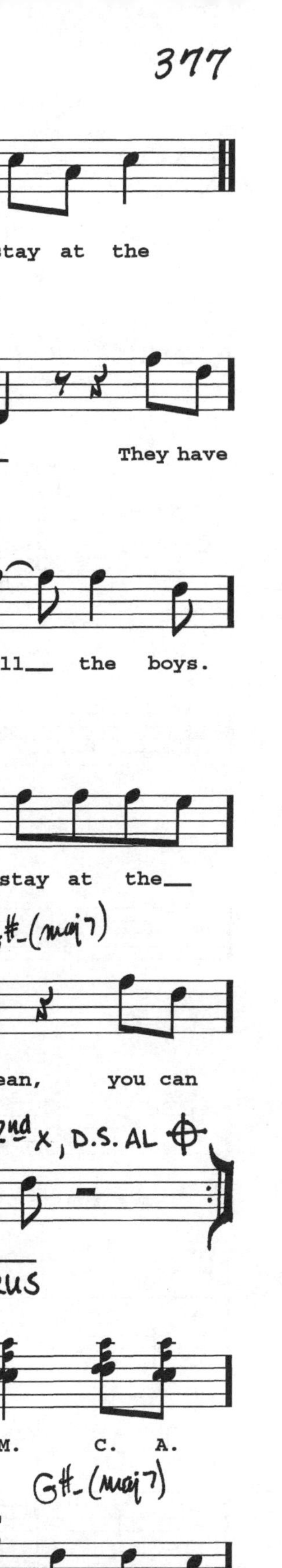
B F#/A# C#/G# B/C# N.C.
a good time.
you to - day.
on your way."
It's fun to stay at the
CHORUS
F# D#-
Y. M. C. A. It's fun to stay at the Y. M. C. A. They have
G#- G#-(maj7) G#-7 G#-6 TO B/C#
ev - er - y - thing for young men to en - joy. You can hang out with all the boys.
F#
It's fun to stay at the Y. M. C. A. It's fun to stay at the
D#- G#- G#-(maj7)
Y. M. C. A. You can get your-self clean, you can
G#-7 G#-6 B/C# 2nd X, D.S. AL
have a good meal. You can do what - ev - ever you feel.
B/C# OUTRO - CHORUS F#
hang out with all the boys. Y. M. C. A.
D#- G#- G#-(maj7)
It's fun to stay at the Y. (Y. M. C. A) Young man, young man, there's no
G#-7 G#-6 B/C# REPEAT AND FADE (W/ LEAD VOC. AD LIB.)
need to feel down. Young man, young man, pick your - self off the ground.

378
(BALLAD)
YOU ARE SO BEAUTIFUL
-BILLY PRESTON/BRUCE FISHER
INTRO
(PIANO)
VERSE
You are so beau-ti-ful to me.
You are so beau-ti-ful to me.
Can't you see?
You're ev-'ry-thing I hope for, you're ev-'ry-thing I need.
You are so beau-ti-ful to me.
A TEMPO
You are so ev-'ry-thing I need.
RIT.
You are so beau-ti-ful to me.

YOU REALLY GOT ME
(MED.)
-RAY DAVIES
INTRO
(GUITAR)
VERSE
(SIM.)
1.Girl, you real-ly got me go-in', you got me so I don't know what I'm do-in' now.
2.,3.See, don't ev-er set me free, I al-ways wan-na be by your side.
Yeah, you real-ly got me now, you got me so I can't sleep at night.
Girl, you real-ly got me now, you got me so I can't sleep at night.
Yeah, you real-ly got me now, you got me so I don't know what I'm do-in', ah.
(Yeah,
Oh, yeah, you real-ly got me now, you got me so I can't sleep at night.
Yeah.)
You real-ly got me. You real-ly got me. You real-ly got me.
TO ⊕
(GTR.)
GUITAR SOLO
PLAY 8X, THEN D.S. AL ⊕
real-ly got me.
(GTR.)

(MED.)
YOU GOT IT
-ROY ORBISON/JEFF LYNNE/TOM PETTY
INTRO
A G D
VERSE
A G D A
Ev - 'ry time I look in - to your lov - ing eyes
Ev - 'ry time I hold you I be-gin to un - der - stand.
G D A G D
I see a love that mon - ey just can't
Ev - 'ry-thing a - bout you tells me I'm your
E G PRE-CHORUS A F#-
buy. One look from you, I drift
man. I live my life to be
glad to give my love
C#- E A F#-
a - way. I pray that you are here
with you. No one can do the things
to you. I know you feel the way
C#- E TO CHORUS A C#7 F#- D
to stay. An - y - thing you want, you got it.
you do.
I do.
A C#7 F#- D A C#7 F#- D
An - y - thing you need, you got it. An - y - thing at all, you got it,

A/E
E
(GTR. CONT. SIM.)
ba - by.
(GUITAR)
An-y-thing you want,
(You got it.)
an-y-thing you need,
(You got it.)
INTERLUDE
A
C#7
F#-
1., 2.
D
an-y-thing at all.
(Do, do, do, do, do,
do, do, do, do, do.
3.
D
A/E
E
D.S. AL
you got it.)
(GTR.)
I'm
OUTRO-CHORUS
A
C#7
F#-
D
An-y-thing you want,
you got it.
An-y-thing you need,
D
A
C#7
F#-
D
you got it.
An-y-thing at all,
you got it,
A/E
E
(GTR. CONT. SIM.)
(GTR.)
ba - by.
An-y-thing at all,
A
N.C.
(You got it.)
ba - by,
you got it.

(MED.)
YOU'RE MY BEST FRIEND
- JOHN DEACON
INTRO
N.C.
D-/C
C
(ELECTRIC PIANO)
CHORUS
D-/C
C
Oo, you make me live.
D-/C
C
What - ev - er this world can
When - ev - er this world is
D-/C
C
give to me, it's you, you're all I see.
cruel to me, I got you to help me for - give.
D-/C
C
D-/C
VERSE
C
G/B A-
Oo, you make me live now, hon-ey, oo, you make me live.
D
F
G
C
Oh, you're my best friend that I ev - er had. I've
Oh, you're the first one when things turn out bad. You
G
A-
D
F
been with you such a long time. You're my sun - shine, and I want
know I'll nev - er be lone - ly. You're my on - ly one and I love

G E/G# A-
you to know that my feel - ings are true. I
the things, real - ly love the
G F F-6 C
real - ly love you.
things that you do.
Oh, you're my best friend.
BRIDGE
D-/C C E+/G
Oo, you make me live. Oo,
I've been
Instrumental
A- C/Bb F F-6 G E
wan - der-ing round. Still come back to you. In rain or shine you've
A- D G6 G
stood by me girl.
Instrumental ends
I'm hap - py at home, you're my best
C 1. 2. F-6 C
friend. Oh,
F-6 C OUTRO D-/C C
oh, you're my best friend. Oo, you make me live.
D-/C C G C G C G C G C
Oo, you're my best friend.

(MED.)

YOU'VE GOT A FRIEND

— CAROLE KING

INTRO

A D5 Esus4 A G#-7 C#7sus4 C#7

(GUITAR) (GTR. CONT. SIM.)

When you're down

VERSE

F#- C#7 F#- C#7

and trou - bled and you need a help-ing hand
a - bove you should turn dark and full of clouds

F#-7 B-7 E7sus4

and noth-ing, whoa, noth-ing is go - ing right,
and that old north wind should be-gin to blow,

A Asus2/4 A G#-11 C#7

close your eyes and think of me and
keep your head to - geth - er and

F#-7 C#7 F#-7 B-7

soon I will be there to bright-en up
call my name out loud, now; soon I'll be knock -

C#-7 E7sus4 /D /C# /B

e - ven your dark - est night.
- ing up - on your door.

You just call

𝄋 CHORUS

A Amaj7 Dmaj7

* HARMONY SUNG 2nd & 3rd X ONLY

out my name, and you know wher-ev-er I am,

B-7 E7sus4 A Asus4 A E7sus4
I'll come run - ning,
oh, yeah, ba - by,
oh, yes I will,
to see you a - gain.
A Amaj7 Dmaj7
Win-ter, spring, sum-mer or fall, all you've got to do is call
F#-7 Dmaj7 C#-7 E7sus4 TO ⊕ A
3
and I'll be there, yeah, yeah, yeah. You've got a friend.
(GTR.)
D A G#-7 C#7sus4 C#7 E7sus4
(GTR. CONT. SIM.)
If the sky Hey, ain't
Gmaj7sus2 G D A Asus4
it good to know that you've got a friend when peo-ple can be so cold?
Amaj7 D Gmaj7
They'll hurt you and de-sert you; well, they'll
F#-7 B7 E7sus4 E7
D.S. AL ⊕
(TAKE 1st ENDING)
take your soul if you let them, oh yeah, but don't you let them. You just call
OUTRO
A D (GTR. CONT. SIM.) A D
You've got a friend, yeah. Ain't it good to know you've got
A D A D E7sus4 A
a friend? Ain't it good to know you've got a friend? Oh, yeah, yeah, you've got a friend.

(MED.)
YOU'VE MADE ME SO VERY HAPPY
- BERRY GORDY/FRANK E. WILSON/BRENDA HOLLOWAY/PATRICE HOLLOWAY
INTRO
N.C.
(ORGAN)
(HORNS)
VERSE
Eb-7
I lost at love before, got mad and closed the door, but you said try just once more. I chose you for the one, now we're hav-ing so much fun. You treat-ed me so kind, I'm a-bout to lose my mind.
The oth-ers were un-true, but when it came to lov-in' you, I'd spend my whole life with you, 'cause you came and you took con-trol. You touched my ver-y soul. You al-ways showed me that lov-ing you is where it's at.
Dbmaj7
E-7
Gb/Ab
CHORUS
You made me so ver-y hap-py. I'm so glad you came in-to my life.
Bb7
INTERLUDE
Thank you, ba-by. Yeah, yeah.

BRIDGE
B
I love you so much, it seems_ you're e-ven in my dreams._ I can
F#
C#
hear,_ ba - by, I can hear you're call - ing me._
B
E-7
I'm so in love with you,_ all I ev - er want to do_ is
D#-7 N.C.
A7 G#7 N.C.
INTERLUDE
D#-
C# D#-
thank you, ba - by, thank you, ba - by.
(HORNS)
E-
D E- D#-
G D
(GUITAR FILL)
CHORUS
E-7
You made me_ so ver-y hap-py. I'm so glad you
A7
Dmaj7
B7
E-7
came in - to my life. You made me_ so
G-6
F#-7
B7
ver-y_ hap-py. You made_ me so, so ver-y hap-py, ba-by,
E-7
A7b5
N.C. RIT.
OUTRO
A TEMPO W/ VOC. AD LIB. ON REPEAT
Gadd9
Cmaj7
I'm so glad you came in - to_ my_ life.

388
YOUR SONG
(SLOW)
-ELTON JOHN/BERNIE TAUPIN
INTRO
Eb Ab/Eb Bb/Eb Ab/Eb
(PIANO)
VERSE
Eb Abmaj7 Bb/D G-
It's a lit-tle bit fun-ny, this feel-ing in-side;
If I was a sculp-tor, but then a-gain, no, or a
I sat on the roof and kicked off the moss; well, a
So ex-cuse me for-get-tin', but these things I do;
C-(add9) C-/Bb A-7b5 Ab
I'm not one of those who can eas-i-ly hide.
man who makes po-tions in a trav-el-in' show, I
few of the vers-es, well, they've got me quite cross.
you see I've for-got-ten if they're green or they're blue.
Eb/Bb Bb G/B C-
Don't have much mon-ey, but, boy, if I did,
know-it's not much but it's the best I can do.
But the sun's been quite kind while I wrote this song.
An-y-way the thing is what I real-ly mean,
Eb F- 1.,3. Ab
I'd buy a big house where we both could
My gift is my song, and
It's for peo-ple like you that keep it turned
yours are the sweet-est eyes
Bb Bbsus4 Bb 2.,4. Ab Eb Ebsus4 Eb
live.
on.
this one's for you.
I've ev-er seen.

CHORUS
Bb/D
C-7
F-
Ab
And you can tell ev - 'ry - bod - y this is your song.
It may be quite sim - ple, but now that it's done,
C-
C-/Bb
A-7b5
Ab6
I hope you don't mind, I hope you don't mind that I put down in words how
Eb/G
Ab6
Ab
Bb
Bbsus4
Bb
TO
wonder - der - ful life is while you're in the world.
Eb
Ab/Eb
Bb/Eb
D.S. AL
(PIANO)
I hope you don't mind, I hope you don't mind that I put down in words how
won - der - ful life is while you're in the world.
(HARP)

Presenting the Hal Leonard JAZZ PLAY-ALONG SERIES

For use with all B-flat, E-flat, Bass Clef and C instruments, the Jazz Play-Along® Series is the ultimate learning tool for all jazz musicians. With musician-friendly lead sheets, melody cues, and other split-track choices on the included CD, these first-of-a-kind packages help you master improvisation while playing some of the greatest tunes of all time. FOR STUDY, each tune includes a split track with: melody cue with proper style and inflection • professional rhythm tracks • choruses for soloing • removable bass part • removable piano part. FOR PERFORMANCE, each tune also has: an additional full stereo accompaniment track (no melody) • additional choruses for soloing.

1A. MAIDEN VOYAGE/ALL BLUES
00843158 .... $15.99

1. DUKE ELLINGTON
00841644 .... $16.95

2. MILES DAVIS
00841645 .... $16.95

3. THE BLUES
00841646 .... $16.99

4. JAZZ BALLADS
00841691 .... $16.99

5. BEST OF BEBOP
00841689 .... $16.95

6. JAZZ CLASSICS WITH EASY CHANGES
00841690 .... $16.99

7. ESSENTIAL JAZZ STANDARDS
00843000 .... $16.99

8. ANTONIO CARLOS JOBIM AND THE ART OF THE BOSSA NOVA
00843001 .... $16.95

9. DIZZY GILLESPIE
00843002 .... $16.99

10. DISNEY CLASSICS
00843003 .... $16.99

11. RODGERS AND HART FAVORITES
00843004 .... $16.99

12. ESSENTIAL JAZZ CLASSICS
00843005 .... $16.99

13. JOHN COLTRANE
00843006 .... $16.95

14. IRVING BERLIN
00843007 .... $15.99

15. RODGERS & HAMMERSTEIN
00843008 .... $15.99

16. COLE PORTER
00843009 .... $15.95

17. COUNT BASIE
00843010 .... $16.95

18. HAROLD ARLEN
00843011 .... $15.95

19. COOL JAZZ
00843012 .... $15.95

20. CHRISTMAS CAROLS
00843080 .... $14.95

21. RODGERS AND HART CLASSICS
00843014 .... $14.95

22. WAYNE SHORTER
00843015 .... $16.95

23. LATIN JAZZ
00843016 .... $16.95

24. EARLY JAZZ STANDARDS
00843017 .... $14.95

25. CHRISTMAS JAZZ
00843018 .... $16.95

26. CHARLIE PARKER
00843019 .... $16.95

27. GREAT JAZZ STANDARDS
00843020 .... $16.99

28. BIG BAND ERA
00843021 .... $15.99

29. LENNON AND MCCARTNEY
00843022 .... $16.95

30. BLUES' BEST
00843023 .... $15.99

31. JAZZ IN THREE
00843024 .... $15.99

32. BEST OF SWING
00843025 .... $15.99

33. SONNY ROLLINS
00843029 .... $15.95

34. ALL TIME STANDARDS
00843030 .... $15.99

35. BLUESY JAZZ
00843031 .... $16.99

36. HORACE SILVER
00843032 .... $16.99

37. BILL EVANS
00843033 .... $16.95

38. YULETIDE JAZZ
00843034 .... $16.95

39. "ALL THE THINGS YOU ARE" & MORE JEROME KERN SONGS
00843035 .... $15.99

40. BOSSA NOVA
00843036 .... $16.99

41. CLASSIC DUKE ELLINGTON
00843037 .... $16.99

42. GERRY MULLIGAN FAVORITES
00843038 .... $16.99

43. GERRY MULLIGAN CLASSICS
00843039 .... $16.99

44. OLIVER NELSON
00843040 .... $16.95

46. BROADWAY JAZZ STANDARDS
00843042 .... $15.99

47. CLASSIC JAZZ BALLADS
00843043 .... $15.99

48. BEBOP CLASSICS
00843044 .... $16.99

49. MILES DAVIS STANDARDS
00843045 .... $16.95

50. GREAT JAZZ CLASSICS
00843046 .... $15.99

51. UP-TEMPO JAZZ
00843047 .... $15.99

52. STEVIE WONDER
00843048 .... $16.99

53. RHYTHM CHANGES
00843049 .... $15.99

54. "MOONLIGHT IN VERMONT" AND OTHER GREAT STANDARDS
00843050 .... $15.99

55. BENNY GOLSON
00843052 .... $15.95

56. "GEORGIA ON MY MIND" & OTHER SONGS BY HOAGY CARMICHAEL
00843056 .... $15.99

57. VINCE GUARALDI
00843057 .... $16.99

58. MORE LENNON AND MCCARTNEY
00843059 .... $16.99

59. SOUL JAZZ
00843060 .... $16.99

60. DEXTER GORDON
00843061 .... $15.95

61. MONGO SANTAMARIA
00843062 .... $15.95

62. JAZZ-ROCK FUSION
00843063 .... $16.99

63. CLASSICAL JAZZ
00843064 .... $14.95

64. TV TUNES
00843065 .... $14.95

65. SMOOTH JAZZ
00843066 .... $16.99

66. A CHARLIE BROWN CHRISTMAS
00843067 .... $16.99

67. CHICK COREA
00843068 .... $15.95

68. CHARLES MINGUS
00843069 .... $16.95

69. CLASSIC JAZZ
00843071 .... $15.99

70. THE DOORS
00843072 .... $14.95

71. COLE PORTER CLASSICS
00843073 .... $14.95

72. CLASSIC JAZZ BALLADS
00843074 .... $15.99

73. JAZZ/BLUES
00843075 .... $14.95

74. BEST JAZZ CLASSICS
00843076 .... $15.99

75. PAUL DESMOND
00843077 .... $15.99

76. BROADWAY JAZZ BALLADS
00843078 .... $15.99

77. JAZZ ON BROADWAY
00843079 .... $15.99

78. STEELY DAN
00843070 .... $15.99

79. MILES DAVIS CLASSICS
00843081 .... $15.99

80. JIMI HENDRIX
00843083 .... $16.99

81. FRANK SINATRA – CLASSICS
00843084 .... $15.99

82. FRANK SINATRA – STANDARDS
00843085 .... $15.99

83. ANDREW LLOYD WEBBER
00843104 .... $14.95

84. BOSSA NOVA CLASSICS
00843105 .... $14.95

85. MOTOWN HITS
00843109 .... $14.95

86. BENNY GOODMAN
00843110 .... $15.99

87. DIXIELAND
00843111 .... $14.95

88. DUKE ELLINGTON FAVORITES
00843112 .... $14.95

89. IRVING BERLIN FAVORITES
00843113 .... $14.95

90. THELONIOUS MONK CLASSICS
00841262 .... $16.99

91. THELONIOUS MONK FAVORITES
00841263 .... $16.99

92. LEONARD BERNSTEIN
00450134 .... $15.99

93. DISNEY FAVORITES
00843142 .... $14.99

94. RAY
00843143 .... $14.99

95. JAZZ AT THE LOUNGE
00843144 .... $14.99

96. LATIN JAZZ STANDARDS
00843145 .... $15.99

97. MAYBE I'M AMAZED*
00843148 .... $15.99

98. DAVE FRISHBERG
00843149 .... $15.99

99. SWINGING STANDARDS
00843150 .... $14.99

100. LOUIS ARMSTRONG
00740423 .... $16.99

101. BUD POWELL
00843152 .... $14.99

102. JAZZ POP
00843153 .... $15.99

103. ON GREEN DOLPHIN STREET & OTHER JAZZ CLASSICS
00843154 .... $14.99

104. ELTON JOHN
00843155 .... $14.99

105. SOULFUL JAZZ
00843151 .... $15.99

106. SLO' JAZZ
00843117 .... $14.99

107. MOTOWN CLASSICS
00843116 .... $14.99

108. JAZZ WALTZ
00843159 .... $15.99

109. OSCAR PETERSON
00843160 .... $16.99

110. JUST STANDARDS
00843161 .... $15.99

111. COOL CHRISTMAS
00843162 .... $15.99

112. PAQUITO D'RIVERA – LATIN JAZZ*
48020662 .... $16.99

113. PAQUITO D'RIVERA – BRAZILIAN JAZZ*
48020663 .... $19.99

114. MODERN JAZZ QUARTET FAVORITES
00843163 .... $15.99

115. THE SOUND OF MUSIC
00843164 .... $15.99

116. JACO PASTORIUS
00843165 .... $15.99

117. ANTONIO CARLOS JOBIM – MORE HITS
00843166 .... $15.99

118. BIG JAZZ STANDARDS COLLECTION
00843167 .... $27.50

119. JELLY ROLL MORTON
00843168 .... $15.99

120. J.S. BACH
00843169 .... $15.99

121. DJANGO REINHARDT
00843170 .... $15.99

122. PAUL SIMON
00843182 .... $16.99

123. BACHARACH & DAVID
00843185 .... $15.99

124. JAZZ-ROCK HORN HITS
00843186 .... $15.99

126. COUNT BASIE CLASSICS
00843157 .... $15.99

127. CHUCK MANGIONE
00843188 .... $15.99

128. VOCAL STANDARDS (LOW VOICE)
00843189 .... $15.99

129. VOCAL STANDARDS (HIGH VOICE)
00843190 .... $15.99

130. VOCAL JAZZ (LOW VOICE)
00843191 .... $15.99

131. VOCAL JAZZ (HIGH VOICE)
00843192 .... $15.99

132. STAN GETZ ESSENTIALS
00843193 .... $15.99

133. STAN GETZ FAVORITES
00843194 .... $15.99

134. NURSERY RHYMES*
00843196 .... $17.99

135. JEFF BECK
00843197 .... $15.99

136. NAT ADDERLEY
00843198 .... $15.99

137. WES MONTGOMERY
00843199 .... $15.99

138. FREDDIE HUBBARD
00843200 .... $15.99

139. JULIAN "CANNONBALL" ADDERLEY
00843201 .... $15.99

140. JOE ZAWINUL
00843202 .... $15.99

141. BILL EVANS STANDARDS
00843156 .... $15.99

142. CHARLIE PARKER GEMS
00843222 .... $15.99

143. JUST THE BLUES
00843223 .... $15.99

144. LEE MORGAN
00843229 .... $15.99

145. COUNTRY STANDARDS
00843230 .... $15.99

146. RAMSEY LEWIS
00843231 .... $15.99

147. SAMBA
00843232 .... $15.99

150. JAZZ IMPROV BASICS
00843195 .... $19.99

151. MODERN JAZZ QUARTET CLASSICS
00843209 .... $15.99

152. J.J. JOHNSON
00843210 .... $15.99

154. HENRY MANCINI
00843213 .... $14.99

155. SMOOTH JAZZ CLASSICS
00843215 .... $15.99

156. THELONIOUS MONK – EARLY GEMS
00843216 .... $15.99

157. HYMNS
00843217 .... $15.99

158. JAZZ COVERS ROCK
00843219 .... $15.99

159. MOZART
00843220 .... $15.99

160. GEORGE SHEARING
14041531 .... $16.99

161. DAVE BRUBECK
14041556 .... $16.99

162. BIG CHRISTMAS COLLECTION
00843221 .... $24.99

164. HERB ALPERT
14041775 .... $16.99

Prices, contents, and availability subject to change without notice.

HAL•LEONARD®
CORPORATION
7777 W. BLUEMOUND RD. P.O. BOX 13819
MILWAUKEE, WISCONSIN 53213

For complete songlists and more, visit Hal Leonard online at
www.halleonard.com

*These CDs do not include split tracks.

1012